A Game of Polo with a Headless Goat

IN SEARCH OF THE ANCIENT SPORTS OF ASIA

Emma Levine

André Deutsch

First published in 2000
This paperback edition published in 2003
by André Deutsch
An imprint of the
Carlton Publishing Group
20 Mortimer Street
London W1T 3JW

1 3 5 7 9 10 8 6 4 2

A catalogue record for this book is available from
the British Library

ISBN 0 233 05041 8

Jacket based on an original design by Button Design

Typeset by Derek Doyle & Associates, Liverpool.
Printed and bound in Great Britain by
Mackays of Chatham plc, Chatham, Kent.

Contents

Dedication and Acknowledgements

Dedicated to my somewhat scattered family –
Mum, Dad, Iain, Simon and Colin

There are countless people to whom I owe gratitude for making the trip go that little bit smoother by sharing their knowledge, time, kindness and hospitality or plain common sense. There are too many to mention in all, but those I wish to specially thank are:

Hamid Arkhund in Karachi for his vital information on sport in Pakistan; Yaqoub Shah and Mohammed Ali for hospitality in Quetta; Hameed and friends in Quetta for buzkashi leads; Mr Akhtar and family for Sibi transport; Farooq Memon for patient donkey racing visits; Asem Mustafa Awan in Islamabad; Ifraz in Lahore; Imtiaz Sipra for access to *The News* library in Lahore; Mr Rana and members of the Pakistani Wrestling Federation for the akhara tour; Shoaib Hashmi for learned information on wrestling; Mr Khalid and family in Bhawalpur; Salim Bukhari and members of the PTDC in Islamabad; Karim in Gilgit; Nasir Ahmed and Wali Ur-Rehman in Chitral; Erhan and the Crazy Turkish Engineers in Quetta; the Camel Crew – Şahin, Cafer, Hoca and Mahmoud – in Selçuk; Şenol for a home in Istanbul; Nihat Gezder for cirit information and hospitality in Erzurum and Kamil for patient translation; Mehmet Ali in Edirne; Alper Yazorğlu and his committee members in Istanbul; Halil Delice, Yasin Dilek and Sali at *Türkiye* newspaper for their help and kindness; Suzy and Mollie for their support in Kaş; Mr Amaglobelli and Irakly in Kutaisi for my first sample of Georgian hospitality; Zaza Gachechiladze and his wonderful staff at 'Georgian Times'; members of the Georgian Olympic Committee for tchidowoba and the banquet; Hank for his hospitality in Bishkek; Kabyl Makeshov and Murat for my first sighting of the headless goat; Bolotbek Shamshiev and Askar Salymbekov in Bishkek; Selima for translation; Uday Deshpande in Bombay; Mr Laloo for archery information in Shillong; Mr Balakrishnan in Calicut; all the Gurukkals I met in Kerala for their valuable explanations and demonstrations of kalaripayattu; Mr A Vinod in Trivandrum, Mr Vashist at Manipur Bhawan; Mr Mufti at Delhi's Pakistani Embassy; Iboyama Laithengbam for his time and endless hospitality in Imphal; Hemanta Singh for arranging sporting visits around Manipur; Dr Sadjjadi in Tehran; Zohreh and Mr Saiid in Esfahan for their fantastic information on zurkhanes; and of course Dr Dawoody for livening up that long, long bus journey ...

Special thanks to my mates in England for their support during the completion of the book and their growing interest in headless goats, to Laura Longrigg at MBA and of course Nicky Paris for endless patience during editing.

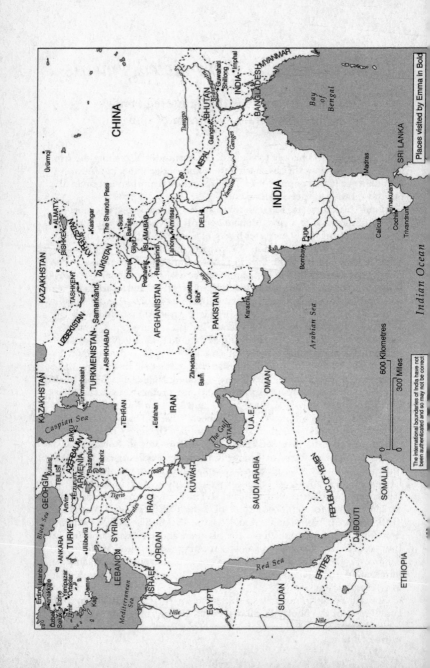

Places visited by Emma in Bold

The international boundaries of India have not been authenticated and so may not be correct

Prologue

Beige, sandy mountains surrounded the ground, which appeared to be worlds away from civilization, although we were only thirty kilometres from Baluchistan's capital, Quetta. A large crowd had arrived and most gathered on the hillside, offering as it did a perfect view over the pitch, which was rough, stony and grassless – hardly a typical match venue.

It was Friday afternoon and way past the scheduled start time. The horses were here and the riders were all strong and fit and even the young boys looked like natural horsemen. A few of them took advantage of the late start and showed off their abilities; making their horses rear up into the air and scattering people around them.

It wasn't safe to emerge from the jeep yet. Foreigners were objects of such fascination – added to which I was the only female for miles around – that we had to stay hidden until the action on the field would distract attention away from us.

Buses and trucks were still bringing spectators from nearby towns, from young boys to turbaned old men with wise, wrinkled faces and thick beards, blankets thrown dramatically over their shoulders. Everyone waited impatiently, fearing the worst. A feeling of doubt began to sink in. We had the venue, the horses and riders, the spectators. It was a perfect day, sunny and clear. But where was the goat?

1

Bedsheets and Borders

'**C**'est un jeu qui est comme le polo, mais sans la balle. Les hommes sur les chevaux jouent avec un, um...' I searched in the depths of my memory, going back twelve or so years to O-level days, to find the French word for a goat. I decided that a sheep would do. She would get the drift, surely... 'un mouton sans la tête.'

To me it made perfect sense: 'It's a game like polo, but without the ball. The men on horses play with a sheep without its head.' But the French lady's slight raising of an eyebrow, as she gazed out of the train window, wasn't as dramatic as the image, so eloquently described, called for. The two Sikh men opposite us, their bright turbans glowing softly in the gloomy carriage, watched us silently.

'Pourquoi?' she replied. Why indeed? Obviously the image of the game of *buzkashi* failed to stir any spirits in her. I lost the enthusiasm to launch into a detailed description of the great Central Asian game (of which many have had their one and only sight in the film *Rambo III*): a kind of anarchic rugby on horseback where teams of men wrestle and race to grab a headless goat and, having done so, hurtle down the field to score a goal. She would be unlikely to appreciate the reason for my journey – a long, lustful desire to see this game wherever it was now played.

My French vocabulary was now exhausted and it just seemed like too much trouble. I gave her my best Gallic shrug and a 'Je ne sais pas', and the subject was closed. She probably thought I was just another crazy hallucinating hippie who'd taken too many drugs. She continued to gaze out of the window and I dreamed of buzkashi in Afghanistan; where men are men and goats are dead.

Our train travelled through two seasons in one day. The Indian

1

Railways Golden Temple Mail left Bombay on a sticky summer's day and arrived in a chilly, late-night Amritsar in Punjab, forty hours and 1400 kilometres later, including the obligatory eight hours' delay. Amritsar railway station is no party and less so at 2 am after a long journey without heating. A cloak of freezing fog came with the descending gloom of the night, and even the gaggle of *chai* sellers with their nasal whines produced little cheer.

I was due to leave the next morning for Pakistan, so decided to risk an only-to-be-used-when-really-necessary Railway Retiring Room, these usually being cold and cavernous with leaky taps in the bathroom. As I wandered around with my huge pack, I caught the attention of a young man waiting with his sister for a delayed train to Chandigarh. He introduced himself as Raj: 'Let me help you with your bags.' Being completely intoxicated, he overbalanced on the stairs, but he supervised the shuffle through dusty bureaucracy in the booking office – four staff, six carbon copies, four receipts, 150 rupees and fifteen minutes – and then into my room, led by an even more intoxicated attendant.

First came the necessary task which guests at the Hilton or Sheraton never have to do: check the sheets. As a frequent guest of unwholesome hotels, I have certain prerequisites to getting into bed and my modest standards rule out pubic hair and rodents. A quick inspection of the sheets revealed enough pubic hair to knit a jumper, and congealed food remains which could feed a family of four for a week.

The drunken duo gazed with dropped jaws when I demanded clean sheets, and the grumbling attendant staggered off for more sheets (minus stains and extras) and then the bed was ready. Raj attempted a lunge at me, saying ruefully, when I dodged his clumsy advance, 'Sorry, it's just our typical Punjabi way of saying goodbye.'

'Sure – I could demonstrate our Yorkshire way of saying goodbye, called "knee in the groin".' And I smiled sweetly at the gently hiccuping Raj as he rejoined his sister, who was still waiting for the Chandigarh train, and then ushered a bewildered attendant back to his bottle, and slept.

The next morning's feeble sun failed to rejuvenate the station. It rained, it was cold and the entire population of Amritsar station, who appeared to be there for any purpose other than catching a train, was glum. Inquiries about the when and whereabouts of the much-heralded train to Lahore were greeted with a mixture of optimism and realism. 'Yes, madam, the train is supposed to leave at 9.30 but usually leaves a few hours late.' A group of optimistic Pakistanis waited on the platform armed with huge brass pots, sacks of dried fruit and bundles large enough to contain entire households. I was not reassured – I could see myself celebrating New Year's Eve, just a few days ahead, right there on Platform 1 – so I decided instead to take the bus.

The last time I had undertaken the cross-border bus trip had been in comfort with the South African TV Broadcasting crew, travelling from the 1996 cricket World Cup semi-final in Chandigarh to the final in Lahore. Little chance of comfort now. My carriage awaited, revving on full throttle (though it was still empty and was certainly not going to push off until full), black clouds billowing around it.

I took the front seat, while those behind me quickly filled up with pots and pans and people, and we lurched off. I was fortunate in not having to accommodate a large farmer, complete with pitchfork, on my lap, as most had to do. A large hole in the under-carriage, right where the exhaust pipe was positioned, spewed smoke inside the bus as we bucketed and rumbled from Amritsar to Attari.

Considering the uncomfortable relations between the two countries, the border crossing is a remarkably affable procedure. My main concern was distracting attention from the plethora of electrical equipment in my bag – a lap-top computer and printer, spaghetti-like wires and a couple of cameras might provoke ideas of 'duty' charges or itemized lists in my passport.

'What's your purpose of visit, madam?'

'Well . . .' How does one begin to explain the reason for this trip? To see the bizarre sports through the continent and espe-cially buzkashi? To see the camel wrestling in Turkey and the Horse and Cattle Show in Baluchistan and bull racing in India and perhaps even see inside a traditional Iranian gymnasium? To see as many wild sports as possible in a year? How could I tell this genial immigration officer that I was lured by a headless goat?

It was the perfect opportunity, right there in the Immigration shed at the Indo-Pak border, to dwell on the insanity of this trip. I pondered over the reasons: brought up in a sports-loving Yorkshire family, I had left England for Asia seven years earlier, and immersed myself in the cricket culture of the subcontinent, entranced by the passion invested in the game there. Throughout those years, however, I also carried the image of a camel-wrestling festival I stumbled across in a Turkish village at the very beginning of my Asian adventures, which planted the seed of curiosity. A few months afterwards, while travelling in Pakistan, I heard about the wonderful game of buzkashi, where men on horseback play polo with a headless goat. That began an obsession to search it out – along with other bizarre traditional Asian sports – which had, until this trip, remained unfulfilled.

So here I was, embarking on a one-year trip to do just that: to travel around Asia to see as many of these sports and games as possible, to learn what people do, and how; to find out if they are games of the past or the future. And I wanted to have fun.

But, for now, there was the more pressing matter of the Immigration officer, pencil poised over his ledger, waiting for my reason of entering Pakistan.

Lamely I replied, 'Oh, you know, just a tourist.'

To avoid being searched, I turned the conversation to cricket and the current series between Pakistan and Australia. As he was about to open the computer bag, the innocent question of, 'So, who's better – Saeed Anwar or Aamir Sohail?' was an easy decoy. By the time we had discussed Inzumam Ul-Haq, I was practically being offered Pakistani citizenship.

A couple of minibuses later and I was in Lahore.

The Royal City Hotel was situated in the middle of a muddy heap where the buses depart at all hours of the day and night, opposite the railway station. It was a safe option out of a mass of cheap hotels, some with rumours of unsavoury owners, drugs planted in hotel rooms, police looking for bribes, and sticky-fingered staff.

It was only for a couple of nights, as I had to get to Karachi to board a flight to Turkey five days later, in order to catch the season of the camel-wrestling festivals. New Year's Day I spent on another cold train for twenty-four hours – the only available ticket for me to reach Karachi in time for my flight. A couple of days in Karachi before my flight to Istanbul provided the opportunity to check out dates of forthcoming festivals: the Sibi Mela – Sibi's Horse and Cattle Show, which usually has traditional local sports as entertainment – and also the famous polo tournament on the Shandur Pass in the northern, mountainous region of the country.

I went to the city's main branch of the Pakistan Tourist Development Council where Mr Khan, unaccustomed to seeing visitors, promised to phone around and check the dates so that when I returned six weeks later, the facts would (in theory) be at our fingertips. He gazed at me a little vacantly when I asked about Sibi.

'Ah yes, Sibi.' He scratched his head as if the name rang a bell. Sibi, in the tribal state of Baluchistan, hardly makes the headlines apart from its Horse and Cattle Show and its roaring summer temperatures of 50 degrees Celsius making it one of the hottest places on earth. 'Well, we don't know about the Show but they usually let us know a couple of weeks before . . .' The same applied for the polo festival – no dates had been confirmed. My schedule for the year – intended to catch the correct 'season' for the sports I wanted to see – would have to remain flexible.

I also went to see the Sind government's director of culture, Mr Hamid Arkhund, who suggested some additional events: he told me about *malakhara*, a specific type of traditional wrestling in the Sind province, and he promised to find out dates of festivals for my return. Cockfighting, he said, was relatively easy to track down in any town and village, as was *kabaddi*, a combination of tag and wrestling, widespread throughout the sub-continent.

The day before leaving Pakistan, I watched a local cricket match in Karachi Gymkhana, a prestigious cricket club whose high membership fees deter all but the crème de la crème of society. In the members' pavilion were silk suits and mobile phones, and on the wall was the plaque marking the occasion of the Pakistan victory over the MCC in 1937, which led to Pakistan's international cricketing status.

On the other side of the ground, the free-for-all section was packed with noisy spectators, more concerned with betting than with enjoying a good game of cricket. Moreover, the gambling here was highly sophisticated and needed a degree in accounting. The grounds echoed with shouts of 'Fifty paise that the next ball will be a single,' 'Thirty paise that this over won't see a boundary,' 'Ten paise that number 6 will be out this over,' while dozens of amateur bookies were calling and waving money in the air.

Every local cricket match in the subcontinent, no matter how tiny or unofficial the venue, has a commentator hooked up to a loudspeaker. At this match, it was a businessman who had spent three years in Scarborough, in my native Yorkshire, who provided a commentary mainly in Urdu with occasional English in whose style one might detect shades of Geoffrey Boycott.

The first team was all out for 85 and he summarized the innings to a laughing crowd: 'That was pathetic. Absolutely pathetic. You saw it, I saw it, we all saw it. Truly awful.' Afterwards, friends who were also watching the match told me that one batsman, who was well on target to win the match easily for his team, was offered money by a bookmaker to be out before he reached 50. He was run out for 49.

With little chance of seeing much cricket over the year, I set off for the cold winter of Turkey and the camels.

2

Drinking with the Devecis

Trying to describe camel wrestling to a novice is like explaining cricket to an American. To the ignorant, it sounds physically impossible, cruel or just silly. It's easy enough to make it clear that it is not man against camel, but camel against camel, but after that there's no real way to explain it unless you act out the motions of two huge camels locked in embrace, each trying to overbalance the other.

My first camel-wrestling festival was in February 1991, when I stopped off briefly en route to India, and visited a small mountain village near Selçuk. The entire day was a feast to the senses; more than just the fights, the whole intoxicating atmosphere of music, food and drink had me hooked, and I had been unable to forget the spectacle. Now I had the opportunity to see more festivals. If I could find out the dates and venues of different village festivals, I could visit one every weekend and end with the largest, most historical, camel wrestling at the ancient ruins of Ephesus.

It was good to be back in Istanbul and after getting from the airport to Sultanahmet I found a cheap room in a pension, overlooking the tram-rumbling main street of Divan Yolu, and went to find my old mate Yilmaz in his shop, for tea and a chat.

Yilmaz is the archetypal 'lovable rogue', lacking in morals and conscience and involving himself in a wide array of highly illegal activities. Yet he is amusing, entertaining, charming and well-dressed, with a charisma which attracts an interesting collection of women.

I had met him ten years earlier, since then his activities had grown progressively less innocent; he was now everything mothers warn their daughters about: a womanizer, drug-smuggler, hit-man, armed and dangerous complete with bullet-proof vest. Drinking tea with Yilmaz was like being in a *Godfather* movie.

'I'm engaged!' he beamed. Not to his current blonde Canadian girlfriend but a 'suitable' match (a distant cousin) arranged by his parents. 'Fuck is fuck, but I have to marry Turkish and have one hundred per cent Turkish son.' The blonde was taking a large quantity of heroin back to Montreal. 'Big money for me, big money for her. Darling, if you ever need money, you can always do the same.' He habitually persuaded girlfriends to take a parcel of heroin to Europe or USA. 'My Swiss girlfriend was the best. She was a stewardess and her airline never check the cabin baggage, so she was getting through every time.'

Eventually I managed to get the conversation shifted from smuggling heroin to the more pressing subject of camel wrestling. The big Ephesus festival was usually held in mid-January, but Yilmaz was worried that fights would be postponed until Ramadan had finished, three weeks later. I hoped he was wrong.

On the more conventional sports front, Turkey was now in the middle of its football season and I wanted to support a team, to forge an allegiance. Three clubs, all from Istanbul, dominate national support: Galatasaray, Fenerbahçe and Beşiktaş. Galatasaray as the most successful I thought boring and predictable; Fenerbahçe's colours, blue and yellow, being the same as Leeds United's (sworn enemy of Bradford City) were therefore taboo for me, which left Beşiktaş. I bought a Beşiktaş black and white woolly hat which would forever mark me a Kara Kartal (black eagle) supporter.

For more information about other Turkish sports I went to see Hüseyin, an officer at Istanbul's Belediye (municipality), who advised me to see cirit (pronounced 'jirit'), horseback javelin, in the summer in eastern Turkey, which would coincide with my return to see oil wrestling in July.

No one in Istanbul knew where or when the camel wrestling would happen, though some said that the Ephesus fight *was* postponed until after Ramadan. Selçuk seemed to be the best place to find out about other, smaller village festivals. So I took the night bus to Selçuk down near the Aegean coast. The twelve-hour journey was livened up considerably by Angie and Ebrahim: she a buxom blonde from Middlesbrough; he a shy Turkish man who spent most of the time with his nose down her cleavage. He was a waiter, she a tourist, and they had met in his restaurant in the resort town of Didim, and, after a few more visits to Turkey, the Northern lass was off to meet his family in the village.

'If they expect me to wear a headscarf they've got to be kidding . . . I mean, enough's enough. I'll have kids, bring them grand-children and that, but I'm not bloody working in the fields with a scarf on my head like all the women do in that village. The Turks are all right really – except those lads in Sultanahmet. All they want to do is get into your pants and get you into their carpet shop.' She had a point there. 'Ooh, they'd take your *eyes* if they could. And the hotels . . . they wouldn't let us share a room 'cos he's a Turk. I told them we were getting married but they don't like it. We had to take a really expensive hotel where they're not as fussy.'

Angie's low-cut shirt revealed a generous amount of flesh and provoked craning necks and bulging eyes from most men on the bus. 'And the men in this country . . . my God you'd think they'd never seen blonde hair before . . . and my God, their eyes are just all over me, you know, on me boobs . . .'

There was an advantage to sitting with Angie. The steward on the bus (usually spotty young men wearing yellow nylon waistcoats and bow-ties, who serve free coffee and small packets of fruit cake) kept returning to refill our coffee cups assiduously and splash us from a bottle of lemon cologne. Angie's bag contained every type of chocolate imaginable, bought in England for her hosts. 'I bought them this,' she said, producing a box of Ferrero Rocher chocolates the size of a small football field. 'And I checked – there's no pork fat in them.'

Twelve hours later and after little sleep, I left the lovebirds and the porkless Ferrero and fell off the bus in an early-morning Selçuk. The sun had barely risen and the town was cold and sleepy. Immediately after getting a room, I tracked down one of the regional organizers, Mahmoud, who owned a shop in the bazaar selling bedding and linens, and he made a couple of calls. He confirmed that the following Sunday there was a festival in the small village of Ezine, near Çanakkale.

At hearing the news I nearly kissed him. The Ephesus festival was indeed postponed until after Ramadan, but he assured me that many smaller village festivals would provide adequate enter-tainment until then.

Lee-shan boarded our bus when we were halfway to Çanakkale, a petite Chinese-Australian woman, wearing make-up and high heels, tight leggings and glamorous sunglasses. She was on her way, like most Antipodeans, to the site of the battle of Gallipoli, just outside the port town of Çanakkale. There was little else to see there, and I must have been the only foreigner to visit the area and *not* see Gallipoli.

We went to a hostel which, because of its inclusion in the *Lonely Planet* guidebook, does little else to earn a good reputation. It offered exactly the same tailor-made package as every other hostel in town: bed, breakfast, guided tour of the battle sites, and a screening of the film *Gallipoli* in the TV room. I declined the tour, breakfast and the film, which provoked a minor stir. 'No one,' said the proprietor, Mr Osman, icily, 'comes to Çanakkale without going to Gallipoli.' 'But have you ever had a guest coming just for camel wrestling, Mr Osman?' He didn't have an answer to that.

In spite of an evening sampling the local night life with Lee-shan, which lasted until 3 am, I still managed to arrive outrageously early for the camel wrestling, the only people present being the organizers and a few police loafing casually around. Cars and trucks started to arrive in a slow trickle and people set up stalls, barbecues and drinks, but there was no evidence of alcohol or camels.

At eleven o'clock, I could hear approaching drummers and a *zurna*, a traditional instrument also found in the Middle East and Indian subcontinent, giving a reedy sound similar to a clarinet. The musicians stood on a truck, driving around the streets to advertise the event. Soon afterwards, the camels began to arrive, with their owners, helpers and supporters, most from surrounding villages. Towards midday, buses came loaded with fans who filled up the wooden spectator stand, some pressed up against the perimeter fence, or perching on top of trucks for a view.

Each village had its own prize camel, and each camel its own fan club, with many villagers travelling throughout the region to support it. These fighting camels were a special cross-breed, called Tülü. The famous ones were household names, and often as well known locally as footballers or film stars. For fighting, they carried, over their one hump, a *havut*, a straw-stuffed wooden frame decorated with coloured rugs and with their names embroidered on the back. Bells hung off their necks and their backs, glittery material was draped along their bodies to adorn them, and each had a large brass bell under its chin which made a solid clang as they walked. Beautifully decorated as they were, they still looked bad-tempered; as they snorted and spat, it was difficult to imagine these clumsy, lumbering things having grace and poise in the arena.

Before the first fight began, the barbecues were already sizzling and the stalls set up – with one product doing a roaring trade: camel-meat sausages. It seemed the height of tactlessness to sell a dead animal when the live ones were the object of such rapt attention. What if a wrestler could smell his dead grandmother on the barbecue? Could a camel smell his own relation? Did he care?

Another important ingredient of the festive atmosphere is the music, provided by groups of musicians playing drum and zurna. They play to spectators, but also, for a small fee, to each camel before he fights, to bring him luck.

Prior to the start, there was an important requirement. In order for the two male camels to work up a sufficient frenzy to fight, it was necessary to give them something to fight for. So a spirited young she-camel was paraded around the arena. This was the mating season – the main reason why the wrestling takes part in winter, another being that they eat less during the colder months and therefore lose weight and are quicker to anger – and even though the Tülü camel can't reproduce, hormones are hormones and the theory goes that, on seeing a female, they get so aggressive towards other males, that a great fight will result.

For the first pair, this theory didn't quite work out. There was lots of drool but not much action, and they were more interested in sniffing each other's bottoms than engaging in anything more aggressive. This went on for a while much to the amusement of the spectators, and the frustration of their owners. But suddenly, there was a sudden burst of action. With a huge grunt, they lunged at each other and, to everyone's delight, locked in embrace. Each used shoulders and necks to shove and push, then heaved away with his front legs to try to overbalance the other, their owners meanwhile shouting instructions to them.

'The relationship between a camel and his owner is very special, very close. A bit like a brother,' one owner told me. But surely even brotherly affection must draw the line at drool. Camels produce saliva not just in a spray of spittle, but in great, gluey masses that emerge from the mouth in long strands and end up everywhere. An obvious sign of an experienced deveci – camel trainer – is a black leather jacket with white sticky mess dribbling down the front. In fact, when a gloop lands on his head, he makes no move to wipe it off. In these circles, perhaps it's the mark of a real man.

These festivals, organized by a local committee, all follow a similar formula. Each participating camel is paired with one similar in size, weight and championship record and another crucial aspect, one I would never have guessed at: just like humans, a camel is right-footed, left-footed and occasionally ambidextrous. So, it's necessary to pair up like with like – the wrong pairing would be like a left-footed person trying to dance the tango with a right-footed one – as you can't really teach a camel to use the other leg.

The festivals all begin with the smallest camels, the animals getting progressively bigger with each fight, and the day ending with the real heavyweights. The larger animals are also the most famous and by the time they're on, the crowd is at its biggest and most excitable. (And,unless it's Ramadan, at its most drunk.) The rules are quite straightforward: a win is achieved by a camel either chasing his opponent away or causing him to overbalance. And, as in human wrestling, a fall can be caused by force or a simple trick. Although it sounds as though pitting against each other two animals weighing several hundred kilos each would end in injury, the sport is not dangerous at all. In fact, the Turks consider this a humanitarian sport. They have great respect for the camel, and wouldn't allow anything which would cause it harm. They take precautions to prevent injury to the beast – there are fourteen rope-bearers (*urganci*) present who will restrain excessively mettlesome camels, or drag the animals apart if it seems necessary; and the camels are muzzled to check any over-enthusiastic teeth. And, as with any sport anywhere in the world, the referees and board of judges are all experienced.

Because the camel is highly respected, gambling on the outcome of the fight is seen as dishonouring the animal – which is unusual, considering that most animal fights (dog- or cockfighting, for instance) take place *only* for betting. I thought of the local cricket match in Karachi just a few days before, where the excitement was generated not by the sport but by the betting. Here, it was the opposite.

The first camels were still heaving and pushing at each other when one, perhaps its concentration disturbed, suddenly bolted. The other chased it, but according to the rules the bout was already won and the rope-bearers caught the two safely and led them out to wild cheering and whistling.

The winner was paraded around the arena by a grinning owner, and shortly afterwards the next pair were led into the vicinity of the frisky female.

This fight got off to a more promising start, and the two beasts were aggressive from the outset. They collided head-on, and, grunting and snorting, pushed with their front legs to try to knock each other over. It was stalemate for several minutes, while they also gave sideways shoves with their necks, which made all the little brass bells clang frantically.

Neither camel looked like faltering, until one of them stuck his head between his opponent's front legs and tried to bite his underbelly, which seemed to me a very cheeky action – if any human wrestler had his belly nibbled, I thought to myself, it would be an almighty distraction. It had the desired effect and as the nibbler advanced his head further towards his opponent's back legs (and heaven knows *what* his intentions were), he used some nifty footwork to push the other's front left leg, sending him staggering sideways. Victory clearly in his sights, he gave a hearty shove with his shoulder which threw the other camel down onto his front knees.

Victory achieved, the rope-bearers rushed to separate the camels, yanked them up and led them out to the excited concluding comments over the loudspeaker. After a short break, the next pair entered and were announced, and so the afternoon progressed.

When each bout ended, a small ceremony was enacted in which a rug was presented to the winner and a blanket to the loser. This feature is one of camel wrestling's greatest appeals, for it rounds off a game that fulfils all the purest sporting principles: a true battle of strength with no financial incentive; participation for pleasure and for honour; financial sacrifice by the owner; no media hype; sheer enjoyment and support from the spectators; and both participants receiving a similar prize. This is a rare example of the true Olympian spirit. When it was time for the final prize to be given to the biggest camel, the heavyweight, it wasn't an excuse for pomped-up formalities, but just the end of another festival and the sign for everyone to go home.

The next day, after Lee-shan – who had created a major stir when she turned up at the camel wrestling with her waist-length black hair, scarlet lipstick, tight red leggings, and chain-smoking

– had gone off to Gallipoli with the tour, I tried to discover the brains behind the local camel-organizing committee. I found Çanakkale small enough to wander around in search of the right people, and I was assisted by a local tour guide, Bülent, on his day off.

Our search took us to a small teahouse in an old corner building near the market. The owner was drinking beer with a friend, safe in the knowledge that as it was Ramadan, few people would be walking through their doors. They invited us in, offered us beer and crisps, and were delighted to hear of my 'mission'.

Tipsily enthusiastic, the boss told us of his love of camel wrestling. His grandfather and father had been trainers, he said, and while he couldn't afford to own a camel, he was a member of the organizing committee. 'I do it for a hobby, not for any money involved. Some people are football fanatics; I am a camel fanatic.' He waved his arm towards the wall in demonstration. Usually posters of football teams adorn the walls in teahouses and restaurants. Here, it was large photos of camels and posters advertising forthcoming festivals.

Even Mehmet's surname, Deveci, was advertisement for his devotion, as it translates literally as 'camel man'. 'In the 1920s Attaturk encouraged everyone to give themselves a family name' – before that it was practically unknown to have one – 'so people usually chose their trade, or something connected with their family. My grandfather trained camels so he wanted to be called "Deveci".'

I asked them where and when they thought camel wrestling originated, which prompted a good-natured but inconclusive argument between them, spitting showers of beer and crisps everywhere.

Camel wrestling, I learned, may be a hobby, but it doesn't come cheap. A camel costs around £6000 or more to buy, food and maintenance costs at least £2000 a year, while hiring a man to look after him comes to another £2000 or so a year. As no money may be made from the competitions, this means that most owners have a decent income, perhaps from farming or business.

Many buy their camels in Iran, Mehmet Deveci said, as they are cheaper there. The best age is around four or five years old when the camel starts to grow his azu – 'big teeth' – which signifies he is ready to fight. It takes around two years to train a camel and often a young one is taught by, or can follow the behaviour of an older one. He talked on about camel wrestling, cracking open more beer, until eventually we took our leave.

I returned to Selçuk the next morning. There, one cold and dull night, Serkan, who worked in the hotel, invited me to a cockfight with his uncle, a regular visitor to fights in the area. The three of us drove to Söke, about fifty kilometres away, to track it down: the venue had already been changed three times, so there were many others driving around on a wild-goose chase. Although cockfighting is officially legal, its venue must have a licence, and, rather than going through the rigmarole of organizing the necessary paperwork from the police, many find it easier to hold the fight without the knowledge of the police.

The fight had begun when we eventually found the venue. This was my first time, and I wasn't sure what to expect, but I wondered if it would be as bloody as the notorious fights in South-East Asia. The small warehouse had wooden seating in terraces which looked down onto the small, 12-by-6-foot sawdust-covered arena. The spectators were all quite well-dressed, with the obligatory cigarette dangling out of the corner of each mouth. Overhead fluorescent strip-lights illuminated the room.

As soon as I sat, in the front row, an old man carrying a tray came and handed me a glass of tea, sent by a smartly dressed middle-aged man in black leather jacket and hat sitting opposite, which instantly put me at ease. Shouted numbers flew around as people placed their bets without, it seemed on first impression, any order or system. Two bookies, who clearly knew everyone in the room, sat at a small wooden table recording each punter's bid in a large ledger, as they were made.

As the fight was reaching its crescendo, which was more flapping around than fighting – perhaps, like camels, they needed warming-up before they got aggressive – the birds flapped, rose in the air together with a flurry of claws and a peck, then fell to the ground again. The two owners stood and watched the fight with a look of concern, each rather like a parent with a young child. Every few minutes one took his bird in his hands, checked under the wings, the legs and the claws, and then took a mouthful of water and blew a spray over the bird to wash it and smooth over any cuts. Obviously they didn't follow the practice of attaching razor blades or metal claws to the birds' legs; it was altogether much less bloodthirsty than I had imagined.

If blood appeared on a bird's head, usually from being pecked, the owner revived it, washing the blood away and putting his mouth over the wound to suck the blood off. I suppose that signified genuine affection for the creatures. Certainly, the owners and trainers of fighting cocks assured me of their love for their birds, and how they would hate to see any serious harm done.

The feathers continued to flutter but more slowly as time went on and the birds grew more tired and battered. In the final few minutes, the punters' shouts getting louder, the birds slowed down to such an extent that they could barely peck and claw. Their owners frantically tried to extract the last ounce of energy, but one cock eventually gave out and put up no fight at all when pummelled by the other's beak, and the fight was over.

The few minutes after the fight was dominated by financial affairs: the bookies paying out fistfuls of lira to the winners. More tea was drunk and cigarettes lit. A few cocks were crowing inside their cages at the side of the room. Everyone prepared for the next fight which, according to Serkan's uncle, promised to be a real heavyweight humdinger.

The birds were released into the arena and everyone settled back with a low buzz of conversation, when a commotion at the door caused the room to fall silent, disturbed only by the occasional crowing. Three large policemen entered and, judging by their expressions, they weren't there to place a bet. Within four seconds, everyone was up and scrabbling towards the exit as if the place was on fire. The police demanded to see everyone's ID, but no one took any notice. If a licence for the venue hasn't been obtained from the local police – or, possibly, a large bribe has not been paid – they can raid any venue. I wondered if we would all be arrested but it ended in an anticlimax when we were all dismissed, and people dispersed into the night. Cars revved off to circle around, meeting up again as rumours flew thick and fast about another fight in the next town.

The following Sunday I returned to Çanakkale and from there went to the village of Özbek for the next camel wrestling. It was a tiny old village, consisting only of fields and small farmhouses. The morning was freezing, and everyone gathered inside the warm teahouse by a blazing fire. There we waited for the camels to arrive, and at last we heard the slow chime of the heavy bell around each camel's neck signalling their arrival. In a procession they came along the tiny street and into the small field, followed by the villagers and musicians. The festival was under way.

The venue and crowd were much smaller than at Ezine, and the atmosphere more intimate – the spectators were nearly all local people. At 10 am, with rain-heavy clouds overhead and a biting wind, the day began, the crowd standing on the football terrace or perched on trucks and trailers. Some had small boys on their shoulders and most wore the *poşu*, the brown and white headscarf which every deveci wears.

I was surprised at how many women there were, especially as the area appeared to be very traditional. Someone explained to me that they were encouraged to come because the men weren't drinking. The women, some quite old, were muffled up well against the cold and sitting separately from the men, in their own trucks and trailers. They weren't only keen and vociferous, but also knowledgeable: one of the committee members told me they were shouting encouragement to the camels, using technical jargon that only true camel fans would know.

The circular fighting area was marked only with flimsy barriers which would hardly have contained a handful of kittens, let alone a couple of rampaging beasts. Several times the fight moved close to the edge, the fence was trampled down and the camels burst into the crowd, paying scant attention to people or vehicles. It looked dangerous but the intrusion was greeted with no more than loud laughter and rapid scattering. Alternatively they would shoo away a fast-approaching camel with a simple flapping up and down of the arms.

Mahmoud from Selçuk was there and invited me to sit in the officials' trailer from where we watched his friend's camel; there was little action, however, which Mahmoud said was because 'These two camels once belonged to the same owner, until he sold the younger one to a friend. Even now, these two hate to fight because they used to live together.'

Towards the end of the day, as the biting cold was getting more severe, a camel owner came over and said, 'Didn't I see you at Ezine?' – the camel-wrestling world's equivalent of 'Didn't we meet at so-and-so's dinner party?' and it gave me a feeling of acceptance. The next step up the social ladder would be an invitation to a camel party, the dinner held for owners and officials the night before each festival.

The following week, I travelled to Kaş in order to attend a festival at Demre, a small town on the south coast between Kaş and Antalya, and supposedly the birthplace of Saint Nicholas, aka

Santa Claus. From Kaş I took the bus along the winding coastal coast to Demre and went straight to the Belediye, the organizers. Musa, who worked in the water department, drove me out to visit the camels who were staying in warehouses normally hosting aubergines and tomatoes. The animals had just eaten and most were sleeping and docile.

'The camels will be coming to our office later,' said Musa. The image of a hundred camels standing in the Mayor's office was lovely, but he meant the parade would begin outside the office. Back in the main square, people were beginning to gather for the parade. Traditionally, the parade of camels was a way of advertising the forthcoming festival – more important in pre-television days – where a line of camels accompanied by the local town-crier and musicians, was sufficient to rouse the whole village's attention. Heads thrown back, the fully-decorated camels were their own advertisement.

At 1 pm the camel parade entered the square, attracting connoisseurs and newcomers alike, including a large number of small boys who played a version of 'chicken', the challenge 'how far can you go up to a camel without flinching?', and competition was hearty. When a camel grunted, snorted, or made any nasal noise which produced drool, the boys screamed with laughter and ran away. Most of the older men sat around the square drinking tea, nodding appreciatively.

Early the next morning, the camels came from all directions to the arena, some by truck, most led along the main road in a solemn, plodding procession. The strong, slow, rhythmical chime of the bell told everyone of their arrival. Passing cars and buses tooted in appreciation, and the owners waved back in acknowledgement. The arena was the local football ground, with the benefit of stone terraces around it to hold everyone. There were many women there, sitting in a separate area.

This festival was quite a large-scale affair, and many stalls selling clothes and food set up early. It reminded me of India, where any gathering of people (whether religious pilgrimage, festival, or cricket match) would prompt local entrepreneurs to set up shop selling postcards of movie stars, plastic jewellery and nylon trousers. Here the selection was more eclectic: camel salami, cassettes of Arabesque music, black şapka – the eight-cornered flat cap favoured by camel trainers – poşu scarves, and football scarves.

I got talking to Izzet, a teacher who had spent several years working in Switzerland and had recently returned to teach in a local school. 'Actually I don't really like camel wrestling that much. It's a bit of a silly sport but I just came to support my local village, as my friends have brought their camels.' He took me over to meet them, where they were petting and grooming their animals. They greeted me warmly, telling me of their chances that afternoon. They even agreed to let me go with them to the next fight, at Ortaklar, travelling with the camels later that afternoon.

Then I received the much-awaited offer. 'We're going to the festival in Yenipazar next Sunday. Do you want to come to our party the night before?' I accepted, excited at receiving the invitation which surely indicated my acceptance into the glorious world of camels.

In a glow of self-importance, I watched the now familiar events. With Izzet's help I was able to talk to spectators, and ask them what they liked about camels and why they were so important. While everyone acknowledged that football dominates Turkey's sporting culture and you're never far away from a Galatasaray, Fenerbahçe or Beşiktaş hat, everyone was confident that the tradition of camel wrestling would never die.

'It's the way we remember our ancestors,' said one man. 'This is how they used to live, when they travelled and worked with camels, and this sport is our way of respecting history. For that reason, it will never die.' Women were equally keen. 'I come here every year,' said a grandmother with her large family of several generations. 'It's a day out, we bring food, we eat, we talk, we like camels. We only support the ones from Demre, of course.'

I was delighted to be introduced to an important character in these events: the man who made the havut, the large wooden frame which the camels wear on their hump throughout the winter and for the fight. There are very few left who make them, and they fear the craft of making them could well be under threat.

We were halfway through the fights when the day abruptly ended with a violently sudden hailstorm. People, camels and vehicles collided as the entire field dashed for cover. It was bitterly cold, and neither humans nor animals coped well with the conditions. Within minutes, the field was waterlogged and mud was everywhere. Officials packed up their equipment and the commentators rolled up electric cables and dismantled tables. Camels were bundled into trucks and everyone tried to leave at the same time. In the confusion, I couldn't find the truck going to Ortaklar, so I settled for diving into a minibus going back to

Demre. At least I had managed to secure the all-important invitation for the party the following weekend.

From Demre I returned to Kaş, and there caught an overnight bus back to Selçuk; from there a short bus ride to Ortaklar took me to the next festival.

I was watching the first fights in the large arena when I met Talat, a carpet dealer. I told him of my desire to travel with a camel entourage back to their village, and he absorbed this information as if it was perfectly normal. He went off to speak to a friend, and returned having arranged for me to travel that afternoon with Ibrahim and his two camels back to Yenipazar, a couple of hours' drive away.

An hour after Ercihan and Hakan had been furiously fighting for their women, they were led, scarves over their heads and knotted neatly under the chin, and protesting furiously, onto the back of a lorry where they had their front and back legs tied so they could not stand up; then they were muzzled and chained to the lorry.

With two camels, a donkey (who always accompanied them to bring luck), three helpers and myself, it was cramped in the truck and I was glad we weren't travelling overnight. It was cold and I soon found that the best way to keep warm was to snuggle up to a camel. As they were tied up and kept still, I could relax and appreciate the warmth of a large, furry camel back. The two young assistants thought I was mad. 'Why don't you travel in the front of the lorry where it's warmer?' they asked. My Turkish wasn't sufficient to explain that, for me, to understand the many aspects of camel wrestling, it was necessary to 'live camel' as much as possible.

As we entered Yenipazar, people recognized the truck and came out onto the streets to welcome them back, eager to hear how they'd got on. Hakan was a local superstar and when we arrived he was led by one of the assistants off the lorry and into the village; on hearing his bell people emerged to greet him and follow him along the road. It was a real hero's welcome.

The procession made its way to Ibrahim's teahouse, where Hakan was tethered outside to be fussed over by his admirers, while, inside, everybody discussed, dissected and replayed crucial scenes over endless cups.

Off-season, Selçuk, a town which revolves around tourism, was quiet, life centring on football with occasional interludes for camel wrestling. Every Friday, Saturday and Sunday night all the teahouses and bars would be packed with het-up and ferociously partisan football fans, gathered round the television sets.

However far from Istanbul, nearly everyone in the country supports only one of the three big Istanbul clubs. If I asked them: 'Why do you support Galatasaray when you were born in Izmir?' they would look astonished at such a stupid question and reply, 'Well, because they were champions last year.' If that logic followed in England, I said, people would change allegiance from year to year depending on who was currently best. Local loyalty holds no importance to Turkish football fans.

One evening during Bayram, a three-day festival marking the end of Ramadan, I bumped into four members of the camel crew (the local organizing committee), who invited me along to a camel party in Bayindir that night. My acceptance into the real drinking world of camel trainers was now but a raki glass away, and I didn't need to be asked twice.

An hour later, all crammed into a tiny car, we arrived at the venue. Dinner had already begun, and a layer of smoke from hundreds of cigarettes lay like a blanket a few feet above the ground. Long tables were laid out in lines in the huge hall, covered with white tablecloths and cluttered with plates and glasses, from which people were eating and drinking.

The organizers ushered us in and made room for us. A glass of raki was poured for me, plates of food appeared; there were *mezze*, or starters, small dollops of dips and salads, masses of cheese and bread and big dishes of chicken and rice. Opposite me were a camel owner's two assistants; young men, about eighteen years old, with beautiful eyes and shy smiles, who whispered in excited tones about the possibility of '*natashas*' (Russian prostitutes) making an appearance later. Next to them were a group of older men who looked like they'd been through a few parties, rough whiskered faces topped with the black eight-cornered şapka.

This was the first time a woman had been present at this type of function, but even with the abundance of alcohol – now that Ramadan was over – everyone was extremely well-behaved. With aid of raki, I was able to overcome language, cultural and camel barriers, fluttering around the tables like the best social butterfly, repeatedly dragged down to sit with groups of old men and drink with them. Most had seen me around at some festival or other, and appreciated that I knew one end of a camel from another.

Entertainment was laid on to follow the meal – first a singer, whose heart and voice were plainly not in it, and whose dress, slit to the thigh, caused shy embarrassment among the men rather than the leers one might have expected. To follow her were two dancers, whom I was taken to meet before their act. They were unattractive women, in heavy make-up and glittery costumes and, most unusual in Turkish women, they were drinking heavily – whisky by the half-pint – which explained to me how women could dance that sexy, sensual bellydance to a roomful of eyes as big as saucers.

To my disappointment, however, camel politics at that point reared its ugly head and my friends, who had got into a row with a rival group, beckoned me away. Still, my next camel party – the one at Yenipazar, was only eighteen hours away.

The next day I made my way to Yenipazar. I was unable to contact Izzet, the teacher I'd met in Demre who had secured me the invitation to this party, but I did meet Talat, who took me to the teahouse-cum-bar where all the camel people had gathered. There we spent a hugely enjoyable hour before setting off for the room over the Belediye building where the party was being held. Its layout of long tables was identical to the previous night's party, and the meal when it came was the same too. Many of the windows were broken and the room was sub-zero. The stage was set up with speakers and microphones, and a band started a sound-check with cheap synthesizers and drum machines. Guests began to trickle in while waiters dashed round in last-minute panic.

Talat and I sat down at the table reserved for important officials. One of these was Ali, commentator for the following day's fight and also MC for the evening. He was a hard-core deveci, aged around sixty with grey hair and bright, shining eyes. During the dinner he kept leaping up on stage, to sing folk songs with the band or recite verses and fables, eloquently and dramatically capturing the romanticism of the whole sport.

When not on stage, he bounded between tables, having his arm pumped by appreciative friends and glasses offered to him. 'This is my life!' he said as we drank raki together. He wasn't, as I had expected, a camel owner, but was a lifelong lover of the camel-wrestling culture. I asked him what made it so special for him.

'It's in our blood; it's our life, our tradition and culture – this is living history . . .' which I could understand clearly. Its roots were deeply set in the past generations of nomadic Turks who used camels for transportation; yet reinforced in the present day by the revelry around us. The sport had a life of its own, not just limited to the action in the arena between two camels, but a spirit which thrived in music, dance, food, drink and camaraderie.

'There are people who only meet at this festival, giving them an opportunity of meeting up as old friends. Camels bring people together, you know.'

At my table were some employees of the local Belediye. The handsome man on my left looked drunkenly, adoringly, into my eyes and offered to drive me back to my hotel, but his difficulty in standing up made me doubt his ability to see straight, let alone have full control of his car. I politely refused his offer which made him angry. 'I am sober enough!' he shouted, banging his fist on the table and sending a plate crashing to the floor and a glass of raki over me. 'Even after drinking two bottles, I'm OK to drive.' 'In my country, you'd be in prison for driving after so much drink,' I replied. 'It's OK,' he grinned, 'I know all the police officers in this town.' I didn't doubt his ability to bribe a police officer, and dropped the subject. Talat whispered to me that he'd see I got home safely. Yet again, it was an early departure, just enough to see some of the dancers' routine and know that I really wasn't missing much.

The following day I made my way to the next camel wrestling. Lorries were parked with chairs set up in the back for a good view, while small groups of people were setting up tables and chairs behind the perimeter fencing and preparing food – something taken very seriously in Turkey.

The first fight was the signal for the barbecues to be lit. Fresh bread was heated, salads chopped and burgers mixed, kebabs skewered and onions peeled – all done by the men. Tea was brewed on wooden stoves and bottles opened. Equal attention was paid to the food as to the fights, but every camel was cheered – especially Ibrahim's Hakan, a star on his home ground. The music grew louder, the players flocking round the drunkest spectators, knowing they were most profitable.

Ali was in great form, on the stage where microphones and loudspeakers broadcast his commentary so it boomed around the field. The commentator's role is not only to inform spectators about each camel – its owner, weight, past achievements and form – but also to create the atmosphere. Ali was perfect for this role and continued from where he left off the previous night, reciting folk tales which glorified the event.

When the last fight was over, those who could still stand after all the overindulgence in food and, especially, raki, ended up at the obvious venue. Ibrahim's teahouse was now packed with supporters particularly as Hakan had won his fight. Ibrahim, looking extremely serious, demonstrated the fight of his prize camel, emphasizing in slow motion that superb left-shoulder shove which had sent the opponent tumbling. It had been a profitable day, the musicians told me as we hitched back to Selçuk, crammed into a minibus with drums and zurnas.

3

The Cup Final

Selçuk was slowly preparing for the great fight: the camel Cup Final, the biggest camel-wrestling event in the country and the most prestigious (even though not the last of the season as such festivals continue to the end of March). The local Belediye and the Tourism Department combined efforts to put on a high-profile affair. Some were cynical about the event, saying it was too big and ruined the authentic atmosphere and was put on only for self-publicity. Locals complained that tourism had hit a slump, and everyone was hoping that the festival would bring many visitors for the weekend.

The nucleus of activity was the Selçuk Kültür ve tourizm Vafki (or the camel office, as it is commonly known), a small department which also organizes folk-dance festivals and demonstrations. The office doubled as a place where friends dropped round for tea and watched and analysed previous fights on video. Die-hard fans did so with the passion and dedication of any sports follower, finger on the remote control to pause and replay a crucial moment of action, praising the owner for his camel's great move.

To the outsider, camel wrestling can appear like another folk festival and opportunity to get drunk, but the expertise and technical knowledge make you realize it requires immense skill and knowledge. As we watched the previous year's final on video, one member of the committee told me about the trainer's input during the fight. 'The camels can understand a few words through training, and so the trainer can call out instructions, like *otur* (sit), *haydi olum* (come on), *yuru* (walk). A bit like training a dog. The camel acts on its instincts and is helped along by instructions.'

The committee puts many voluntary hours of preparation into the camel event of the year. Every camel owner wants to participate but the selection procedures have to be strict. 'We have to check out every camel who applies to enter. We can only pick around ninety, so we have to go for the most successful and the most popular. We want a camel to participate that's going to attract a few hundred spectators.' There is no prize money, but every participant, win or lose, gets around £30, which covers little more than expenses.

In spite of growing interest in football and basketball, and the increasing ownership of cable TV, camel wrestling has become more popular in recent years. 'Ten years ago,' said one deveci from Antalya, 'there were around a hundred fighting camels in Turkey. Now, there are over six hundred. It means that there are more festivals, and better attended. Before, they were only in small villages and now they are more popular in bigger places.' The media has also played its role in popularizing this national culture.

Selçuk's is the most famous and prestigious, mainly because its venue is the antique stadium of Ephesus, and people come from all over the country to attend. In previous years the hotels and pensions were fully booked, and shops and restaurants did a thriving trade. This year, it was a little more subdued.

The night before the fight I went for a quiet dinner with some of the camel crew. The evening was transformed when the guests at the next table, buoyed up by another music group, got up to dance. Encouraged by a couple of bottles of raki, they threw plates on the floor, which was greeted with whoops of joy from other diners and anguished looks from the staff. The tempo grew faster, the dancing wilder, the pile of broken crockery higher. The host of the boisterous group, who it seemed owned a restaurant on the outskirts of town, then invited us to a party there that night.

We grabbed a taxi in the pouring rain. It was a small gathering, appearing all the more so as we were sitting in a cavernous, empty restaurant, around just one table. The only other woman was Nena, a Russian woman who didn't particularly appreciate my inquisitive friendliness. ('Natasha,' explained my friend in a whisper – in other words, don't ask too many questions.)

An argument soon broke out between the host and his friend. The host delved in his pocket for his gun and brandished it around; silence fell and the music stopped, though probably because the musicians wanted to listen in. The two men's voices rose to a furious level, then calmed down, the quarrel apparently settled. Then suddenly the gun went off, giving me, at least, a terrible fright. To my relief, though, the gunman was shooting into the air in a good-natured way – a kind of party trick that is customary here especially at weddings, a macho display of celebration.

There's nothing like a pistol-shot to unsettle your guests, so when another argument broke out, this time between Nena and her client, it was the signal for us to make an unsteady exit.

The hotel I had been staying at was undergoing repairs, and I had moved to another; however, my late-night returns to this hotel had inspired fury and hatred from the young hotel manager, who was convinced that I was the whore of Babylon. He especially resented me speaking to his Australian girlfriend, presuming I would lead her astray. The atmosphere eventually sank to an all-time low, and such was the very visible hatred demonstrated to me by the staff that I felt it was best to get out. The decision was received very quietly, though the dizzy Aussie warned me that 'Jimmy hates you and says he's going to damage you. He thinks you're dangerous.' One doesn't take words like that lightly, even though I thought it unlikely that he would kill me in my bed. However, better to scoot to some anonymous alternative.

I had arranged to meet Dizzy Aussie that night in the old teahouse in the main square, the kind frequented by old men playing dominoes and with an atmosphere calm enough to dissipate the most serious of death threats. She had been forbidden to see me, so we had to meet on neutral ground. But after I'd waited some time it became clear she wasn't going to show up, and, a little concerned (she was also getting frightened of her man's tempers and threats of violence), I crept round to the hotel.

She was standing on the second-floor balcony, watching for me. 'Don't come back here,' she whispered frantically, in tears. 'Jimmy says he's going to find you and kill you.' The scene befitted a gangster movie. 'I don't know why he hates you, but he's furious and says he's going to get a gun. I'm scared what he'll do to me if he knows I've talked to you.'

Scared of him though she was, Dizzy Aussie wouldn't leave. There was little more I could do than return to the teahouse and spend a surprisingly relaxed evening watching football on the TV, putting death threats from local boys down as one of those pesky things one has to deal with occasionally. However, I did look over my shoulder several times as I returned to my new hotel and, there, every noise in the corridor got my imagination going.

The sunlight of the next morning brought a feeling a calmness. By 1 pm, the main square was filled with locals and visitors, waiting for the parade to begin. As it was Saturday, the streets were busy with shoppers in the bazaar, while most Selçuk people were there for the event of the year. Some older men, sitting in bars most of the morning, were already drunk and there was a carnival atmosphere, with the shoe-shiners and poşu- and şapka-sellers doing good business. There was a large collection of musicians, in their predictable trios.

Before long came the slow, deep drone of the first bell as the camels started to arrive from their accommodation about a kilometre away. They came thick and fast, and the parade began: in a long line the camels went along the main streets, buses and cars tooting in appreciation. Children, old men and women, gathered along the pavements or just waved from their windows, while others followed the slow procession along the main street, circling the town, through the market, before returning to the square. The parade over, the camels ambled back to the huge warehouses where they were being kept. The floors were laid with straw, and the devecis busied themselves feeding and soothing their beasts. An old, bald toothless deveci I had met in Yenipazar took me to see Rambo, strongly fancied for his fight the next day.

With great emotion, he spoke of the unique trusting love which bonds the camel and master. He demonstrated this by turning towards Rambo's significantly larger, hairier face and allowing him to kiss his lips in a long, slobbering smooch. There was drool everywhere. It looked revolting, but no one could doubt the old man's dedication. After creating such harmony between man and beast, though, he shattered it by showing me his left ear. Part of the lobe had been bitten off, the result of affection going perhaps just a bit far.

The party that night followed much the same pattern as the others I'd attended, down to the menu – obviously one didn't come to such parties for a culinary surprise – but on this occasion, apart from the folk dancing which some of my friends performed after the dinner, there was a collection of money from the guests; an appeal which I presumed went towards the costs of the festival. A long speech from the Mayor, who presented small plaques to everyone, completed the formalities.

The evening continued predictably with the usual singer, belly-dancer and good-natured drunkenness, the only difference being that the folk-dancers and I got into trouble with the police for making too much noise at the restaurant to which we had proceeded after the party.

Eight o'clock the next morning found me walking along the streets, empty of traffic, in the wake of three large lumbering camels making their way to the ancient amphitheatre of Ephesus. The beauty of the walk, the winter sun peering through branches of leafless trees lining the street, the silence broken only by the chimes of the bell, was for me tinged with sadness as this would be my last parade with the camels.

The walk to Ephesus took nearly an hour, and by the time I arrived it was already filling up. Every spot on the steep, trackless, grassy hill surrounding the arena offered a perfect view. I watched groups of people setting up their places, while the area outside the arena, reserved for restaurants, was being laid out with huge tables and spits. Already kebabs were being grilled and as usual camel sausages were selling well. Lines of smoke caught in the sunlight as they rose from the many barbecues. Topping the whole scene was a ring of armed soldiers standing on the surrounding hill tops, guns resting against their shoulders.

As the smell of roasted meat filled the air, the fighting began with the usual pomp, and with plenty of cheering and partisan support: camels had come from all over the country, as had the spectators. My friends on the camel committee looked the part, transformed into their best *cisme*, poşu and şapka, all worn with attitude.

Everything was much the same as at previous venues I'd been to, but bigger, better organized with more of everything – more businesslike restaurants, more professional clothes stalls, more photographers and TV cameras (the national media usually carried a small feature on this festival), more protocol, with the extrovert Mayor hosting the VIPs in a special covered tent, and definitely a better perimeter fence. But, as with any large-scale event, the intimacy and cosiness I had experienced in Yenipazar and Özbek was missing – it was like being accustomed to your local third-division football team and going to a Premier League match.

Even the camels seemed to appreciate the splendour of the

ancient, almost sacred venue. 'The camels know, and feel the history of the place,' one deveci told me. 'It makes them fight better. They have an intuition that it's the most important camel-wrestling venue in the world.' Whether camels have such intuition is arguable, but they were definitely encouraged by the huge support. One bout between two heavyweights continued for nearly half an hour, quite the best fight I'd seen between two skilful, attacking and evenly matched animals. When it ended, the whole crowd gave them a standing ovation, with wild appreciative cheers.

The grander, more formal atmosphere meant that there was surprisingly little drunkenness. On the other hand, the cooking was taken most seriously and the barbecued feasts were more sophisticated. I was offered tastes of everything as I wandered around, and even as I walked inside the arena to take photographs, hands poked through the fence proffering glasses of raki and kebabs.

Naturally most of the people I'd met at other venues were there: Talat was in the 'restaurant section' cooking kebabs on a spit and his brother was serving at the tables; Ibrahim was skulking around and fussing over Hakan; Ali though not commentating today was reciting poems and stories to a delighted group of friends, and the toothless old deveci (minus the earlobe) was now drunk as Rambo had finished his fight. He gave me a huge kiss on the cheek and presented me with a poşu, ceremoniously tying it around my head in the proper manner. It was a marvellous souvenir.

The day finished with the biggest fight of them all. Last year's champion, Çakar, from Söke took on the might of Ercihan from Tire. Çakar was an old favourite; now thirteen, he had eight years' wrestling experience behind him. His owner, from Demre, owned three highly respected camels and like most camel owners, was rich. Never once, however, did any of these men brag about their money. Owning a camel gives you status, and a prize-winning camel bestows honour on his owner, on which there can be no price tag – the more wins, the greater the honour. To own a camel already means that you have money, and the lack of prize money means that it's not the financial incentive which has increased the game's popularity.

As their immense heavyweight status demanded, Çakar and Ercihan were met with huge cheers when they entered the arena, both camels inspiring respect, admiration and partisan support in equal amounts.

This confrontation, the grand finale, was a guaranteed crowd pleaser: little time wasted on sniffing or wandering about, they almost instantly fell into a clinch which developed into a titanic struggle. It was a class act which held everyone's attention as first one, then the other, took the advantage, both displaying strength and skill in attacking moves – like the classic leg-lock to overbalance the opponent – and in self-defence.

The fight lasted nearly fifteen minutes, until Ercihan finally won through, which brought forth great cheers from the spectators on the hillside and a fresh burst of music. As always, the prize-giving ceremony was remarkably unceremonial and informal: even the big heavyweights receive similar prizes: for Ercihan there was a rug; for Çakar a blanket. The two owners and the camels received hearty pats of congratulation, and, with no further delay, people began packing up. It was the perfect end to the day. The sun was still shining as the arena emptied, busloads of spectators revved out of the field and camels were led back to the camel house, then on to trucks to be driven home, while hundreds of people filed along the street, back to the city centre. The restaurants began to pack up, the last bottles of raki were emptied, and the remaining smoke from the barbecues fizzled out. It was over for another year.

Back at the camel office, the devecis were having a final cup of tea and the usual post-mortem on the afternoon. I made a last-ditch attempt to get a lift up north in a camel truck, with a romanticized image of leaving my last festival nestling into the neck of a large (tied up) Tülü as we drove off into the sunset. To my disappointment, it remained a romanticized image. So I had to take the predictable coach service from Selçuk to Istanbul. Still, I had my imagination: it wasn't really an air-conditioned coach with the spotty young man in a yellow nylon waistcoat serving plastic cups of coffee, and the occasional night stops in late-night restaurants drinking hot soup. I was actually leaning against a couple of safely tethered Tülüs. They were covered in wool blankets and we all sang folk songs to keep us going through the night. We stopped occasionally, bumping into musicians in late-night bars, drinking raki with them and re-enacting the fights of the previous day. Call me an old romantic, but that's what I dreamed of on that bus back to Istanbul.

4

Evening Blood and a Taste of Goat

The camels' bells were still ringing in my ears on that late-night flight from Istanbul – until the plane landed at Karachi airport at 4 am. Since the late 1980s, Karachi has had troubled times, pockets of the city exploding – sometimes quite literally – with murders and gun battles between rival political factions.

The streets considered unsafe at night, I waited at the airport until sunrise. Eager immigration officers bounded up to 'practise their English', wiping out my plan to snooze for a couple of hours. The usual 'Are you married what does your husband do how much money does he earn how old are you how many children do you have' questions were quickly dealt with. Then a Mr Karim came to pour a round of green tea, served in little bowls, and announced, 'My heroes are Saddam Hussain, Idi Amin and Colonel Gaddafi. Are you married?' I felt it polite not to comment on his choice of heroes.

Later that morning, after checking in at my usual hotel, I returned to the Tourist Office where Mr Khan probably hadn't had any visitors since I had last seen him seven weeks earlier. He had no further news about the Sibi Mela – the Horse and Cattle Show – which usually falls between early February and mid-March (it was already the middle of February), but he promised to investigate. That night I received an excited call at my hotel.

'The Mela starts tomorrow!' he shouted down the line. 'They've changed the date three times already,' he wailed, 'but I think this is definite.' The Sibi Mela is an annual agricultural fair where farmers from all over the country come to buy and sell livestock. There are also many 'best of breed' awards, plus ample entertainment to keep a few thousand people amused for around a week, including competitions and demonstrations of traditional sports, which was what attracted me to this week-long event. After the Mela, I planned to travel around Baluchistan's capital and explore other parts of the state, which remain predominantly tribal.

The main lure of Baluchistan was the possibility of seeing buzkashi, the horseback game with the headless goat originating in Afghanistan and Central Asia. An earlier visit to Pakistan's North-West Frontier Province – home to millions of Afghan refugees, who had played buzkashi every Friday – had, alas, proved fruitless. Now I was hoping that the Afghani population in Baluchistan still played buzkashi, and that I might track them down.

Mr Arkhund, Sind's director of culture whom I also went back to see, promised to send a musician friend of his to meet me off the bus in Quetta, Baluchistan's capital, and arrange onward transport to Sibi which was another four hours away. So that evening, instead of lounging on plump sofas in the Sheraton hotel café watching cricket on the big-screen TV as planned, it was the less luxurious seating of the night bus to Quetta. Armed with a tiny handful of contacts – a tribal leader, a high court judge and a farmer – it was a journey into the unknown.

Being a foreign woman in Pakistan presents difficulties – you can be on the receiving end of all too many eyes that undress you, straying hands and muttered suggestions (I once had a man walking behind me down a Karachi high street, who had whispered 'Will you fax me' three times before I realized what he was saying.) But there are some advantages, too – such as when, on the bus trip that evening the ticket-seller gave me two seats, as it is improper to seat a man next to a woman he doesn't know. In Pakistan, women rarely travel without a male relative. One friend told me, 'We won't let our sister take the bus to the next village alone. She must go with a brother or cousin.' A foreign woman travelling alone in Pakistan provoked surprise, whereas people in India were more accustomed to it. On the fourteen-hour journey having a double seat compensated for the penetrating smell of glue and lack of ventilation on the bus.

The predictable in-bus entertainment – Bollywood movie soundtracks played at full volume on a sound-system requiring urgent help – little as I enjoyed it, gave me something to occupy my mind with, and the opportunity to ponder why, although India and Pakistan are supposed to hate each other, there is a great love of Indian films in Pakistan. But this was a minor distraction from the rapid temperature drop. The other passengers had blankets, woolly hats and thick socks. Each man sported a hearty beard with the effect of a facial rug, and a large cotton turban which wound several times around the head; all good preparation for the frosty night. I had no such luxury. Out of the window, in the night's growing gloom lit only by a feeble moon, I could make out the silhouettes of leafless trees standing, solitary, in the harsh environment of the desert scrub. The occasional stone village gave the only hint of habitation as there was hardly any traffic, save for a few overloaded trucks. It was easy to believe that Baluchistan, although covering over 40 per cent of the country's area, contains only 5 per cent of the total population.

At one of the highly inconvenient (for women, at least) 'toilet stops', I tried to put on a pair of leggings to help against the cold, but it proved too difficult. After several unsuccessful attempts, I gave up and drank lots of tea to thaw out, and such is the hospitality of the Baluchi people that no one would let me pay. 'You are our guest here,' was a phrase I would hear numerous times. Even in the small restaurant in Khuzdar – a village no more than a wind-blown group of huts, which feeds the Quetta-to-Karachi passengers – a large, smiling manager came over as I tucked into dhal and spinach.

'Is this your first trip to Baluchistan?' I told him yes. 'Welcome to our state. You are from England? Oh – from Bradford? My uncle is there – I have visited England many times.' (Perfect English is often spoken where you least expect it, and moreover someone has always got a relative living in Bradford. I often get questions like 'My brother is Mr Shah. Do you know him?') He wouldn't accept any money. 'No – you must not pay for this. This is your first time in Baluchistan and you are our guest. You come alone?'

During the overnight bus journey, the terrain never altered; a vast whiteness of stony sand, a moonscape with small icy ponds. We stopped for tea at sunrise under the most exquisite peach glow soaking into the sky, with wisps of steam rising from the ice.

As we pulled into the depot at 9 am and bleary-eyed passengers stumbled out, a small man with a shy smile quickly darted onto the bus and carried my bags off. He then brought me to Mr Arkhund's friend Mr Akhtar, a Baluchi musician whose singing was famous throughout Pakistan.

Arrangements were briskly made with the pomp and precision of an army manoeuvre: 'You will go to the Muslim Hotel and take bath. Then you will take breakfast. Then you will take rest, and we will come for you at twelve o'clock and we all go to Sibi together,' Mr Akhtar told me, pleased at the chance to use his organizational skills. It would been rude to demur.

A great deal later than twelve o'clock, a small white minibus pulled up in the courtyard of the Muslim Hotel with a driver and Mr Akhtar, apologizing profusely for their delay. 'We're now going to collect my family – all coming to Sibi.' We drove to the outskirts of the city, crossed the railway tracks and came to a large house and hooted. I expected to see his wife and perhaps three or four kids appear. But, like a line of busy ants, an army of people came running from the house and piled in the back of the minibus. All shapes, sizes and generations of people climbed in, laughing and laden with bundles; the great-grandmother clutching her shawls, Mr Akhtar's sister carrying enough food for everyone, his brother's wife holding their week-old baby. Here were Mr Akhtar's own eight children and his extended family of parents, grand-parents, brothers, their wives and children.

Once people, bags, food, clothes, crates of water and musical instruments were loaded, we were off. We played cassettes of tradi-tional Baluchi music. 'This is like camels marching through the desert,' Mr Akhtar explained softly, his black eyes shining, and it was true – when you listened it was possible to hear the slow, grace-ful steady plod of a line of camels walking. I described to him the wrestling I had seen in Turkey and showed him a photograph of two fighting camels. He translated for the others and they laughed at the picture; his grandmother, especially, shook with mirth until tears ran down her face.

Sibi is the second largest town in Baluchistan after Quetta, with a population of around 100,000 which was substantially, if temporarily, increasing as man and beast arrived from all direc-tions on every type of transport for the festival.

I was immediately whisked through a series of well-meaning officials in the town, all determined to force endless tea and food down me. The final house belonged to a member of the local council who insisted we had tea, sending his son to buy samosas and cakes. We sat in the living-room, with other male guests and family members. Typically, as a foreign woman, I was treated as an honorary man, and had access to both male and female 'sides'. Like most traditional households in Pakistan, no woman was allowed to be seen by a man in the house unless he was a direct blood relative. So the women stayed in a separate part of the house, forbidden to male visitors.

After the tea was drained from the pot, I was escorted to the back room to meet my host's daughters. They had dressed in their smartest clothes for the occasion, with lipstick and reddened cheeks. My clothes looked dreadfully shabby in comparison and I tried to hide the mud on my trousers and dusty boots.

They were excited to meet me and amazed that I a) was travelling alone, b) wasn't married and c) liked cricket. Although kind and inquisitive, conversation was limited after 'Are you married?'. Women like these rarely venture outside their segregated courtyard, other than to go shopping, and in their small world I was a curiosity to be peered at and analysed from all angles. They blew the dust off an old Instamatic camera and we had a photo session with every possible combination of eight people.

Eventually I was taken to my accommodation, which the organizing committee insisted on providing for me. It was a basic room which shared the bathroom with the adjoining room. No sooner had I lain down for a doze, than another official arrived and insisted that I left.

'Madam, this place is not suitable for you. There are many,' he paused to find a suitable word, then said in hushed tones, 'bachelors, staying in this building. We want to take you somewhere safer.'

So he brought me to the State Guest House, which for the mela was reserved only for VIPs. The modern stone building had a lawn with a well-kept rose-garden and flowering trees, complete with armed guards on each floor and a lovely old man who cooked and served guests in their rooms. It was impressive, considering they had such little notice of my arrival.

Before I had settled in, Mr Akhtar said, 'I think we should go down to the police station to register. It is advisable.' In my experience, whenever it was 'recommended' to register and I went to the local police station, no one seemed to know what to do. And, if the area is supposed to be unsafe, what use is registering if you're kidnapped in the middle of the night by armed bandits? Sibi was no different. My arrival at the police station provoked complete surprise; the dazed officers there were keen to make us tea but thereafter puzzled as to what to do. A young officer asked 'Where are you from?' and 'Are you married?', licked the end of a stubby pencil to write my answers on a scrap of paper, and this appeared to suffice as my registration.

Eventually I met the mela committee, the local politicians who organized the event. Although this was the first day of Sibi's biggest event of the year, things were remarkably casual in the office with visitors sitting drinking tea around the glass-topped table in the Deputy Commissioner's office. 'You are welcome,' said the DC, pumping my arm, and more tea appeared. I asked for the schedule of the festival and the sports events. 'Actually, this year we're not showing many sports. Lack of budget, you know.' That was no surprise, given Pakistan's worsening economy. The big mela in Lahore, due the following month, had been cancelled and the Prime Minister had just forbidden people to hold lavish celebrations for weddings. 'Usually we organize camel races and bull races, but we can't afford to hold them this year. The only thing is a competition of nezabazi [a traditional sport which translates as tent-pegging] on the final day.' So all the travelling and effort to reach there on time was only for a short display of one sport, four days later!

The nezabazi was scheduled for the final day of the mela, another three days away. The main purpose of the mela, the biggest and most significant event of year, is agricultural with farmers coming from all over Pakistan to buy and sell livestock: bulls, cows, sheep, goats, and camels. They had set up camp in surrounding fields, which had been divided up according to animal, in simple tents next to their tethered beasts. Early in the morning, after the animals had been fed, a thin layer of smoke hovered above the field as everyone lit fires for making bread and tea for breakfast.

Like most village melas, the entertainment was in another large field, with food, stalls and a circus. There were tea stalls, sizzling meat, bottled cold drinks of every hue, sticky halva and assorted *chaat* (spicy potato snacks). Music blared as the steam from a thousand rice pans rose, peanut vendors shouted, photographers arranged large family groups into stiff, formal poses in front of painted façades of palaces and gardens. A postcard vendor had an eclectic collection of heroes on offer – from Saddam Hussain to ousted Prime Minister Benazir Bhutto, Che Guevara and ex-cricketer Javed Miandad.

In the next field was a trade fair with dozens of stalls promoting local and national agencies, companies and Baluchi crafts. I went to meet Mr Malik, a friend of Mr Arkhund, who ran a local handicraft display. We sat for tea with Mr Aziz, a large middle-aged businessman from Quetta, who explained to me Baluchistan's *jirga* system, the rule by tribal law.

The system is run by a committee of men, usually village elders, who resolve disputes, carry out the law and punish those who break it. 'For example,' he said, 'we have a strict arranged-marriage system here in Pakistan. Parents choose the partner and usually the couple don't meet until their wedding. But if two young people fall in love and try to run away together, jirga law permits us to kill both. This is fair.'

I was astounded by his compliance, assuming that most city people felt tribal law was obsolete. 'But if your daughter fell in love with a man not of your choosing and ran away, what would you do?' 'Well,' sighed Mr Aziz apologetically, 'she would have to be killed of course. After all, jirga system is our tradition and we must keep it.'

'Rubbish,' snorted an impatient Mr Malik. 'The jirga system is outdated. Stuff the tradition – I'm a humanist and we have to break away from this. It shouldn't run our lives. Would you really let your daughter be killed?'

They had a heated but good-natured discussion on tradition versus modernism. Mr Aziz asked me about love and marriage in the West. In conservative, religious societies such as his, most people are baffled by the practice of 'choosing your own partner', which seems to them so extraordinary that they are ready to believe anything they're told. 'I have heard,' said Mr Aziz, 'that you in the West have parties where you swap your partners. My friend told me that in Europe, married couples can change their wives for the night. Is this correct?'

In spite of my denial – and my pointing out that most married Pakistani men see no harm in sleeping with other women, and enjoy a freedom that women don't have – Mr Aziz was still convinced that we in the West live a life of immorality and free sex.

The next day was Ladies' Day, when men are strictly forbidden

– a relief for me from the distracting collection of males aged from five to forty-five following my every move. The stalls enjoyed good trade, the women being better customers, and glass bangles and kitchen goods, especially, were sold by the box-load. The circus drummed up business by a deafening racket of people with megaphones linked up to loudspeakers, standing on wobbly wooden platforms, supported by bamboo scaffolding. Fairground attractions used heavily made-up and flirtatious women in high-heels to lure in the crowds, smooching and singing into their megaphones. Their conservative *shalwar kameez* [trousers and tunic] were incongruous with the scarlet lipstick and garish blue eyeshadow they were wearing; their dancing was slow and sugges-tive, gyrating hips and pouting lips, and they called out lewd remarks much to the hilarity of the women watching from under-neath.

One invited me behind the curtain of the Freak Show with an enticing wink. It was then that I realized that they were men, or, more specifically, eunuchs. In Pakistan, the 'third sex', or *hijras*, have a low status in society but with a certain mystique surround-ing them. 'Neither men nor women – just miserable people', as one man described them to me. Some travel with circuses, and some work as prostitutes in the cities.

I moved to the circus ring. The women in the audience looked more relaxed than when with their menfolk, dressed up with jingling bangles and big earrings; even the young girls wore make-up. Some were smoking with a carefree attitude, which I was sure they wouldn't be allowed to do in public with their husbands. The circus wasn't quite Billy Smart. There was a passable acrobatic troupe in glittery costumes and a clown who performed predictable stunts. A doped-up lion obliged with unenthusiastic leaps and jumps onto platforms. Two years before, a lion had escaped into the audience and attacked two men, but there wasn't any excitement this year. The audience loved it all, and chewed sugar-cane sticks and peanuts excitedly.

The animal field was now quieter. The camels were especially placid; they had short brown fur, and were much smaller and possessed none of the dramatics of their frothing, snorting Turkish brethren.

Dr Qurban Ali, from the Veterinary Research Institute in Quetta, showed me around some of the prize animals. He explained that the mela's original purpose was to encourage the best breeds of local bulls and horses. The first Horse and Cattle Show (its official name) was held in 1885, the Commissioner, Sir Robert Sandeman, having suggested that a Horse Show be held every year. This, he envisaged, would serve two purposes: the tribal sadars (leaders) from all over the region could meet once a year to exchange ideas and information; and it would help promote horse breeding and trading.

The first mela was a resounding success, mainly for trading horses by the Punjab Remount Department and the Bombay Cavalry. Later, the demand grew for load-bearing animals, so the local administration added the cattle of the Bhag Nari breed. Use of horses declined with the building of canals, and cattle increased. These days, the Bhag Nari bull is still the crème de la crème of animals, and the government subsidizes farmers who maintain the pure breed. Much is still at stake for the 'best-of-breed' awards, as a farmer wishing to sell his best animal knows that winning the first prize will push its price higher.

A chief from a nearby village, a top breeder and a regular at the mela, was sulking that morning because his bull only won third place. We sat on the dry earth outside his tent as he boiled up water on the wood-fire to make tea. Some of his villagers, he told us, had left an hour earlier to watch a bull race in Lehri, several hours' drive away. There were around twenty bulls participating in Lehri that day, and his friends had hired a lorry and gone. 'They all made good sales today,' he told us. 'Now they go and spend some of it at the races.' Bull racing is a common rural sport in Pakistan and India, usually organized at festival time, or for when farmers have more free time and the fields have been ploughed. One or two bulls are attached to a wooden cart, on which a man stands and 'drives' the bulls, racing them against another cart usually for a couple of kilometres. Aside from entertainment, the main interest lies in gambling.

I was tempted to join them and considered hiring a vehicle and driver but was dissuaded. Opinions were mixed – some said that it was dangerous to travel between villages unless in a large convoy with at least four gunmen, while others snorted at such caution and claimed they ventured freely. Mr Malik's advice was not to go: there was a renewal of fighting between two tribes, he explained, and frequent attacks took place on the road to Lehri.

At the stables, preparations were in hand for the nezabazi the next day and I spoke to two young men from the Cadet College team who were grooming their horses. One of them, articulate and well-educated, said he wanted to play nezabazi 'to be a trained horseman which will give me charisma'. This harmless ambition seems incongruous when the bloodthirsty origins of the game are considered: the roots of nezabazi probably lie in an old form of entertainment called tent-pegging, consisting of a group of horsemen swooping on enemy camps, pulling out all the tent-pegs at the gallop then wheeling back round to stab the occupants floundering under the fallen tents. Also known as *shab-khun* in Urdu and Pashto, which translates as 'evening blood', it was usually conducted by Afghani warriors who, waiting for dinner and bored, chose, after a couple of drinks, to pass the time by slaughtering a few enemies.

The formalities on the final day began with a parade of the prize-winning animals, led by their owners with enormous pride on their faces. The excited crowds were packed into the wooden stand which ran along the entire length of the field, with VIPs on a balcony. The bulls came first, pure white with fierce yet noble elegance, followed by the slightly less daunting figures of cows and calves, then snorting, stamping horses of every shade, loping camels, goats, lambs and rams. The farmers were dressed in their best waistcoats and turbans, and the animals were adorned with coloured scarves, bits of tinsel, embroidered collars and bells. Most of the crowd were agricultural people and showed their appreciation of the quality of the animals with generous applause.

Then it was at last time for the nezabazi. As the horses cantered up, I met the two students from the previous day, Ameer and Habib. 'Our team is the least experienced of the three taking part, but we are confident of doing well. The other teams are the Police and the Army – they have *too* many horses and so many years of experience. But, Inshallah, we can beat them.'

It began with a flourish. One rider from each team lined up at the starting point; Habib, kicking off for Cadet College, held his head up confidently. At the gunshot, all three galloped down the field towards the halfway point where three rectangular pieces of wood were propped up in the ground, a red ribbon tied to each of them. Each rider held a long spear in his right hand and tried to spike his wood without slowing down. Habib was successful in spearing the wood but then it fell off before he had reached the other end of the field. The other two riders, their experience very

41

much evident, still had their bits of wood on their spears when they reached the finish. As each rider managed to spear the wood, a huge cheer rose from the crowd.

Then the next three lined up and did the same. When all three riders from each team had had his turn, they repeated the process, thus allowing everyone two goes. At the end, the total points were calculated, with the Army team getting nearly maximum points. Small prizes were awarded to all participants, warmly encouraged by the spectators. The College team, taking into account their inexperience, did well and ended up not far behind the two others. Ameer had his opinions as to why his team did less well. 'The other teams had extra horses so when they played another round, they were more fresh. We only have one horse per player, so we are at a disadvantage. We wanted to learn to play polo but you need much better and stronger horses for that.'

He wanted to study in England. 'I am trying to go to an English university, but can you get expelled if you drink alcohol? In Pakistan they do this, and also if they catch you with a girl in your room, they also expel you.' He looked worried, and I tried to reassure him, without actually saying that those crimes are almost compulsory at universities in the UK.

Nezabazi has no real place in Baluchi sporting culture but it is enjoyed in India and Pakistan by the upper classes, mainly the Army, the Police and the more reputable colleges, many of whom also play polo. It is usually considered a somewhat regal sport, a test not only of riding skill but also of aim and balance, its 'evening blood' origins forgotten or ignored.

A close relative of nezabazi is pig-sticking, an old hunting sport in which horsemen attempted to spear a wild boar on the run. Its most recent heyday was from the late nineteenth to the mid-twentieth century, when British officers in India helped spread its popularity. It dates back to the early nineteenth century in India, when planters in Bihar hunted the sloth bear with dogs. To avoid a painful death, the bears quite sensibly retreated to the forests where it was impossible to ride. The sport of boar hunting was then taken up which spread to Bombay and Calcutta, and the riders organized themselves into 'tent clubs', riding out in groups of five or six. It became an obsession with British officers, primarily because of the lack of fox hunting, and tournaments were organized. The riders dressed like jockeys and used a three-metre-long spear, thrown like a javelin.

Hunting and catching a wild boar whilst on horseback required great skill. The wild boar is strong, vicious, fast and heavy; often weighing over 100 kilograms. Their curved tusks could rip open a horse, and undoubtedly a man also. The riders hunted in a line a few metres apart and on seeing a boar would decide if it was huntable or not (even in this bloodiest of sports there was some conscience), sparing a sow or very young boar.

When the leading rider came alongside a boar, he had only a fraction of a second to take aim and thrust his spear into the boar's heart. If he missed, those curved tusks could be turned on his horse, perhaps on him too.

It was time for the closing ceremonies, and in an intriguing mélange of cultures the Baluchistan Reserve Police band marched onto the field, all dressed in shalwar kameez – with Scottish tartan shawls thrown over their shoulders. Then, rather than the rousing collection of marching tunes I had expected to hear, they played, on the bagpipes, a selection of popular Hindi film songs.

To conclude the mela, after extensive closing speeches, was the presentation of prize money and certificates to the winning farmers. The officials and spectators left and the farmers clustered around waiting to be called to receive their prizes. Dr Ali came over to me and whispered, 'Would you help us present some prizes? It would be a great honour for us – the first time to have an English lady.' So I handed over the prizes to grinning old farmers, with Instamatic cameras flashing and popping at each handshake and announcement.

An hour before I was due to return to Quetta on my final morning a local boy asked if I wanted to go to a batir fight, beginning shortly. Not even knowing what a batir was, I went with him into town. We walked into an old teahouse, and into a babble of activity. We were taken up a flight of semi-broken wooden stairs which came out to a narrow platform overlooking the main room. From there, we had a good view of what was holding the attention of a cluster of men sitting on the ground, all wearing shawls and cotton turbans with a piece of material hanging down to one side. Most were old and bearded, and nursing a small sparrow-like bird. They had, I learned, for years been coming to this teahouse every morning for the daily fights. The batir, I later discovered, is a small relation to the partridge, and commonly used as a fighting bird in Baluchistan.

It was gloomy inside, with a light bulb partially hidden by a massive ceiling fan. The first batir fight was just beginning, two of the tiny birds being alternately pushed and coaxed into the middle, the punters placing their bets, when the boy tugged my sleeve. 'Your friends have come to take you outside,' he said. My lift to Quetta had arrived. I was reluctant to leave just as the action was unfolding. 'Don't worry,' he said, 'you will see this all over Baluchistan. It is our most famous sport!'

5

A Foreign Attraction

It was difficult to know how to dress for dinner at the home of Baluchistan's most famous tribal chief. Remove all remnants of nail-polish? Cover up and wear a large scarf? Smart clothes? Conservative? Feminine? It was a simple choice – I had only one clean pair of jeans and warm jumper left, and struggled to find a pair of socks without holes.

Mr Arkhund had suggested that I meet Nawab Akbar Bukti, Chieftain of the Bukti tribe (one of the biggest in Baluchistan), who Mr Arkhund thought would, with his knowledge, status and charisma, be an ideal introduction to the area. He would know about bull racing, Mr Arkhund hoped – and perhaps buzkashi.

A couple of hours after I'd arrived at my hotel in the centre of Quetta a jeepload of gunmen marched in to collect me, provoking dropped jaws from the reception staff. Turning off the main Jinnah Road, we stopped on the corner mounted high with sandbags with armed watchmen peering behind them. Four more guards stood by the house. This man didn't take any chances.

With the drama of a hostage transfer, I was hustled inside the door to a huge living-room with a blazing fire and a deep red carpet. There was no one there, and a servant directed me to the long cushions arranged along three sides of the square room. Otherwise it sparsely furnished, with a tiny table in one corner on which were four telephones. Photographs, presumably of the Nawab, decorated the white walls.

After a few moments the Nawab entered the room. He was tall and slim with thick white hair and beard, dressed in pure white shalwar kameez and waistcoat. He stood straight and dignified with a walnut wooden walking stick in his hand.

'Madam Emma, I am delighted. Please, be comfortable and let's talk.' As he sat down, two phones began to ring. Holding one against each ear he dealt smoothly and skilfully with both, a note-book at hand and scribbling notes. The following day he would be returning to his village for several weeks – this was last-minute work before he left town. I was additionally grateful for this dinner invitation.

'Now,' he said eventually turning to me, 'what is it exactly you want?' My request now seemed curiously trivial and inconsequential. I described my search for the region's traditional sports especially buzkashi, and he listened silently. As I spoke, there was a knock on the door and a tall, turbaned and heavily-armed man entered. He touched the Nawab's feet and relayed a tale of woe which probably caused all thoughts of goats, dead or otherwise, to disappear from the Chief's mind.

After a discussion, the man brought from his pocket a brick-sized wad of 500-rupee notes, counted it out and gave it to the Nawab. They shook hands and he left. 'That is one of my tribes-men who has brought money from another member. The man had to pay a fine of 200,000 rupees [around £2200] because he had promised his daughter to one man, then later changed his mind and she married someone else.'

'But that's a lot of money – how could he afford it?' I asked. He shrugged, unconcerned. 'It is a lot but he knew the price you pay for this crime. He shouldn't have done it. The fines are fixed and if he can't afford that – well, that's his problem.' Judging by his home and surroundings, the Nawab obviously didn't suffer any financial problems.

He elaborated on some tribal laws, which have ruled the Bukti people for hundreds of years, beginning with its most crucial aspect: when killing is OK, and when it's not.

'Of course, I first learned to use a gun when I was seven years old,' he said modestly yet with a humorous glint in his eye, in all likelihood trying to provoke shock. It was probably his standard opening line with foreign journalists. I responded with a dead-pan 'Oh', as if he'd told me that the sun rose every day, and continued, 'How old were you when you first killed a man?' He feigned shock: 'Oh, I've never killed a man,' and the subject was closed.

Tribal law revolves around honour of the tribe and the family. If someone breaks that honour, you are free to kill him or, even generations later, kill a member of his family. (Two of the Nawab's

sons had been killed, and another opted out of tribal life, preferring to run his own business in Karachi.) 'But it is strictly forbidden to kill a man in your own home. It is also forbidden to kill a
woman or child.' I was safe on two counts then.

On forgiveness: 'If a man is due to be killed and his wife comes
to my house to plead for his life, I have an obligation to honour
her plea. Then I place a shawl over her when she leaves so as to
protect her honour.'

On being old enough to die: 'Once a boy starts to wear shalwar
kameez, he is considered old enough to die. Sometimes, he tries
to look younger to save his life, but then you look at his waist. If
he has the mark of elastic from the trousers, you know he is old
enough.'

On women: 'We have much higher morals and respect the
women in our society more than they do in Punjab. We would
never kill or molest them. We give them so much respect that we
cannot look at a woman who is not our relative. They must keep
themselves completely separate and cover their faces.'

On adultery: 'In an adultery case, both partners have to die. If
a married woman goes with another man, her husband can shoot
her. If it is a single woman with someone else's husband, her
father can. But as it is not acceptable to kill a woman in our society, she is obliged to do the decent thing and hang herself.' The
definitions of adultery are far stricter than a spot of illicit nookie,
too: 'If a woman is seen looking at another man, that is considered adulterous.'

Soon afterwards, other guests arrived and sat down. They were
all bureaucrats, clutching papers and documents, discussing local
politics and urgent business before the Nawab left for the village.
At a suitable pause, I asked the assembled gathering their knowledge about local Baluchi sports.

The Nawab eventually commented, 'They all like watching
cricket these days. Oh, that and bird-watching.' He chuckled at his
pun and no more was said. The food arrived on big metal trays,
placed on a starched white cloth at our feet. The other guests
gathered around to sit on the floor.

For once, no one asked me if I was married, but I asked the
Nawab about his family. 'I have five sons,' he said but he had previously mentioned sons-in-law so I asked how many daughters. 'I
have five sons,' he repeated. I asked again, and he explained. 'In
our tradition we give our women great honour and so we don't

mention them.' It really wasn't the time or place to bang the feminist drum, so I didn't respond.

After eating, the Nawab told me proudly about his grandson, who could handle a Kalashnikov by the time he was three years old. He summoned him to be introduced. He was a tall, broad-shouldered eighteen-year-old, with a beard and immaculate white shalwar, who in broken English explained how he was looking forward to going to study at university in England. Definitely following in the footsteps of his grandfather, who had spent many years at top public schools in England.

The other guests suddenly stood up and left and the Nawab brought me a huge photograph album, filled with black-and-white pictures dating back to the 1930s. They were of him with his tribal members, with family, pictures of him hunting, at weddings, at dances with young beautiful European women on his arm (a different woman in each picture) and even at a garden party at Buckingham Palace, one of several occasions where he had met the Queen.

They revealed a lifestyle far beyond the means of the rest of his tribe, but there were also several cheerful pictures of him in prison uniform. 'What were you imprisoned for?' I asked. 'Oh you know, just insurgency against the government,' as if it was a speeding offence.

As I took my leave I thanked him heartily for his hospitality but he reprimanded me. 'We never thank anyone for food or hospitality, because it is taken for granted. When I returned from my trip to London to Buckingham Palace, I had to sit and tell my people about the trip. They were all amazed that I had to stay in a hotel and had to eat in restaurants. They assumed that because I had an invitation to London, I would be able to stay with the Queen for a few days.'

I felt a little guilty that English hospitality now had a bad name thanks to the Queen. I was escorted back to the hotel, none the wiser about Baluchi sports but wiser about the life of the Bukti tribe, and very grateful to have been born in Bradford.

My visit to the Tourist Office was even less conclusive than to the Nawab's. People in tourist offices, whilst well-meaning and polite, have little necessary knowledge for the job. The officer in charge didn't know about traditional games but put me in touch with Mr Fida, who knew about dog fighting, cockfighting and buzkashi, and promised to enquire further. Mr Fida advised me to visit Mr Yaqoub Shah, at the Baluchistan Culture and Tourism Cell. 'After Pakistan won the cricket World Cup in 1992, and with everyone in Pakistan watching TV, people are only interested in cricket now. When I was young growing up in my village, we used to play lots of games: *khosai, yenda, baddhi*, but these days the children play only cricket or else watch it on TV,' said Mr Shah, sorrowfully.

Televised cricket has been the most important sporting cultural phenomenon to hit the Asian subcontinent. Already popular in the region for decades, the spread of satellite television and endless 'made for TV' one-day tournaments – and of course Pakistan winning the World Cup – relegated other sports to distant memory. Even hockey, once thriving in the subcontinent, has suffered.

Most of Baluchistan's indigenous games have vanished, except one: fights. In this area, watching duelling cocks, batirs, chakors (another cousin of the partridge), dogs, bears and other combinations is a popular pastime.

My expert in this subject was a wonderful man called Mr Mohammed Ali who owned a gold shop in Liaqat Bazaar. He was in his mid-forties, short and broad with neatly clipped grey hair and moustache and always wore a white shalwar kameez and black waistcoat. Speaking a smattering of English, he was determined to show me the best of Quetta's animal fights.

'We can see batir, chakor, cock, dog and dog, dog and bear.' I asked him the difference between them. 'I don't like animals fight. Only I like pigeon racing for my hobby. Animal fight no good. Dog and dog,' he screwed up his face in disgust, 'very bad, very cruel, dogs just fighting each other. No-good people that watch. No good. But dog and bear -' a beam spread across his face – 'very beautiful. Two, three dogs against one bear tied up. Very good.'

Our first trip was to a cockfight in the Huda district of Quetta. It was held in a field attached to a massive farmhouse with a pigeon-coop on the roof. Mountains surrounded us, grey in the distance against a clear sky.

A small ring of spectators clustered around as the owners prepared their birds, and began to cheer as the birds received their 'pedicure', their claws sharpened with a razor-blade. Then, the owners took a mouthful of cold water and blew it all over their bird's body. This was done with as much loving care as I had seen the devecis treat their camels.

Throughout the fight, the owners stood among the spectators but close to the action and shouted encouragement, as did the punters when they weren't shouting out their bets. Cocks waiting to fight crowed with impatience, eager to be let into the action or else to escape. A man came round with glasses of green tea, and small boys picked their way through the crowds selling peanuts. The fight was totally unlike the one I saw in Turkey; here, as well as sharpening the birds' claws, they made the birds fight until one of them could not move.

After the fight, one bird had blood gushing from a wound, and its owner took water in his mouth and washed the wound in his mouth. I couldn't decide whether it was repulsive or moving.

Attracting the most interest were the chakors, though in fact they fought with far less conviction than the cocks, with none of the squawking and fluttering, clawing and nipping of the roosters. Instead they spent most of the time avoiding each other and pecking the ground. Their fate was not lucky: either fight their fellow chakors, or end up as chakor casserole – a speciality of the area, Mr Ali told me.

The host, the owner of the house, walked around greeting everyone. 'He is no-good man,' growled Mr Ali, as soon as they had finished greeting each other. In Baluchistan, there are set formalities for greeting. Two men will shake hands, occasionally hug, put hand on heart and fire a volley of rapid-fire questions at each other, at the same time answering the other so it's impossible to tell who is asking and who answering. They ask after the other's family members, their life, job; if one had just been away, he would ask about the news since they had last met. It is usually a lengthy procedure.

Mr Ali's smile left his face. 'Crooked man – he getting all money from no-good things. Smuggling, robbery, dishonest. Bloody bastard.' The 'bloody bastard' had reason to look happy: he was raking in the rupees every Sunday by charging the bird owners for hosting the fight, taking a cut from all the book-makers, and charging a small entrance and parking fee. 'Bird fight horrible – I show you dog and bear tonight.'

I prepared myself to see a bear attacked by two dogs, but after a huge dinner in his home – with twenty of his family members (and the usual barrage of questions on the theme of 'Are you married/why not/when/who will you marry and how many children') – the non-immediate-family members having disappeared,

Mr Ali settled me down with his wife and children, and got out a video, solemnly announcing, 'My dogs.' The video showed a bear tied to a tree so he could only use his paws. The two dogs, charged up and ferocious, were goaded on by the crowd. For a victory, the dogs must get the bear on his back, as in wrestling. If they fail to do so during a set length of time, the bear wins. Usually, though, the dogs are the victors, and the dog owner earns money from punters.

A small bear costs around 100,000 rupees (getting on for £1,200), and because it's usually the bear who ends up the worst off, the dog owners pay the bear owner for the 'privilege' of fighting.

The next morning, Mr Ali with his two youngest sons, impish as monkeys, took me through the hail, wind and rain to a small shed nearby. The interior of the shed was gloomy and in shadows, lit only by a few bulbs dangling by long wires from the wooden slatted ceiling. A large circle of men sat cross-legged on the floor, all wearing turbans, all with beards and blankets cast over one shoulder. Each had, clutched lovingly in his hands, a small bag made from curtain material. Every so often one or another of them would open it, peer inside and fondle the contents with a look of warm paternal devotion. In these bags were their batirs – apparently also good in casserole or soup.

Before the fight started, there was a tremendous discussion as each man weighed up his friend's bird. Expert eyes and hands scrutinized every feather, eye and beak, judging the quivering little bird's fighting ability, which signified its value. The intensive haggling indicated that the buying and selling trade amongst batirs was healthy (something to do with the season) – and far healthier than the Karachi Stock Exchange.

The eventual fight was a tremendous anti-climax. The tiny, fragile, sparrow-like creatures merely flitted around each other, half-heartedly pecking at the ground, their sharpened beaks failing to inflict any damage. There was more excitement amongst the punters as everyone wagered their bets than among the birds.

The entire morning was thus spent; dazed in a haze of marijuana smoke in which bloodshot-eyed young men sat abstractedly, dreaming the day away. I hoped the economy of Quetta was not entirely dependent on this gathering. Mr Ali wasn't impressed with their lack of work ethic. 'These – no-good men,' he said, casting a discerning look over the huddle of cross-legged bird-watchers. 'Not safe here.' He seemed more concerned about the safety of my bag than the fact that his two young sons were inhaling lungfuls of smoke.

According to Mr Ali, there are two varieties of people in the world. 'Some work hard, have business, family, nice house, work for their children. The others – no-good people – smoke hashish, no working, only sitting gambling, smuggling, using black money.' He promised to take me the next morning to see another bunch of 'no-good people' at a dog fight.

Dog fighting is popular all over Pakistan, and especially in Baluchistan and Punjab. Huzda, heavily populated with Afghanis, holds a fight in the small village of Kuchla every Wednesday, as most of the men were butchers and for some reason (which I couldn't grasp from Mr Ali's explanations) it was their day off.

There was another strike on the Wednesday, closing everything, in protest against the census that the national government was carrying out (the strikes now averaged at least one a week). As he visited each house to ask how many people lived there, the enumerator was flanked by a couple of armed guards for protection. The local people objected to this census, fearing that when the officials realized the high population of Afghans, it would disadvantage them.

Armed police were everywhere in the city, and soldiers drove around in armoured trucks with the barrels of their guns pointing at every passing vehicle or person. 'Don't leave town,' Mr Yaqoub Shah warned me. 'Don't even leave your room today.' Recently there had been attacks on these officials and locals didn't need much reason to start a fight.

It wasn't the ideal day to visit a tribal village for a dog fight. However, the presence of Mr Ali's two youngest sons reassured me that people were being a little over-cautious. Halfway to Kuchla, a series of ominous shudders and rattles emerged from the bowels of Mr Ali's old car. Finally, it stopped altogether.

'Bloody bastard,' muttered Mr Ali. He tinkered around unhopefully for a few minutes; then we pushed the car to the side of the road while his sons played marbles on the back seat, and decided the plan of action.

As a car approached, Mr Ali stopped it and negotiated with the driver, who agreed to take us to the fight and bring us back. After Huzda, the car left the road for a series of barely passable muddy tracks at which point the man stopped the car, pointed us in the direction and suggested we walk the remainder.

Just below mountains, a large, rough piece of land between a village and the railway tracks contained a couple of hundred men and few dozen dogs of various breeds. They sat in a large circle on the ground in their usual turbans and shawls and beards, many of them holding dogs on ropes, watching a fight in the middle. The scene looked like a sort of Crufts-from-Hell.

Our arrival caused quite a stir. Eyes shifted from the dogs to us, and about a hundred small boys made their way over. The most efficient way of dealing with an undesired swarm is to keep on the move, so I set off on a slow circuit of the crowd. As I was doing this I saw two dogs being led into the middle of the fighting area (just an open space within a six-deep ring of people). They immediately began to snarl, leap, bite, claw, and rip at each other's face. In a short time there was lots of blood, which provoked a frenzy of barking in the other dogs, chained up, awaiting their turn. The spectators watched with appreciative eyes; the more blood, the louder cheers. A few more feared senior members of the community (the men with biggest guns) sat at the front of the circle, sitting on mats or, for the more senior, carpets. Peanut sellers did the rounds as did bookies collecting their money.

The swarm following my every move was growing; it was neither hostile nor aggressive, but as a white woman at a dog fight isn't the norm here, I was an irresistible sideshow for them. Eventually, a mountainous Afghani with large paunch, heavy black beard and broad shoulders, became my unofficial bodyguard and producing a big stick (crowd control is fairly simple in Baluchistan), whacked anyone who came within a few feet. But Mr Ali had a better idea. He spotted a jeep parked at the edge of the arena and told me to get inside. 'My friends,' he said. 'Safer here.' So we watched the remaining fights from the inside of the jeep with the windows wound down, in clouds of thick smoke from the endless joints of the two 'friends'.

These Afghan chiefs possessed the highest seniority, as indicated by their jeep. Their beards were thick and black, their eyes soft and brown, and with smiles they offered me joints; one even pulled out of a pocket a brick-sized lump of best hash to take home (which I refused). Mr Ali wandered around, clearly uneasy. His sons were also in the jeep, still playing marbles, oblivious to the thick clouds of hash.

When one pit-bull nearly had his ear ripped off, producing more blood and cheering and a fresh round of barking from the other dogs, I decided that it was time to leave, and went to find Mr Ali, who had gone in search of the man supposed to be driving us back. We eventually found him sitting calmly in his car, and set off.

'Did you enjoy?' asked Mr Ali on our way home. I didn't know how to answer. He replied for me. 'This dog fight – no good. But dog and bear – really beautiful.' I decided to leave it at that. Mr Ali's logic was unfathomable.

I needed to go to the police station to extend my visa. This entailed first finding out on what days the police station was open. Quetta's working week seemed to consist of approximately three days thanks to a combination of strikes, on top of confusion as to whether Friday or Sunday was the day off. Until a couple of years previously, Pakistan had observed Friday (the Islamic day of rest) as the day off, but this was changed to Sunday, following the international norm. However, different areas of Quetta operated on different holidays, resulting in confusion. Some shops would close on both days, plus the afternoon before.

I eventually found the police station open, and requested an extension of my visa, a task which tested the limits of patience, tolerance and logic. Large, jovial DS Gramkani, who was in charge, gave me the low-down: 'To get an extension, you need to first register. To register, you must bring this form filled out four times and four photographs. Then come back when we have registered you and I must send your extension request to Islamabad, and they take a few weeks to decide. Then we let you know if you get the extension.'

Once that was over, I could turn my attention to the task in hand. I decided that I'd seen my quota of beasts in combat, it was time to make more inquiries about buzkashi, which was proving difficult to track down. Eventually I was introduced to a film-maker, Hameed, who had made a recent film which included a scene of buzkashi, so I enlisted help from him and his friends. Hameed knew some of the local star players and we arranged to have tea with them in the Sadarbahar Hotel.

The 'hotel' was actually a small cramped Afghan teahouse with a ladder to a balcony so low you had to stoop to enter and then sit, cross-legged on the wooden platform. It was the perfect vantage point to watch the activities downstairs, mainly consisting of people drinking tea from small pottery bowls and eating plates of oily mutton and dhal, scooping it up with pieces of naan. A garish mural, predominantly blue, depicted a highly improbable summer landscape in unnatural colours.

The five of us were guests of the owner, Sadar Mohammad, the main organizer of local buzkashi. He was everything I imagined a *buzkash* (a player of buzkashi) to be – tall and broad, with blue eyes, a black beard, a thick turban and a heroic demeanour. He and his friends sat down with us and talked about their love of the game.

'It takes,' he said, speaking softly in Pashto, 'strength and stamina to play. You need to be a good horseman, strong and confident, but also need the physical strength to lift up the goat. Most players begin in their early twenties.' As they spoke about the greatest horseback sport (in my opinion) with the drama and dauntless qualities of a timeless Afghani tradition, we could see WCW wrestling on the tiny colour television on the ground floor. You couldn't avoid Americana even in an Afghan teahouse with the best buzkash in town.

This cultural conflict prompted me to ask them the chances of the survival of buzkashi, given the growing invasion of TV culture and especially cricket. Mr Mohammad looked down at the TV set with contempt,and looked back with a smile. 'Our game will never die,' he said simply.

His main concern was that its authenticity would be ruined by the intervention of people wanting to hijack its success. Local bigwigs, he told us, promised they would help finance them, but they were concerned that these people would use it for their own advantage. Buzkashi is expensive and usually the host of a celebration – a wedding or the birth of a son – supplies the goat and pays the horsemen a fee. For the ordinary man, the game is out of financial reach and rarely possible unless sponsored, so monetary limitations were the biggest threat to its future.

I was lucky, he told me, because that afternoon there was a match in the nearby village of Nawakilli. The dreamed-of experience was just approaching, and I confirmed and reconfirmed the details several times. My friends assured me they knew the village and location of the ground, and it seemed that nothing could stop us now. The lure of the headless goat looked like being satisfied.

I could barely contain my excitement when they collected me that afternoon. With us was Dr Faisal from Lahore who was in town for a few days, and curious to see buzkashi. We drove to Nawakilli, a few miles outside Quetta but well out of city life. The traffic began as motorbikes, cars and buses, battered old trucks and trailers; then became more sedate with horse-drawn carts, bicycles and small three-wheelers.

We soon arrived at the venue, where there was already a large crowd. It was perfectly clear and sunny, the late-afternoon sun casting superb toasted hues on the sandy mountains in the background. Several horses had already arrived, and young men were cantering around, meeting friends, and people were patting the horses and looking over them with appreciation. Males of all ages made up the crowd – either women were not interested, or it wasn't acceptable for them to watch buzkashi.

More spectators arrived and the excitement grew with the numbers. But every time we tried to get out of the jeep, a crowd gathered round within seconds, making it impossible to move, let alone get around and take pictures. As at the dog fight, it was curiosity rather than animosity but it was intimidating as well as a hindrance. Even Dr Faisal was getting hot under the collar. 'Oh my goodness,' he kept saying, looking worried and fidgeting with his tie.

'We should wait until the game starts, and then people's attention will be taken up so they won't be as interested in you. How does it feel to be a sex symbol?' Hameed asked with a mischievous grin. 'Awful,' I replied. He had a solution: 'Next time, we'll get you a *burqah*, so no one can see any part of you – not even your eyes.' This is the usual attire for women in the more conservative areas of Pakistan, and parts of the Middle East. It is a long, tent-like garment which is put over the head and covers the entire body, even the face. Only a mesh over the eyes allows the wearer to see.

The two teams were complete and cantered around on the playing area, which was rough and stony. It was now well after 4 o'clock and a cloud of doubt was growing among my friends. 'Do you think they've cancelled it?' I asked in a small voice. Even Hameed looked worried. He went out to ask around and returned shortly afterwards, not looking happy. 'It seems that the goat hasn't arrived.'

The news sank in. This was like a football match with no ball. 'The man who had promised to bring the goat and slaughter it hasn't come. Maybe no one has paid for it.'

A mauling at the weekly dogfight in Kuchla, a tribal village near Quetta, Pakistan.

Above: Two heavyweights going for the clinch in their fight in Selçuk, Turkey.

Below: Spitting image: camel drool is an essential part of the event.

A first-round winner is paraded to the crowds in Selçuk.

Oil wrestlers perform the peşrev – the ritual preparation before a fight.

A rear-end view of the kispet, the leather breeches worn by all oil wrestlers.

Hulking heroes: posters of past wrestlers adorn
the walls of every Pakistani wrestling house

Gripping the trouser belt is a predominent move.

The essential item for every game of ulak tartish:
the newly beheaded goat just before kick-off.

A game of polo with a headless goat: ulak tartish
in full swing near Bishkek, Kyrgyzstan.

A demonstration of mallekhamb – yoga atop a pole or rope – in Bombay, India.

A village game of mukna kangjei – a unique combination of hockey and wrestling in Manipur, India.

I would have been happy to pay for it myself, but now it was too late. People drifted away back home. I wanted to stay until the last minute in case the goat made a late entrance but once the horses started to ride away, I had to admit defeat. The goat, dead or otherwise, had had the last laugh.

To make up for the bitter disappointment I decided to see some *rhiji*, Baluchi traditional wrestling, that afternoon, as there was regular practice every Friday in Sadiqshahid Park. As we drove past I asked Hameed to drop me off so I could watch some action. He looked concerned. 'We should come with you – maybe it's not safe for you alone.' I scoffed at his caution and my protectors drove off, leaving me alone.

At least this event had a promising beginning, with rhiji appearing to be underway. Rhiji is a variation of *kushti*, the traditional wrestling style of the subcontinent. It is only in more recent times that the free-style and Graeco-Roman methods of wrestling were adopted for international competition. Rhiji is more specific to the Afghani areas, and closely related to Mongolian wrestling.

Inside the park, a small leafy enclosure with a few trees and benches dotted around, there were several pairs of competitors engaged in bouts, watched by hundreds of people. Anyone could participate, and the competitors were matched by size and weight. There were no prizes or gambling – the wrestlers participated for the honour of winning, while those watching were there for a straightforward appreciation of the sport.

In rhiji, like in most wrestling, a win is achieved when one competitor gets his opponent down on his back twice. The competitors were topless and wore loose baggy trousers, and around their waists a *patu*, a belt made from a long piece of twisted material. The knack was to wrap your hands around your opponent's back and inside his patu. Locked into this clinch they then had to trip each other up using only their legs.

They were locked together in pairs, clasped with hands at the back and moving their legs slowly, reminding me of a beginner's class in ballroom dancing. It was oddly graceful, cautious, waiting for the right moment for the kill and very similar to other types of Asian wrestling, sumo, for instance. Bent at the waist, they moved together like crabs. Then, suddenly one gave a ferocious kick and the other, before he had time to think, was flat on his back. Several bouts were being fought simultaneously, each one with a referee keeping score. When one competitor was floored, as signified by the referee, the crowd murmured with appreciation but there was no applause.

The force with which many of them were whacked to the hard stony ground must have resulted in injuries but it would have been way beyond their pride to admit to being hurt. After picking themselves up off the ground, they staggered back to their places, probably hiding severe concussion and broken limbs. A group of old men, all ex-wrestlers, invited me to sit with them, which I was glad to do. It was safer here, as respect for elders meant that no one would dare approach me.

As the sun began to set signalling wind-down time, a few hundred pairs of eyes turned towards me, so I decided to leave before the wrestling finished and get out before being followed. I packed up my camera-bag, but it was too late. The action suddenly finished and to my dismay, after a brief round of applause, the attention was now firmly attached to me. The five old chaps couldn't do anything as an enthusiastic bunch of men swarmed forward. Excitement mounted as they crowded around, and arms and hands reached out with calls of 'Hello, missis, where are you from?' Such friendliness, whilst perfectly manageable in small groups, is not appreciated when it's a mob.

I tried to force a path through the crowd which was growing larger and noisier by the second. Approaching the exit, I spotted several three-wheeler auto-rickshaws waiting for passengers. I thankfully leapt into one as the crowd followed me outside. 'Jinnah Road!' I cried out to the driver but one look at the approaching mob convinced him that this was a high-risk customer and he shook his head and pointed to one of his mates.

I dived into the other, just as we were surrounded. Hands darted inside, grabbing at me and my cameras. It was all, I kept telling myself, in good humour and just curiosity. But the thought of raging hormones possibly sending the sexual inquisitiveness of these men out of control was frightening. The driver sensed the urgency in my scream of 'Jinnah Road and get your arse in gear!' as the door kept being opened and more hands grabbed me, but we were now completely surrounded and there was no way the flimsy vehicle could force its way through.

He too decided this was too much trouble for a 15-rupee fare and started flee the mêlée, but I dragged him back by his collar with some well-chosen obscenities and he returned to his vehicle, brought out a big stick from under the seat and whacked it around randomly. We drove away, leaving behind us the crowds, for whom it was perhaps the most exciting day's wrestling they'd seen for months.

6

Duelling Donkeys and Macho Playground Tag

Although I had enjoyed Baluchistan, I felt a sense of relief as I stepped off the night bus on to the streets of Karachi. Shortly after I arrived at my hotel, a message came from Mr Arkhund. He had told me about a unique sport famous here, yet little known outside the Sind province – donkey-racing, which is taken utterly seriously in Karachi. The message was confirmation of a donkey race that afternoon on Clifton Beach.

I arrived an hour before the scheduled start, and scoured the beach for four-legged beasts, but the only ones around were a couple of sulky, spitting camels giving rides to petrified children while proud parents photographed them. I was eventually directed to a gaggle of people standing opposite the Red Onion restaurant on the sea-front. I made my way to them and was told that the race would start 'any time', which seemed unlikely, although it was certain that something was going to happen, sometime.

Soon after, a scrawny moth-eaten grey donkey arrived pulling a small cart with an old man sitting on it, who got down, tied up the donkey and joined his friends for a chat. Then more arrived, all of the animals looking bedraggled and unenthusiastic; surely, I thought, these can't be racing.

At that point a man with a large black moustache and natty waistcoat beckoned me into a small yard, and there stood a donkey, pure white, elegant and strong with a healthy face and sturdy long legs. It was surrounded by many admirers, petting and stroking this thoroughbred with appreciation. 'Champion,' his owner proclaimed to me as he caressed the long white ears proudly.

There was no one to explain what was happening so there was nothing for it but to wait and see what developed. I saw several more grey transport donkeys trundle up pulling broad wooden carts, loaded with spectators. Then a sleek car screeched to a halt in the midst of the gathering crowd, and the driver emerged with a mobile phone (incongruous in the setting) and began the real business: the betting. More unofficial bookies (without phones or cars) also began to take bets and there was a loud babble of excitement.

It was long past the scheduled start-time of 4 pm by now, and signs of preparation began only when the second racing donkey arrived with a flourish. Spectators began to organize themselves, noisily and chaotically grouping together, arguing over taxis and piling onto motorbikes and Suzuki jeeps. The vehicles then lined up on the roadside, some of them driving down the road just a few hundred metres away. It all seemed quite extraordinary.

No one spoke English and unable to fathom out what was going on, I followed the others and stood on the roadside in a good viewing position, although I was the only one on foot. I was offered standing-room in several trucks and planned to leap onto the back of one, once the race began.

Now the street was silent, anticipatory, for several minutes. Just as my attention wandered to gaze at the sea, there was a sudden burst of activity. The noise from the roadside spectators grew to high levels, as two donkey-carts approached us at full speed. Their drivers, shouting frantically, were perched on top of the tiny carts and whacking at their animals' bottoms with sticks to steer them.

As soon as they appeared, my camera was zooming in on the two racers but as I did so there came a roar as engines revved up, choking fumes filled the breezy sea air, every horn was blown and amid whoops and yells of delight, all the vehicles had driven away, in the wake of the two donkeys now well out of sight.

I had missed any chance of a lift, and was completely alone on the roadside with just the sunset and four men digging a ditch for company. There was a deathly silence, the action gone. Next time, I vowed, next time.

Clearly I needed an expert to enlighten me. That came in the unlikely figure of Mr Farooq Memon, a small, shy journalist, who had researched Karachi's donkey-racing culture and was eager to introduce me to the stars of the alternative race-track.

Perched on his tiny motorbike, we cruised the streets of the Lyari district in the south-west of Karachi, the oldest and poorest area of the city. This was donkey territory; where the transportation of people and goods was done primarily on donkey and bullock carts. They dragged vegetables from wholesaler to bazaar, concrete pipes to building sites, and fridges to homes. The occasional camel cart loped along the crowded streets, towering over cars and bikes.

It was a slightly unnerving journey as we dodged trucks and wobbled around pot-holes, piles of rubble and half-completed repairs. Every so often, Mr Memon would turn and give me an apologetic smile, a shrug, and say, 'Sorry – our roads are not like yours in England.'

We were going to meet Juma, a famous local lad and experienced jockey. 'He says he's the best jockey these days, but it's not easy to decide who is champion. I think,' Mr Memon continued tactfully, hesitantly, 'that many men call themselves champions.'

He had given me a crash-course in donkey-racing, outlining the basic facts. 'There are two main types of donkey-cart racing: the first and best-known is called free-style, which uses a small cart, faster donkey and one jockey. This is the more serious race. The other uses the regular cart used for transporting goods, which is for fun, done with friends as a social activity.'

The small racing carts are handmade from rosewood by specialists, mainly in Sind and Baluchistan. Each craftsman decorates it in his own style, using *chamakpatti*, the light-reflecting coloured plastic also used on most trucks and buses in Pakistan which gives its decorative element to the cart, as well as making the cart visible at night.

Mr Memon got lost in the maze of small back-streets, and we constantly asked people for help. 'Where's Juma the donkey-jockey?' he called out but this vicinity was home to three different donkey-jockeys all called Juma. We eventually found the correct one, sitting on a rope *charpoi* and drinking tea with his mates.

He was a young, slim man who confidently assured us that as recent races proved, he was the leading jockey, riding on his favourite donkey, Kaputar (which translates as 'pigeon'). We asked him how long the sport has been around, and he gave a shrug and looked up to the skies.

He spoke in Sindi, and Mr Memon translated for me: 'We don't know exactly – people will say that they always remember it but no one knows for how long. It is part of Karachi life, everyone from here knows about it.' Buying and training a donkey requires substantial investment. The best animals are from the Kelab region of Iran, where a two- or three-year-old can cost £95 to £160. Then, it has to be trained by a specialist. A racer costs between £2 and £7 a day in food and care, and as it is never used for commercial work the only income from it is in racing.

Training takes around two years, beginning on open land or desert, then progressing to the more challenging city roads. Apart from showing fitness and speed, the donkey must be able to manage the rough surface of Karachi's streets and know how to monitor other traffic. Once these skills have been mastered, the donkey is shown to a top 'donkey-wallah' and if he performs well, can be resold as a fully-trained animal for up to £380.

Before a race, the donkey's food and care are carefully monitored and administered, as with all top athletes. Loving care is dispensed lavishly and during training he is fed green apples, milk, almonds and special herbal remedies.

Most owners we spoke to emphasized the aspects of the sport that go far beyond winning and making money. As all trainers, owners, jockeys and fans know, a winning donkey is a source of pride to the owner and his friends. Each donkey has his loyal supporters, rather like the wrestling camels in Turkey. Stressing that it is more than sport but a way of life, owners talked to me of their deep devotion to their animals, *ghadha shoq* – literally donkey love.

For a race, there has first to be a challenge from a *mohalla* – a housing estate or area – from somewhere in the city. So, for example, Korangi's champion will challenge Orangi's, and once accepted they arrange a race and the route is chosen. The jockeys' friends and supporters collect money to support their donkey and pay for the extra preparation costs. A trustworthy and experienced person from each 'side' is selected to take extra care as watchman, and prevent foul play on the racers.

'Owning and training a donkey is not something that you can take lightly. For many, it's a first love from childhood and during race-time some devotees neglect their own family. When I was younger I didn't even care for my food, as I spent all my time with my animal. My mother and sisters tried to stop my ghadha shoq, saying I should get a proper education instead of earning money from this profession. But I became a racing champion and earned good money from it,' said Mr Ghani Manglo, a retired champion racer.

Mr Memon told me of the political connection. Donkey-wallahs are working-class and politicians are always keen for their vote. In the Lyari equivalent of kissing babies, Zulfikar Ali Bhutto's first election campaign had processions of donkeys to show support. When his daughter Benazir returned to the country after a long exile, a large parade of donkey-carts greeted her at the airport. When Karachi was suffering law and order problems in 1985, the Chief Minister and his Cabinet arranged a large peace rally of donkey-carts through the city.

It was difficult to see a race, as the fixtures were unreliable, there being no organizing committee to take responsibility for them. Information about a race is passed along the grapevine and often, the grapevine breaks or is just inefficient. Juma and his friends assured us of a race the following day.

'They promised me it's at 3 pm,' said Mr Memon as he picked me up on the now-familiar motorbike. 'But you know – maybe it's not so reliable.' The poor man knew for himself the reality. Arriving at Juma's place at the designated time, there was confusion. 'Well, we're not sure if it's going ahead now. One of the owners says that his donkey is injured, so maybe they cancelled.' Everything was remarkably haphazard and it had suddenly become a non-event. 'There may be another race over in Muach – perhaps Teen Bhai (Juma's closest rival) is racing there.' Mr Memon and I decided to take the chance, and drive the 30 kilometres there.

When we got to Muach there was an ominous absence of donkeys, people, vehicles and donkey-race trappings. Everyone we asked looked blank or confused until we eventually found someone who told us it had been postponed to the Saturday.

On Saturday afternoon, Mr Memon's son Iqbal and Iqbal's cousin, Yaqoob, both in their late teens, picked me up in their friend's battered car. Neither had any previous knowledge of donkey-racing, cricket being their preferred sport. This race was also to start in Muach, but this time we arrived to see many Suzukis, bikes, vans and people waiting in a restaurant car park, while excitement was building up. This race, they told us, had two important Karachi jockeys competing but that was the only information we could glean, other than that the route followed the road back towards the city, ending seven kilometres away at the hospital.

We drove off to find the best viewing spot, which turned out to be the crest of the hill so we could see the approaching race. I asked the lads if we could join in the 'Wacky Races' and follow the donkeys, and they loved the idea. 'We'll open the car boot, you climb inside and point your camera towards the race. As the donkeys overtake us, we'll join the cars.' 'But will you try and get to the front?' 'Oh yes, that's no problem.'

The two lads who had never been interested in this Karachi sport were suddenly fired up with enthusiasm. We waited for eternity on the brow of the hill, me perched in the boot with a zoom lens pointing out. Nearly one hour later I was beginning to feel rather silly when the only action was a villager on a wobbly bicycle, who nearly fell off as he cycled past and gazed around at us.

Several vehicles went past, and some donkey-carts carrying spectators. 'Are they coming?' we called out to them. 'Coming, coming,' came the reply. I was beginning to lose faith in its happening, but the lads remained confident.

Just as I was assuming that the race had been cancelled, we spotted two approaching donkey-carts in front of a cloud of fumes and dust created by some fifty vehicles roaring up in their wake. As they drew nearer, Yaqoob revved up the engine and began to inch the car out of the lay-by. The two donkeys were almost dwarfed by their entourage; but there was no denying their speed – the Kibla donkey is said to achieve speeds of up to 40 kph, and this looked close. The two were neck-and-neck, their jockeys perched on top of the tiny carts using their whips energetically, although not cruelly.

The noise of the approaching vehicles grew; horns tooting, bells ringing, and the special rattles used just for this purpose (like maracas, a metal container filled with dried beans). Men standing on top of their cars and vans, hanging out of taxis and perched on lorries, all cheered and shouted, while the vehicles jostled to get to the front of the convoy.

Yaqoob chose exactly the right moment to edge out of the road and swerve in front of the nearest car, finding the perfect place to see the two donkeys and at the front of the vehicles. This was Formula One without rules, or a city-centre rush hour gone anarchic; a complete flouting of every type of traffic rule and common sense.

Our young driver relished this unusual test of driving skills. It was survival of the fittest, and depended upon the ability to cut in front of a vehicle with a sharp flick of the steering wheel (no lane discipline here); quick reflexes to spot a gap in the traffic for a couple of seconds; nerves of steel, and an effective horn. There were two races – the motorized spectators at the back; in front, the two donkeys, still running close and amazingly not put off by the uproar just behind them. Ahead of the donkeys, oncoming traffic – for it was a main road – had to dive into the ditch and wait there until we had passed. Yaqoob loved it. We stayed near to the front, his hand permanently on the horn and his language growing more colourful with every vehicle that tried to cut in front (I understood the worst Urdu obscenities).

The road straightened and levelled, and everyone picked up speed as we neared the end of the race. But just as they were reaching the finishing line, the hospital gate, there was a near pile-up as the leading donkey swerved, lost his footing and he and the cart tumbled over. The race was over.

And then the trouble began. I assumed the winner was the one who completed the race but it was not seen that way by everyone. Apart from the two jockeys and 'officials' (who, it turned out, were actually monitoring the race) there were over a hundred punters who had all staked money on the race, and therefore had strong opinions. Some were claiming that the donkey had fallen because the other one had been ridden too close to him. Voices were raised, fists were out and tempers rising. Everyone gathered around one jockey and official, while the bookmakers were trying to insist that the race should be re-run.

Yaqoob and Iqbal were nervous of hanging around a volatile situation. They agreed to find out for me what was happening, ordering me to stay inside the car as they were swallowed up by the crowd. They emerged some time later. 'It's still not resolved,' said Iqbal, 'but it's starting to get nasty. I think we should leave.' As we drove away, Yaqoob reflected on his driving skills. 'I really enjoyed that,' he said as we drove off at a more sedate pace. 'But I don't even have my licence yet because I'm underage!'

They both found this hilarious, but I was glad he hadn't told me before; an inexperienced, underage driver causing a massive pile-up in the middle of the high-stakes donkey race could have caused problems.

The next stage of my journey was Islamabad, to see a kabaddi tournament. In contrast to donkey races, of which little is known outside Karachi, kabaddi is one of the subcontinent's most famous traditional sports and has been gaining popularity all round the world in recent years. (The International Kabaddi Tournament in 1996 was held in Birmingham, England.) It has been described by the English journalist David Hunn, writing in *The News*, Lahore, as 'a pretty silly sport, that rouses millions of Asians to a fanatical frenzy. Kabaddi is a macho form of playground tag'. An accurate if dismissive description.

Unlike cricket, which is an English sport adapted to the Asian lifestyle and mentality, kabaddi is the pride of the subcontinent and, rising from humble village roots, is an integral part of the nation's sporting life. 'It reflects a philosophy of simple living and high thinking,' claims one encyclopaedia, and these qualities are still reflected today, even in the rather imposing stadium with TV coverage and international teams.

The Kabaddi Association Handbook puts the game rather grandly into context: 'Games provide not only an emotional outlet to a number of people but also rid the participants of animal spirits and excess emotions . . . There is no other sport except kabaddi which uses the individual and the collective potentialities of man. It develops a strong physique, determination and sense of responsibility. This is probably the most economical means of keeping an individual hale and hearty, because it does not require any costly costumes or equipment.'

The Kabaddi Association has organized many competitions and championships, and thrives as much in Pakistan as in India. The biggest breakthrough came when kabaddi became a sport included in the Asian Games, and they still hope that one day it will be part of the Olympics.

I had only ever seen informal games on the warm sands of Chowpatty Beach in Bombay, and on the Esplanade in Calcutta. I remembered seeing several young men in their underpants running to catch their opponents, who tried valiantly to escape, and a long continuous chant of 'kabaddi kabaddi kabaddi' and lots of people gathered to watch them giving their enthusiastic support.

There were four teams taking part in the tournament: two from Pakistan, one from India and one (to my surprise) from Canada. The stadium was far from full, but there was a great deal of noise, especially from the group of musicians in traditional costume who stood at the edge of the playing area, drummers beating frantically. Every time a point was scored, the music and cheers grew louder. For a game of tag, it was taken pretty seriously.

This was circle-style kabaddi, played in a circular area marked on the field, with a team of four on opposite sides. One player, called the 'raider', has to pass across the halfway line into the opposing (the 'anti-raiders' or 'antis') team's half of the circle, touch a player, and return to his side without getting caught. Simple, but a couple of factors make this rather more challenging.

First, one of kabaddi's most famous characteristics is that the raider must during his raid mutter a continuous 'kabaddi kabaddi kabaddi', without taking breath. This is called the cant. Secondly, during the whole procedure the four members of the opposing team are doing their best to catch him and bring him down to the ground. If the raider manages to touch an opposing player and be safely back in his own half without losing the cant, he then scores a point for his team. If the antis succeed in holding him down or bringing him to the ground, then they score a point. (There are, however, certain rules and restrictions to ensure the players' safety – for instance the raider must not be brought down in such a way that he hits his head on the ground.)

It was one thing to watch it in a village field or on a beach; quite another in Pakistan's capital city, where the atmosphere was completely different. But what was more interesting was that the entire team from Canada all had the surname 'Singh' and were all migrants from northern India. So here was an added dimension: a sport which through migration has spread its popularity into America, Britain and Canada.

'The world is getting smaller. This sport is one of the most important ways of remembering our culture. These sporting events keep a nation of Punjabis alive wherever they are from. Each *gurudwara* [Sikh temple] in British Columbia and Vancouver runs a sports club, and has a kabaddi team. Some of the best players are sponsored privately by companies,' said the coach of the Canadian team, another Mr Singh.

Most of the Canadian team who I spoke to echoed his words. Some added that although they weren't particularly religious, they kept in touch with their local temple for sports such as kabaddi. 'I left India sixteen years ago,' said one member, 'and if it weren't for this team I would really feel homesick.'

On the second day I was able to get accustomed to the rules

and skills of certain individuals, but the more I watched, the more I was struck by its absurd simplicity, and amazed that such an unsophisticated game could still be so popular. Its beauty surely lies in its simplicity, a game which evolved as a village sport needing no equipment. Yet it has always been looked upon as an aid to the development of manly, war-like skills; some would even go as far as saying that its emphasis on man-to-man contest helps train people to be warriors. I noted that, while speed is the most important aspect for the raider, kabaddi does use some of the skills of wrestling in bringing and holding down the raider. However, looking at the top players, many of them of average build, it's clear that the most important skill is speed and reflex.

'*Pakistan zindabad, Pakistan zindabad,*' bellowed the crowd, which was substantially larger on the second and final day, as they watched a final which saw a Pakistan team clash with India. It was what the spectators and the media wanted, even though much less of a dramatic clash than if it had been cricket. Each time an Indian attacker was successfully brought down, especially when it was one of the broad burly Sikhs, screams of joy came from the onlookers and the musicians burst into tune.

Television cameras were covering the tournament live and the crew and the many journalists gathered there let impartiality be forgotten and they screamed Pakistan to a 73 points to 46 victory, which saw the crowd erupt in delight when the final whistle blew. The band began a rousing burst of folk songs, swamped as the crowd ran down the stadium steps and flooded the field, carrying their team on their shoulders and dancing.

Other enthusiastic crowds fresh in my memory, I made a quick getaway, marvelling at the success of this village game which has evolved into an international sport.

7

Real Bruisers

The Pir Batho Mela was in full swing when I arrived. I had touched down in Karachi just a few hours earlier from Islamabad, and Mr Arkhund (an astounding source of valid information) had already told me about this festival, which promised animal races and malakhara.

Malakhara, he explained, was the original Sindi wrestling, now performed only at melas and village competitions. The sport, of unknown origin, is believed to be as old as the history of the state and is an important cultural and historical part of the heritage of Sind.

Unfortunately, we arrived too late to see the camel racing, and there was only one bull race left, of which I just caught a frustratingly narrow glimpse – a few seconds' worth, just enough to catch sight of two bulls attached to each cart, on top of which a man was standing, barely visible through a cloud of dust.

The races had finished for the day and the crowd dispersed to the other attractions, very similar to those at the Sibi mela. There were rows of stalls and the usual goods for sale, the typical selection of food (which here looked very unappetizing) and muddy-coloured chai.

It was hot, too hot to amble aimlessly, but once the sun had descended to a comfortable level and the burning heat diminished, the start of the malakhara was announced. It was held in a field with a high barrier round it – presumably to prevent people watching from the outside without buying a 2-rupee ticket – and spectators sat on the ground in a ring. The commentator had already reached feverish excitement, even though the wrestling had not yet begun.

The wrestlers wore the baggy trousers of their shalwar kameez, with the bottom of the trousers pulled up and tucked into the waist, looking like short baggy bloomers which ballooned from their bottoms. They were topless and wore a turban on their heads. Before the fight, they carried out a sacrosanct ritual particular to this sport. Each took his *sundhro*, which is a very long piece of green material, and with the help of his opponent twisted it into a long rope. Then each wrestler wrapped his sundhro round his waist and tied it securely.

A few old musicians lounging in the shade started up on their *davul* (a kind of drum) and zurna to introduce the first wrestlers. The rule of this form of wrestling, which is quite unique, is for each man to aim to get his hand inside the back of his opponent's sundhro, and then throw him to the ground from that position. (Some believe that this is the origin of sumo.) Other than this move, the arms may not be used to perform any type of wrestling grip, the legs being more important and used to trip and overbalance the opponent and eventually floor him.

It was very different from the rhiji I had seen in Quetta; much faster and more of a frantic scrap, with several matches continuing simultaneously on the field. They darted, each trying to grab at the other's waist, snatching their necks, trying to spin them round to overbalance them. The pair nearest to me grabbed each other's arms, trying to fling each other around, legs kicking in a kind of clumsy waltz; after a few minutes of this, one eventually got his hand in the other's sundhro, grabbed it, pulled it and flung his opponent on his back. He hit the ground with a tremendous wallop.

Such force meant that the fallen wrestler suffered not only defeat, but also it seemed to me severe concussion. He lay motionless on the ground with no one overly concerned except me. The victor went over, slapped him around to revive him and poured water over his face, so if he didn't die by knock-out it would probably be through drowning. A couple of other wrestlers, who had finished, came over to massage his face and neck. Gradually, he regained consciousness and blearily opened his eyes, realized his defeated situation and to restore some semblance of wounded pride he staggered drunkenly to his feet and swayed away. This, I came to realize as the afternoon progressed, is an extremely common end to a fight.

On winning, every victor completed a lap of honour, stopping by the spectators who offered him money, a practice which has remained unchanged for generations. There was one small area where the guests sat on rugs, rather than the grass, indicating that they were VIPs and wealthier than the others, and all the winners made it their first port of call. This is typical of a malakhara competition, where no committee presents prize-money.

There are two rounds to each fight, and the overall winner is the one who wins the second round. Permitted tactics include a leg-lock, to entangle the leg between the opponent's and trip him. A lift and spin means just that: lifting the opponent by his belt and spinning him in the air to try and throw him. In order to prevent being thrown, the defender can put his leg in his attacker's crotch. And an attacker can place his foot on his opponent's foot, holding him in his crotch and pushing him down.

A fair sport, I thought as we left the field, the driver chewing his umpteenth packet of red *paan* and trying to speak with a mouthful of blood-red spittle. A sport which not only demanded great strength and force, but also a skull made of rubber. It was a hugely interesting contrast to the kabaddi which I had seen just the day before, a few hundred kilometres away; one attracted great coverage, publicity and international honours; one was limited to village fairs and although attracted great local interest, would never reach any fame beyond the boundaries of Sind.

Enticed by further rhiji and malakhara, my next venue was Lahore where the *akharas*, or traditional wrestling houses, are surrounded by a glorious history. Wrestling is a sport that was never taken seriously in England, most people's knowledge limited to Saturday afternoon TV during the 1970s and 80s, where Big Daddy sat on the head of an even bigger chap, with screaming schoolchildren at the ringside. More recently, American WCW has a growing fan-club in Asia thanks to satellite television.

But traditional Asian wrestling holds a proud place in the sporting and cultural history of those countries stretching from Mongolia through Central Asia, across the subcontinent to Iran and Turkey. Nowadays, although it has declined in popularity, there are still the remains of a great tradition, even if they fight without the television coverage and glamour of Western wrestling.

Lahore has the highest number of akharas (a Persian word meaning 'arena') from the days of pre-Partition with India, and kushti (traditional wrestling) is still learned there. Ifraz, secretary to the Punjab Cultural Department, offered to take me to Iqbal Park to see the weekend kushti practice.

Before that we visited the Chirgan Mela, or Festival of Lights, held at the shrine of the Sufi saint and poet, Lal Hussain, on the outskirts of Lahore. Ifraz thought there might be a display of kushti, as it is routine in religious and cultural melas.

Chirgan Mela, a Sufi festival, is the celebration of the anniversary of Hussain's death. The Sufis are one of the sects of Islam who take on the mystical side of the religion, although they claim not to be separate but to transcend all the different sects of the religion, their emphasis being on personal spiritual development.

Many Muslims are critical and take a cynical view of them, including Ifraz. We entered and stumbled slowly through the crush of pilgrims which led to the shrine. Inside the grounds of the shrine, the focal point was a huge blazing furnace around which men, women and children were praying, singing and dancing.

A truck arrived from which two men handed out free milk and tea. They were mobbed as a horde of stampeding village women produced shopping bags they had hidden inside their clothes, and grabbed as many free samples as they could.

There was the unmistakable smell of marijuana smoke oozing from groups of people lolling around on the grass, passing around joints the size of snooker cues. Very stoned-looking men with long matted hair were swaying, waving their arms. If the music was a little louder it could have been Glastonbury. The atmosphere was certainly festive, as a mela would suggest, but in a style I wouldn't associate with Islam. Ifraz was clearly unimpressed and tutted with disapproval at their display of celebration. 'They don't really know what they're doing. This isn't permitted in Islam.' 'But if they consider this part of religion, isn't that OK?' I asked him, getting rather confused. He answered with a defiant 'No' and I thought it best to close the subject. There was no evidence of kushti – perhaps potential wrestlers were already too stoned for any action.

'We should go to Iqbal Park – we'll find it there.' So we returned to the centre of Lahore and back to the park at the edge of Lahore's Old City where I used to watch local cricket. Dedicated to physical exercise and sports rather than botanical wonder, with little of nature other than grass and a few trees, the entire park is filled daily with compact and cramped but furiously competitive games so that it's impossible to see where one game ends and the next begins.

We headed to the Muslim Health Club, a large, shabby wooden hut at the edge of the park, with a covered area outside it where exercise equipment was stored. Old, faded posters on the wall depicted wrestling heroes, men with serious expressions and legs like tree-trunks, grimly holding trophies of their success.

A few young men doing warm-up exercises introduced us to Salahuddin, the *khaleefa* (leader, or literally 'star') in charge of the club, an ex-wrestler who had won glory for the country in national games. 'Every day, morning and evening, I come here. At 6 am, we have training for two hours before people go to their office. Then in the evening, people come after work.'

Salahuddin was now in his fifties, a huge, sturdy man carrying a few extra pounds in a slight paunch which hung over his waist. It provoked me to comment on the substantial girth that most *pehlivans* (the word for wrestler, probably of Persian origin) carried around with them, if the posters of them were accurate.

He roared with laughter. 'The pehlivans were as famous for their daily diets as they were for their strength and their honour,' he told me, and went on to describe the daily intake of some of Lahore's better-known characters. The legendary Rahim Pehlwan Sultaniwala, for example, would scoff 2,000 almonds, condensed soup made from 8 kilograms of meat, two whole chickens and a quarter-kilo of ghee (clarified butter). His daily exercise burned up most calories: ten miles of jogging, 2,000 arm exercises, 3,000 leg exercises, digging and scraping the akhara, then finally practising kushti with forty others, simultaneously.

Salahuddin had won many medals for Pakistan and was Asian champion in the 1970s. He showed us photos of himself, looking more streamlined but with the same surly expression that all wrestlers wore, amiable as he was. 'There are some people still very keen on kushti, but there is no money in it these days. And how can we compete with that?' He jerked his head towards the cricket matches.

'Wrestling is really losing out these days, mainly because it hasn't been commercialized like other sports. TV wrestling isn't really a sport, it's just *noora kushti*.' He spoke with a scowl on his face. Noora kushti is a term meaning fixed fight, a choreographed bout.

It was a sentiment repeated often: a keen sportsman could

easily go into cricket and in the face of potential fame, fortune and your face on every soft-drink billboard as a cricketer, there was little prospect for the long-term survival of the akhara. Kushti may be a gruelling sport demanding stamina and strength, but it lacked glamour. For Salahuddin, however, a daily work-out at the akhara was a part of national heritage. 'The akhara is part of the history of this city: great pehlivans like Bholu, Gama and Abid came to Lahore after Partition, and were great heroes to the people. At that time, wrestlers earned prestige in society and were respected by everyone. They went to the akhara every day to train, and their *dangals* [wrestling bouts] were enjoyed by many spectators. These days, there are fewer akharas open in Lahore and fewer people following the sport.'

Salahuddin remembers the days when pehlivans were heroic figures in the community, before and shortly after Partition. If one walked down the street, housewives would send their sons out to get blessings from him. The pehlivan was a symbol of virtue with qualities of humility, and they would always pray after rising early every day and embarking on a series of tough physical exercises.

As we talked, a small, lean pehlivan, wearing only a loin cloth, had an enormous wooden block attached by ropes around his shoulders. He dragged it around the akhara, an earthy pit of some twenty feet in diameter, walking in concentric circles to flatten the soil. When he had covered the whole area, he attacked the soil with a large spade to churn it up, and then repeated the whole process with the wood again. It reminded me of the tale of Sisyphus, doomed to pushing a heavy boulder to the top of a hill to see it roll back down again, and then push it back up for all eternity.

Several more pehlivans began their work-out. It was a far cry from plush gymnasiums with wall-to-wall beautiful bodies posing in front of the mirrored walls whilst riding electronic exercise bikes. The Muslim Health Club had a couple of broken mirrors propped up against the peeling plaster outside walls; several young men lay on the wooden floor (which surely put splinters in bottoms) performing dozens of sit-ups and press-ups in unison. A few dumb-bells balanced against the wall were the only weights around, as this fitness regime emphasizes exercise without equipment.

A pair of wrestlers entered the akhara, smeared each other with a little oil and then with soil, to give a better grip. They wore tiny loin-cloths tied tightly between the legs, so there was no clothing to grab onto. As in other forms of wrestling in the subcontinent, they would grasp their opponent's waist, and try to get him onto his back. This was part of their daily practice and Salahuddin watched and occasionally called out advice. Everyone had a turn, swapping partners until everyone had gone through enough practice.

By the time they had finished it was getting dark and the park was deserted of cricketers. One young pehlivan had been squatting on the concrete floor for the previous hour, crushing a few kilos of almonds in a large wooden bowl with a huge mallet until he'd made a thick paste, to which he added water, milk, black pepper and coriander seeds. This was *sardai*, the special drink all pehlivans drink every day. They offered me a large metal cup – it looked repulsive, but tasted surprisingly delicious. I drained the cup to the amusement of everyone, and I got the feeling they knew something that I didn't.

I asked Ifraz what was so funny. He looked a little awkward and he and Salahuddin had a very long discussion. I was getting impatient: 'Ifraz – what's he saying?' In a rather convoluted manner, he explained that it related to a theory – unclear whether fact or fiction – that pehlivans were supposed to abstain from sex in the approach to a fight. Some (the stricter ones) would abstain for forty days. The belief is that losing sperm meant losing energy and manhood – so most pehlivans were celibate for large periods of their life.

Then, of course, the fear was that they would become impotent, so energy-giving drinks such as these were given as a kind of antidote – supposedly being aphrodisiac. Much to my relief, having drunk a whole pint of the stuff, I didn't have the urge to rip off anyone's loin-cloth. In fact the drink had absolutely no effect on me at all.

A couple of days later, I had the opportunity to visit the akhara where the legendary Bholu and his family used to practise every day. 'The death of Bholu Pehlivan may well mark the end of an era in Pakistan,' claimed Lahore's *Dawn* newspaper when Bholu died in 1985. His family provided the most noble wrestling lineage in the subcontinent and the names of Gama, Imam Baksh, Aziz Baksh are sacred to anyone who enters an akhara.

This akhara, in a small back-street in the old city, is a humble venue showing no signs of the eminence which the pehlivans once held, although there was more equipment than in the Muslim Health Club with weights and bench-presses. On the walls were similar posters of old wrestling stars, rather than the old photographs of the Bholu and others of the illustrious wrestling dynasty I had hoped to see. Apart from the graves, placed discreetly at the side of the akhara, within the walls, no one would know its significance.

'In my father and grandfather's era, there was great pride and prestige for a pehlivan. It was an honourable and noble sport of which each generation was eager to carry on the legacy. But really, the akhara is dead – it died when Bholu died in the early 80s. The wrestlers now have no financial support from any institution,' said Abid, who showed us round. He was the nephew of Bholu Pehlivan and grandson of Imam Baksh, but gave up training in his twenties and now runs a foreign exchange office in town.

After the legendary heroes of Rustam and Sohrab from Iran, two of the world's greatest wrestlers, the sport was picked up in the subcontinent mainly by Muslims. The rajas and maharajas were great patrons, giving monthly wages to the better wrestlers, and each royal house had one. Aziz Baksh Pehlivan was an employee of the princely state of Datiya in northern India, and a state wrestler. He and two of his sons, Gama and Imam Baksh, earned world fame and were recognized as all-time heroes.

A proud memory for every Pakistani wrestler is the occasion when Gama flattened the European Champion, Zbyszko, in London in 1909. The return fight was in Patiala in India, where Gama again defeated the Pole to the appreciation of a huge crowd including Maharaja Bhupendra Singh of Patiala. This prompted the Maharaja – an eccentric character who also gave his support to cricket (including building the world's highest cricket ground in Chail, northern India) – to patronize wrestling.

Bholu was one of Imam's seven sons and after being taught by his uncle and reaching a high standard, he gave the sport's image a great boost throughout the subcontinent. After Partition in 1947, Bholu's entire family migrated to Lahore, where they set up akharas. He was awarded the Mace of Honour in 1949 and became Rustam-e Pakistan (champion of Pakistan), and continued to beat foreign competitors in other countries. But in order to enter the international ring, Bholu had to learn free-style.

His heart had always been in *desi kushti* (traditional wrestling) and he lamented the fact that during the 1960s and 70s, the art which was intrinsically a subcontinental one, was slowly dying, for which he blamed lack of government support. His dream was to open more akharas in every town and city to promote the art. Things descended to an all-time low when Japan's best martial artist, Antonio Inoki, came to Karachi for a *dangal* in 1979 and beat Bholu, which was seen as bringing great shame on the family even though he was in his late thirties and at less than peak fitness. Bholu never recovered from that humiliation and the next time Inoki came, he sent his nephew to fight. The match was adjudged to be a draw, but people didn't take the result seriously and accusations of 'noora kushti' flew.

The arrival of foreign wrestlers to fight in Pakistan caused many of the traditionalists to wince. 'Even this time, when Inoki has come with a team of wrestlers having funny names like Billy Crusher or Flaming Flying Dragon, the exhibition shows have nothing to do with the game of wrestling itself,' reported *The Statesman* of 13 August 1984. 'As expected, the performances of these so-called world-renowned grapplers only reminded people of the wrestling drama they watch every Friday on TV.'

But the virtues of the pehlivan and the tradition of sending a small boy to train in the akhara not just to learn physical skills but also to make him a better person, seem to have disappeared. These days many wrestlers have chosen a lifestyle which would make Bholu and his ancestors turn in their graves. Rumour has it that there is a greater demand (and greater money) in Lahore for a wrestler to be employed by local mafia, using their strength and size to intimidate; indeed, many are reputed to be involved as hit-men and to extort debts repayments.

One of Bholu's brothers, Aslam, sadly illustrated the demise of the honourable wrestling tradition with his death in his thirties, in 1989. 'Unfortunately, during the last years of his life, Aslam fell victim not only to several physical ailments but also to some extremely debilitating trends in the environment,' the *Pakistan Times* tactfully reported. Word has it, though many deny it to preserve his honour, that Aslam died from heroin addiction.

I was given another tour around some old akharas courtesy of three committee members from the Pakistan Wrestling Federation. The federation has come under criticism from many pehlivans for failing to ensure the continuation of desi kushti, their efforts instead going to competitive, international style.

Many khaleefas feel that money should be given to maintain the akharas in good condition and also pay the khaleefas, who survive on minimal payments, a reasonable wage. For their part, the Federation claim they are trying to improve the status of wrestling in general, and need more money for the upkeep of the akharas. I felt that more than just financial help is required – the image of desi kushti needs renewing, interest in it needs revitalizing.

It was a whistle-stop tour, starting with the Police Training Club, where officers have access to good sporting facilities. Many institutions, like police, army services and major industries have on-site sports facilities and usually their own wrestling team. Then we visited Akhy akhara, the oldest in the city thought to be around seventy-five years old, overlooked by the Lahore Fort. Ikram akhara was our next point, famous for its graves of prominent pehlivans. No sporting activities are carried out there these days and it had the atmosphere of a cemetery; the only life evident was a couple of dozen men sitting on the gravestones, playing cards and gambling with one-rupee notes. Most wore a glassy expression and the smell of marijuana was probably just the tip of it. 'No-good people here', said Mr Rana of the Federation grimacing, reminding me of Mr Mohammed Ali in Quetta. It was sad to see a place where such great and noble sporting activities had been performed, degenerated into such dishonour.

The Champions akhara was more positive: inside, the walls were covered in posters and, whether from yesterday or half a century ago, all displayed the same style of well-built man: posing to show those unmistakable chunky thighs and thick-set calves, the standard grave expression which announced 'I'm macho and take myself awfully seriously', the substantial waistline and the skimpy briefs. In thick arms he usually held lovingly the *gurz*, the silver or bronze mace of honour awarded to wrestling champs. The khaleefa, Abdul Rasheed, showed us some of the pictures, including ones of himself when he competed with some of the great fighters.

A number of pehlivans were exercising – the same formula of jogging around the akhara soil in circles, then basic stretching exercises, push-ups and sit-ups – then began their kushti practice, supervised by the khaleefa. A couple of dozen men and boys, relatives, other pehlivans or simply outsiders, were sitting around the sides watching. Most men attend the same akhara as their fathers and grandfathers, so there is a strong family tradition.

At the end of their session, the man who had been grinding almonds in a wooden bowl prepared the sardai, and they poured a huge glass for myself and Mr Rana which we knocked back before saying our farewells, and driving off. In the car, Mr Rana winced. 'This sardai gives my stomach many problems. When I drank it before, it gave me loose movements. Maybe you have the same?' That was really what I wanted to hear just before embarking on a twelve-hour bus journey.

8

Camel? What Camel?

Mr Rana took me to my bus to Bahawalpur; from there I would take another bus to Uchch Sharif, in southern Punjab. Ifraz, after a series of long and complicated telephone calls to various parts of the country, confirmed a mela in Uchch Sharif. 'Go directly to the Magistrates' Office and they will take you to the mela. It lasts for three days and has camel-racing on the first day, and bull-racing on the second. The Magistrate, Mr Ashraf, knows your programme and has arranged a vehicle for you.'

It all sounded blissfully well-organized and I was looking forward to the races. Camel-racing in this country doesn't have the notoriety of its more wealthy counterpart in Saudi Arabia and Dubai, where young boys, some as young as six, are kidnapped or 'bought' from poor families in India and Bangladesh. They are tied to the camels' backs and forced to race, which often ends in injury or the death of the boy, and is all done for high-stakes betting. The racing in the subcontinent is never brutal, the camels are ridden by adults and is done merely for entertainment with little financial gain.

The bus rides were uncomfortable and arrived late, but at least the sardai did not live up to Mr Rana's gloomy prognosis. I arrived in the Magistrates' Office at Uchch Sharif at 10 am, two hours later than he was expecting me.

Mr Ashraf was an untidy middle-aged man, who looked somewhat harassed when I eventually burst into his office. 'I'm terribly sorry for the delay – are we too late for the racing? Do we have to leave now? Is it bull-racing today? What time does the mela start?' I babbled rather incoherently.

He looked baffled. 'What bull-racing?' My heart began to sink and I had the feeling of déjà-vu. 'What mela? What are you here for? We were told that you came to see the archaeological ruins. I have organized a vehicle to show you around.' Panic. I mentally put Ifraz on a painful torture instrument.

During a terse discussion I tried (unsuccessfully) to keep my cool, and he tried (unsuccessfully) to control the situation. It transpired that by the time the messages filtered from Ifraz to the Magistrate via four other people, the contents, like the best Chinese Whispers, had completely altered. From the original 'going to the mela to see the races' it had become 'going to see old ruins'. Worse, there wasn't a mela, anyway.

He tried to placate me with tea, lemonade and a plate of salty biscuits. I phoned Ifraz to shout at him, but he had 'forgotten' ever having told me about a mela, and then blamed everyone else for getting it wrong.

Mr Ashraf drove me out to the shrine of a Sufi saint, where there was something of a mela. Throngs of people were there, it was just not the sort of mela I'd been expecting. 'Camels? What camels?' said a puzzled hawker selling postcards of Indian movie stars and Pakistani cricketers at the entrance of the shrine. 'This is mela but there aren't any animal races. But here – look at this.' He jerked his head in the direction of the field below us to a half-built stadium. 'There's a really big camel and bull race in two weeks.' His eyes lit up at the prospect. 'Madam – you must come to see it. Lots of bulls. Biggest race of the year. Very fine!' That information wasn't really welcome as I wouldn't be able to attend the event.

Mr Ashraf's interpretation of the garbled message was based on the fact that most visitors to Uchch Sharif do come to see archaeological sites. In AD 711 the town came under Muslim influence, but was hotly fought over until the Mughal emperor Akbar eventually annexed Uchch to the Delhi Sultanate and it became an important cultural and literary centre. There are some extremely impressive remains, including the tomb of Bibi Jalwindi and the Mausoleum of Baha al-Din uchi, boasting well-preserved internal mosaics.

I wasn't really in the mood to appreciate such impressive historic and aesthetic wonders, though. However, more hopeful news came from Bahawalpur. A Mr Khalid at the Bahawalpur Arts Council suggested there might be an agricultural mela in his region the following day and would I come over? So, back to Bahawalpur I went.

I followed his directions and found the Eidkah mosque, striking with its yellow minarets, and then his office where I was greeted by an embarrassed Mr Khalid, a small, skinny man with a serious expression set in a hollow face. He was feeling guilty as it transpired he was the crucial link of the Chinese Whispers game.

'I am so, so sorry about this. I do not know where this information has come about this Uchch Sharif mela. I received the message that you were coming but,' he shrugged, 'what has happened I don't know.' His tone lightened. 'Now, I have been on the phone to everyone and we have some good news. Tomorrow they tell me is a donkey race, and the day after that is a bull-racing festival in a nearby village. Will you stay for two more days?' After having come all that way, I didn't need much persuading.

The next day we drove out to a village to see the 'confirmed' donkey race which, as I could have told him based on my Karachi experience, did not happen. Hopes now rested on the bull race, rumoured to be the following day, which became a little more likely after we met some bull trainers in town. One young man from the village, who worked in Bahawalpur, assured us that everyone had been training their bulls for this special festival. The day and the venue seemed pretty concrete but the time of starting varied dramatically, depending on who you asked, anywhere between 9 am and 3 pm.

The next morning we were joined by Mr Khalid's friend and we drove 50 kilometres to Bahargoth Asrani to join the Jindu Shah Pir mela, timed to celebrate a successful harvest. They were due to harvest a bumper crop of wheat a few days later and a day of bull-racing was the traditional way of celebrating this. We arrived at the village at eleven o'clock; then, weaving along small paths and mud tracks, we eventually drove into farmland, with rich fields of glowing yellow and assorted shades of green. Eventually we rose up from a low path into a field filled with hundreds of people, the blast of a sound-system and, unmistakably, bulls.

We parked the car alongside trucks from which magnificent white bulls were being led out. Owners busied themselves grooming and preparing their animals, and people clustered around each one examining the animal and murmuring observations. Most people were at the near end of the field by the road, waiting for the preparations to be completed.

One of the organizers brought us into the field, a charpoi appeared from nowhere and we were given space at the front, just out of reach of the inevitable crowds of children. Tin cups of water and tea appeared – heavens knows from where as we seemed a long way from tea-making facilities.

Before the start of the race two huge white bulls, marigold garlands around their thick necks and twined about their horns, were paraded around the field (now lined on three sides with spectators), along the track where they would be racing. A band of musicians and drummers played to honour the bulls, accompanying the procession and encouraging a troop of followers to dance and sing along with it.

There were two 'tracks' side-by-side, each a wide strip around 300 metres long, on freshly-ploughed soil which wasn't an easy running surface. Each bull, having been admired and petted and cheered on by admirers, was then harnessed to his cart, standard sturdy, heavy wooden carts. The bulls didn't appreciate this and there was a great deal of foot-stomping, snorting and grunting, as they tried to shake free of the harness.

They were lined up at the starting point, the end away from the road so most people were near the finish line. Just before the race began, the riders mounted the carts as the announcer blared introductions through a crackly microphone. Then, with noisy cheers of encouragement, they were off.

Two clouds of dust rose from the eight extremely large and powerful hooves churning up the earth, through which it was possible to catch the silhouette of two men standing on their carts, feet planted well apart and crouched slightly forward for balance. They cracked their whips to catch the bulls' huge rear ends, calling out and shouting frenetically. As they got closer to the finish, the roar of the spectators grew louder. Their speed was impressive; the two were neck and neck most of the way and then, to a great cheer and a crescendo of crackles from the announcer's microphone, they crossed the finish line only a couple of seconds apart. The entire race had taken less than a minute.

The noise level diminished slowly and the bulls were unharnessed. The spectators gathered around the victor, who, accompanied by the musicians, paraded around the field again, this time nearly swamped under scores of congratulatory hands and flowers thrown by the spectators. The owner and the rider then collected money from the spectators, who held out ten-rupee notes, stuffing them down the shirt of the owner. It surprised me to learn that there isn't any betting here; the only money around was voluntary 'donations' from the crowd, with often a little going to the loser too.

A total of sixty bulls present meant there were another twenty-nine races to go. All the races followed the same pattern – a parade, music, a survey of the track, the race, post-race celebrations and another parade. Each bull belonged to one of a group of farmers from the region, and at the end of the mela the group with the most victories is declared winner. The champion bull is declared, based on the fastest time of completing the course. Some bulls are bought and trained only for the purpose of racing, but most are used also for farming and transport.

More people arrived as the afternoon wore on, and they told me the best part of the mela was in the evening during the final races, when the alcohol would flow. As one organizer explained, 'We will start our party at nightfall, drink and dance and sing until morning. Will you come?' Exactly the sort of evening I had in mind, but Mr Khalid reminded me that I had a flight to catch from Lahore the following day.

As we drove back to Bahawalpur, Mr Khalid smiled for the first time in two days – probably because he was relieved to see the back of his guest with unusual demands. He put me on a minibus to Multan, nearly three hours away, from where I had to get to Lahore, for my flight the next afternoon. I was still his responsibility until leaving, so he bought me a ticket for the front seat, and with a huge smile, waved me off.

Two bus journeys got me to Lahore at 3 am, and well after that I arrived back at my hotel, to be greeted by a delighted bunch of reception staff who were always entertained by my activities. Dying for a few hours' sound sleep, I collapsed into bed but was soon disturbed by a small noise. After I'd heard it several times, a small movement got me on the alert.

I was nervous – guests, whether on two legs or on four, are not welcome. The television's cable clattered, and there it was, in all its glory, a four-legged, furry fiend sitting on the TV set. There was only possible and practical thing to do in such an emergency: get help.

'Hello, this is Miss Emma calling from room 204. I have a rat in my room.'

'Ji?'

'A rat. On the TV. I mean, sitting on the TV.'

'Ji? Ji?'

'Oh bloody hell. A rat – a BIG MOUSE. Please come and get rid of it – *jaldi, jaldi, jaldi.*' Hurry, hurry, hurry.

'Ah – a mouse? OK, we come.'

By the time this exchange was over, the big mouse had leapt off the TV and disappeared. The two receptionists, Imran and Asem, purposefully marched with tools necessary for the job: a hammer (small) and a tin of air-freshener (large). I stood on the bed (in case the rat took a bite out of my toes) in a rather unsuitable pair of black silk pyjamas, watching them.

'OK,' said Imran with the hammer, the younger and more gung-ho of the two. 'Where is he?' The rat had gone – probably scooted into room 206 for peace and quiet. They made a quick search of the cupboard, the floor and bathroom, but saw nothing; they then looked at me suspiciously. 'Are you sure? There is no mouse here. Maybe you make mistake? No mouse ever come this hotel.' At that stage I couldn't be bothered to show them the small scattering of droppings in the cupboard. 'Anyway, Miss Emma – very very sorry – maybe you change rooms?' We trooped along the corridor to another room, all carrying my belongings, and we must have made an odd trio; one in black pyjamas, one carrying a hammer, and one with the all-important can of air-freshener.

9

Poles in the Park

Another overland trip and I was back in India, where my plan was to spend the next month before returning to Pakistan for the polo season in May.

Bombay was much hotter and stickier than it had been three months earlier. India's second-largest city and considered the most Westernized, it is famous as a cultural and commercial centre, for its textile industry, and for 'Bollywood' and cricket. The local film industry is legendary for producing more films than Hollywood but with the emphasis on quantity rather than quality. Each film follows a set formula, containing bloody gun-battles which can switch to dance sequences amidst forests and mountains at the drop of a sari, and a love triangle consisting of good-looking impoverished hero fighting moustachioed villain over beautiful rich heroine. As with every popular culture it's predictable and hugely well-received.

Then there's cricket. Bombay has the most skill, enthusiasm and support in the country, and boasts innumerable clubs, tour-naments, coaching and areas for makeshift venues. Shivaji Park in the Dadar area of Bombay is the equivalent of Iqbal Park in Lahore and known as the nursery of Indian cricket. The park is special to every cricket lover, not just because some of India's best-loved players emerged from here – Sachin Tendulkar and Sunil Gavaskar to name but two – but here, five-year-old boys go for daily practices with their fathers; schoolgirls and the Bombay women's cricket team are coached here, and office workers exchange briefcases and ties for bats and pads to practise twice a day before and after work. A plethora of cricket matches take place back-to-back and at the end of the day, middle-aged ladies wearing saris and trainers, or young overweight businessmen with designer sportswear, set out in a purposeful jog around the massive circumference of the park. The entire area is a gathering of sporting activity literally from dawn to dusk.

Bombay is home to several important Indian indigenous games like *kho-kho*, *kabaddi* and *atya-patya*, many of which are played in Shivaji Park. Sports clubs ring the outside of the park, from the Bengal Athletics Club to the Maharashtra Kabaddi Association and the Bombay Tennis Club. Some are housed in old wooden pavilions crying out for a coat of paint, others have bright façades and fresh signboards. In the western corner is the Shri Samartha Vyayam Mandir, opened in 1945 and run by sixty coaches who train students in gymnastics, kabaddi, kho-kho and the Maharashtrian masterpiece, *mallekhamb*.

It was mallekhamb which had brought me back to Bombay, as one of the few cities which still promote this unusual sport. Mr Uday Deshpande is the beaming, balding chap who runs the Shri Samartha Vyayam Mandir. As it's an unpaid position, he crams in another job and then comes to the club every afternoon and evening.

He explained the meaning and origins of mallekhamb. *Malle* means man of power or strength (its origin is also seen in 'malakhara'), *khamb* means pole – hence 'strongman's pole'. The art of mallekhamb, traced back hundreds of years and one of the most ancient in the field of physical culture, combines will-power or inner strength with perfect physical fitness. The result is tricks, balancing acts, gymnastics and yoga, on a pole.

The tiny cramped office was packed with books, trophies, empty tea cups and a constantly ringing telephone, and Mr Deshpande was up to his bespectacled eyeballs in paperwork and children. The former for a forthcoming trip to Europe to perform a display of mallekhamb; the latter was a few hundred small children taking part in a sports course during their school holidays.

'We have more people coming to this club than any other in India,' he said as we drank tea and munched sesame bars at his crowded desk. 'Around three thousand students come every day, making us the largest non-government sports institution in the country – perhaps even the world.' He attempted very politely to turn away people who wandered into his office – parents of his students, young children, officials, coaches – and eventually gave up, offering everyone tea instead.

'Right now we are running a course for children of all ages, one of six camps a year, encouraging general health and fitness. We teach them some gymnastics, basic fitness, indigenous games, but mainly it is to encourage them to enjoy sports and to eat a healthy diet. We give them nutritious, energy foods.' He waved his hand at the dish of sesame bars.

Practitioners of mallekhamb claim that it boasts the most benefits, both mental and physical, of any sports. Like yoga it promotes suppleness, muscular strength and tone, and exercises every organ and limb of the body. But equally important is the development of concentration, promoting a calm mind and relaxed breathing.

That afternoon was the closing ceremony of their week-long course, with demonstrations, speeches and prize-giving. Outside the club-house in the park, anxious parents arrived holding the hands of little Sandeep or Sunita – aged between five and fifteen – dressed in their sportswear. Parents – mostly mothers but a few fathers clutching mobile phones (in India, as most places, it is important to be seen with your phone) – arranged themselves noisily in the rows of wooden chairs on the dusty grass, in front of the large stage set up especially for this. As they shuffled impatiently, the VIPs eventually made their late arrival, garlands were handed out and the obligatory speeches commenced.

It began with martial arts, with the smallest children giving a display of judo and karate. Then the music became more and more dramatic, and a string of small boys wearing loin-cloths leapt on to the sturdy pole which was attached to the ground on the stage. Jumping, smiling, lightly leaping over each other, they arranged themselves into a pyramid shape on the pole, their rubber limbs defying logic. And of course, as with the most difficult of tasks, they all did it with consummate ease.

In different combinations, boys leapt up the pole, struck a pose whilst balancing, then light as a feather sprang down again, each move greeted with a series of 'ooohs' and applause from the audience. A tiny boy, who looked no more than six years old, shimmied to the top of the pole and lay on his front with only his belly on the tip of the pole, and stretched out his arms in the *mayarasana* position (which looks a bit like the classic Superman pose) and received a great round of applause.

In another variation of mallekhamb these exercises are performed on a rope instead of a fixed pole; it is practised by learners as it's easier, and it's possible to wrap the rope around your limbs and body for extra support. Girls from a local school for the blind performed, feeling their way up the rope, then winding it around ankles and calves, and then hanging off it.

'The main problem in teaching blind people to do this,' their coach told me, 'is that really you need a physical demonstration in order to learn about the positions. You can watch how each position is done, and then copy. Blind children can only *feel* their way around the pole or the rope. In addition to that, blind students are never taught any sports, so aren't used to doing physical exercise.'

Two young men with large swords strapped to their backs and two knives to their arms then ran onto their poles without pausing for breath, leaping in and around each other, jumping off the pole, twisting, turning their torsos around the wood with not a drop of blood in sight.

Without a doubt, however, the day belonged to the computer operator. I had met Rajesh Narkhede earlier in the day in Mr Deshpande's office, sitting in a tiny room attending to an ailing computer. He worked there most days, he told me, and I had assumed, as he sat there in his shirt and trousers, that he was an office worker. But just a couple of hours later and the man was transformed. As the finale to the display, there was a drum-roll and dramatic music blared out of the loudspeakers, and in ran Rajesh. He wore nothing but a pair of luminous orange underpants, a massive smile and shining eyes.

Carrying two flaming torches like an official Olympic torch-bearer, he leapt up the pole – a gravity-defying feat as he could use neither of his hands – and performed a series of twists and turns, using only his legs and chest for support. If anyone's attention had wandered over the last half-hour it was brought smartly back.

Rajesh was quite a hero on the local mallekhamb scene. Although only in his late twenties, he had been an expert for several years and had received the Shiva Chchatrapati State Sports Award in 1992, after being the national champion for three years. Competing in mallekhamb is like any gymnastic or artistic sporting event, with marks awarded for levels of skill, technique and polish. But Rajesh told me fire torches (which he has performed with for twelve years) aren't used for competitions and he does 'fire tricks' only for demonstrations, one of only several people in the country who can do this. He retired several years ago from competition, and is now coaching. 'Once you've won this lifetime award, you've reached saturation level. But I get pleasure now out of coaching young people. It's a very important cultural and historical tradition, and it should never be forgotten.'

Most fans of mallekhamb see the importance and necessity of preserving the art. After all, when such a skill has been practised for possibly two thousand years (it is mentioned in the stories of Krishna) and definitely since the twelfth century, no one wants to see it disappear. In contrast to some traditional sports, where interest has diminished or become localized, mallekhamb remains popular, and with Mr Deshpande's encouragement, awareness of it has been spreading to other countries.

More than a sport to promote a supple body and healthy heart, it has a much deeper significance which is ingrained in Hindu philosophy. 'The Hindus believe that life comes from Brahman, the infinite, eternal source of light, and that all the creatures on earth have been separated from this light. The aim of life is to achieve nirvana, passing the soul back to Brahman,' Mr Deshpande explained.

'This takes more than one lifetime to achieve. Once a soul has been born as a human being, there are four traditional ways of working towards nirvana: the first by renouncing worldly things; the second by seeking truth and knowledge; the third through traditional activities and games, and the fourth through religious devotion.' He added that other Indian traditional games also reflect Hindu philosophy and way of life. Even chess, ludo and snakes and ladders (all of which are thought to have originated in India) are 'games of life' and part of the progression back to eternal light.

Originally, all the exercises on the pole were performed by wrestlers, and it is still recognized as the ideal way for the wrestler to train and keep his muscles strong and supple. It was also used as part of military training in Maharashtra (the state of which Bombay is the capital) when the Hindus were fighting the Muslims. Women fought alongside men and began to take up mallekhamb, which would explain why women and girls are as active and interested in it as men.

Each different display encourages skills and qualities. The pyramid, apart from looking pretty against the Bombay skyline, is a team performance with every participant depending on the others, for a slip-up by one could bring the whole thing crashing down. Therefore mutual trust between all members, in addition to strength and precision, is vital.

Often they have knives strapped to their bodies, based on the times when mallekhamb was used in military training and it was necessary to be able to scale enemy walls fully armed. Apart from increasing the skills required to climb the pole, the presence of knives also demonstrates traditional attacking and defensive positions. Mallekhamb has its own internal philosophy and its reflection of the Hindu meaning of life is summed up thus: 'The way of the warrior is not just to defeat the external enemy but to control the internal aggression of one's self so as to be free to achieve the nirvana.'

A more earthly game – like cricket – is seen as an end in itself and an escape from the pressures of everyday life. You might be a world-class fast bowler but this isn't going to improve your soul, which, the Indians argue, demonstrates the main difference between Eastern and Western philosophy. Some criticize the Western approach to sport, accusing its competitive emphasis of putting pressure on children who excel in a sport, to the extent that their schoolwork or other activities suffer. This can, some argue, sap their energy and produce one-dimensional adult sportsmen and women, rather than well-rounded human beings.

Mallekhamb is said to produce the latter and children who practise it from an early age tend to improve their academic performance. It encourages discipline, self-awareness and relaxation, which can extend to other areas of life.

The Shri Samartha Vyayam Mandir has been active for over fifty years and, more than just a sports club, it is, as Mr Deshpande writes in its brochure, 'relentlessly working for the cherished goal of the propagation and popularization of the indigenous activities'. His cause is well-known throughout India, and they are often called to give demonstrations to groups and institutions – even for events as unrelated as the 37th International Mathematical Olympiad in Bombay in July 1996, to which the Tata Institute of Fundamental Research invited them to give a display to their foreign guests.

Through displays and competitions, mallekhamb is gaining popularity in India, and beginning to be known in other countries. The Mallekhamb Federation of India has conducted national championships since 1983 and was officially recognized by the Government of India several years ago. On the subcontinent, becoming 'official' can mean the survival or death of an institution. Mr Deshpande considers this their greatest achievement as government recognition in Indian sport has many advantages, such as financial assistance, cheap railway travel for the practitioners, employment prospects at sports centres and eligibility for Arjuna awards (the national award for service to sports). Funding for competitions should – in theory – be available, although after their status was confirmed, the ever-tactful Mr Deshpande was quoted as saying, 'The financial assistance unfortunately is not yet forthcoming from the government. That is the reason why the organization is looking for a sponsor for the forthcoming Mallekhamb National Tournament.'

Mr Deshpande sees the time, not far away now, when mallekhamb will be included in the Asian Games, and possibly the Olympics too. To his delight it has made some impression on other countries. 'In 1988 the Director of Indo-American Yoga Vedanta Society was passing Shivaji Park, and saw mallekhamb being practised. Fascinated, he approached us to learn more about it. We showed him a video and photographs, and he displayed them back in New York. A couple of years later Gabor Czento, a Hungarian, was also enthralled, collected information and came to Bombay to learn it here. He stayed for three months learning and has been back for three consecutive years to master it.'

Maharashtra is far and away leader of the national championships, with Bombay its hub, for historical as well as practical reasons, but there is also the Maharashtra Mandal, a flourishing centre in nearby Pune (Poona). It was built in 1921 from public donations. 'My father would cycle twenty kilometres to get just one rupee. Just *one rupee*,' said Mr Damle, son of its founder S. V. Damle, who now runs the club. It began as an akhara and then acquired facilities for mallekhamb and in later years, gymnastic exercises.

'I remember when every small village in Maharashtra had dangals, where local wrestlers would have competitions against others from neighbouring villages. Then, every year we'd have a jutra [a mela], with 75,000 rupees going to the winner.' Like in Pakistan, kushti has lost some of its status in society, as Mr Damle remembers. 'Wrestling is more than a physical exercise or sport. It is part of everyone's life, in the streets, wherever you are. If you are a wrestler, you can stand boldly in all aspects of life with modesty. But these days, people are not so interested.'

The Maharashtra Mandal has good facilities for mallekhamb, a sport which Mr Damle sees as keeping in the spirit of his father's intentions. I saw the daily practice of young teenagers who come after school for a couple of hours' training. There was a high proportion of girls and young women, and some of the more experienced ones had welts and calluses on their hands from rope burns.

'Sometimes, when we are moving quickly over the ropes, running our hands over them and doing advanced moves, the rope burns our hands where we grip. I have been coming here for four years, every day, and so my hands are like this.' Ravinda showed me her hands. 'My elder brother also used to do this, and I came because of him. Now, many of my friends come also.'

I found it pleasantly ironic that this was the town famous for Osho, the self-appointed guru (now deceased) who set up the commune with a contrived collection of doctrines and escapist mind-games and an exclusive holiday camp to which people flocked from all over the world determined that this was the 'real' Indian experience. Yet if they had ventured a couple of miles down the road to the Mandal, they would have seen something which is far more relevant to Indian people, philosophy and religion.

10

The Guru

From Bombay I went to Delhi, 10 degrees cooler and a face full of fumes the instant you step outside. The city has one of the highest pollution levels in the world – a combination of leaded fuel, ancient vehicles, no regulations on waste from industries and a thick cloud which hovers permanently over the city.

Around 6.30 am on a chilly morning I left my hotel for Guru Hanuman's akhara, a one-storey stone building with a small yard, situated in the old, north side of the city. In the yard, under an iron roof supported by several stone pillars is the red-earth wrestling pit, inside which were a dozen grunting, sleek, oiled bodies beneath faces streaked with mud. Around the outside of the pit on the stone ground, young men were applying the oil to their limbs and torsos and beginning, like in the ones in Pakistan, a series of push-ups.

A middle-aged short, burly man in a tracksuit shouted instructions to them, getting impatient if they weren't putting in enough effort. Two boys were bashing almonds in a wooden pot, and another was boiling a vat of milk. Watching all these activities was a bald, enormous old man with a huge smile revealing just three teeth. He sat at the edge of a charpoi wearing a big white *kurta* (the Indian long shirt and loose trousers) watching the wrestlers and occasionally calling out advice to them, while from time to time they came over to him and touched his feet in respect.

On the outside walls of the stone rooms were rows of old photographs and newspaper articles mounted in an uneven line; and hanging up were medals and several gurz, like those I saw in Lahore. That wall told so many stories, of the great and noble pehlivans that were part of the life of old Delhi, and typical of akhara 'training', on which many parents send their wayward sons to improve their physical strength and the purity of their souls.

Guru Hanuman was a legend in his own right, named after the Hindu monkey-god who is the role model for every sportsman. Most akharas and sports clubs in India have a statue or symbol of Hanuman at the entrance, and many perform a *puja* – lighting incense or giving an offering – before any activity.

'I have devoted my life to the promotion of wrestling. It must never die – I want to live until it is the national game of India,' said the man who is approaching his hundredth birthday. The major challenge, of which he is fully aware, is trying to make wrestling more popular than cricket which is about as easy as telling Indians to stop drinking tea. Guruji must be the only Indian who wants to ban cricket.

'I want the BJP-led allies [the right-wing Hindu fundamentalist party] to restore wrestling to its former glory, to the status it enjoyed during the days of the *Mahabarata*,' he said in an interview in the *Times of India*. 'Priority should be given to *rashtriya* [indigenous] games. They should be allowed to grow in our country. I will also request BJP government to ban foreign games like cricket, tennis and golf for some time to make wrestling and kabaddi prominent.'

He sees these 'foreign imports', especially cricket, as having a detrimental effect on his own sport. While cricket's facilities are widely available and well sponsored, I couldn't see how banning cricket would force everyone's attention to turn to wrestling. I asked if he was serious, and he remained adamant. 'Wrestlers don't have any decent facilities and no good organization,' he said softly in Hindi.

A major reason is related to social class and image. Many people involved in sport had said to me that kushti, like other Indian traditional sports, is seen as a village institution and therefore lower class. For those eager to join a sporting elite, and those anxious to break out of their urban boredom or poverty, playing cricket is the obvious answer. Kushti really can't aim to compete on the same level.

One of Guruji's suggestions was more realistic: to try and encourage companies to sponsor major dangals, which are especially popular in the villages. They may not be as glamorous as Bombay or Delhi, but villages are where most of India's population lives. Like many people involved in any sport, he has little faith in the administrators. 'The Wrestling Federation of India has done nothing to help us. It is full of people who know nothing about the sport.'

Cricket isn't the only part of mainstream Indian culture that he disapproves of; he also forbids his wrestlers to watch movies. 'The song and dance sequences affect young minds,' he said, which supports the theory that wrestlers are supposed to be celibate and of pure mind. Guruji has never married, although journalist friends told me that he put out several stories in the press that at the age of ninety-six, he was going to marry a Frenchwoman six years his junior. A week earlier a Punjabi athletics official at the Veterans Sports Meet in Bombay, had told me that Guruji had already married. 'Guruji is in his nineties and his wife is an Australian lady in her thirties. She speaks no Hindi and he speaks no English.' I asked the man how he thought they could communicate. He looked at me solemnly. 'Love is love, madam. Who needs words when there is love?'

Whether he started the rumours as a joke, or they just began to circulate, Guruji is actually one of Delhi's most famous bachelors and likely to stay that way. But, he pointed out, 'in earlier times, men lived till the age of two hundred and were eligible for marriage aged one hundred. Therefore, I will marry at a hundred.'

Born Vijay Pal in Childwa, Rajasthan, he lost his parents at an early age and was brought to Delhi as a child for schooling, spending several years in Haridwar in Northern India. He lived at the temple and participated in every wrestling match there, mainly for survival, as he earned one rupee for every win. It was there that his reputation grew and he earned his nickname of Hanuman.

He returned to Delhi in 1919 and started a fruit shop near the Birla Mills in the main vegetable market. This location was fortuitous, for Jugal Kishore Birla of Birla Mills, a family business, gave him space to start an akhara for teaching kushti to young boys. That was the same place where we were sitting that morning.

If anything, his mission to teach, promote and popularize traditional wrestling is stronger now than ever. He claims that Mahatma Gandhi appears in his dreams every morning, telling him to restore wrestling to its former glory through *satyagraha*, the passive resistance which Gandhi used against the British to gain Independence.

Guruji has gone to some lengths to achieve that. In 1997, he protested the exclusion of wrestlers from the Arjuna award list for the previous three years. In true Gandhian style, he threatened to hunger-strike until he died in front of the Rashtrapati Bhawan (the Indian government). This provoked the desired response. After he had fasted for three days, the Union Minister for Sports and Youth Affairs promised to attend to the problem of Indian wrestlers. Chief of Shiv Sena, one of the right-wing Hindu funda-mentalist parties, Bal Thackerey offered his support, as did thousands of pehlivans throughout India.

Guru Hanuman proudly tells the story of the night he was given the Padma Shri Award (a national award for services and entertainment). Next to him at the ceremony was a lady getting the same award and he found out that she was Vyjayantimala, a famous dancer. Disgusted that he was put into the same category as her, he told Indira Gandhi to take back the award, and asked her in fury how the Indian government dared give the same one to a sportsman and a dancer. But Mrs Gandhi, whom he had met several times, persuaded him to retain it. On hearing the story, I couldn't decide if he was highly principled or just a complete cultural snob.

When the practice and exercising session ended, I prepared to leave, but Guruji grabbed my arm and pulled me back.

'You must stay for lunch,' said a smiling young man who was in charge of cooking the potatoes and dhal. 'What time do you have lunch?' I asked. 'Oh, we have it now.' It was only ten o'clock, but the Guru had been up since four.

The cook ladled steaming potatoes from his vat on to tin plates and added a pile of rotis. I had to send half of mine back. 'But you must eat it all,' he said in an injured voice. 'Guruji eats every day thirty to forty rotis, many litres of milk, fruit juice, dry fruits, nuts and grapes.' I took a look at the old man, tucking into his pota-toes and wolfing down four rotis at a time. He sent a boy out to buy half a kilo of *jalebis,* a sticky, orange-coloured fried syrupy sweet, which he offered around. Everyone politely declined, so he wolfed down the lot in around five minutes. No wonder he had only three teeth remaining.

The coach, Mahasingh Rao, joined us while we ate. He has been the coach for fifteen years, employed by the Sports Authority of India. He said that all the pehlivans are either employed by the police or services, or pay a nominal amount to live in small dormitories in the akhara. Most of them hope realistically for a few local victories, then to progress to free-style and get employment through their skills.

Some have achieved great laurels. Pride of this akhara is ex-pehlivan Sudesh Kumar, a Delhi police inspector who won two gold medals in the Commonwealth Games, and came fourth in the Munich Olympics. Satpal won a Gold in the Asian Games and Prem Nath a Commonwealth Gold. But for most of these boys – who range from ten years old to late forties – it's the Sunday dangals outside the Jami Masjid in Old Delhi that offers the main chance of glory.

They invited me to join them for dangal the following Sunday outside the Red Fort in the heart of Old Delhi. As I was leaving, Guruji tugged again on my hand, dragged me into his room, shoved two packets of biscuits into my hand and waved me off.

We had arranged to meet at 3 pm – an hour before the dangal was due to start – on Sunday afternoon at the akhara, and I arrived early. The place was in slumber, and the sound of snoring from the rooms did not sound promising. I was still waiting at the akhara at 4 pm, with the familiar feeling inside that this was yet another waste of time, when two sleepy pehlivans emerged from their rooms.

'Coming, coming,' they promised. 'He telephone – they coming.' Half an hour later there was still no sign and as I was leaving to go alone to the Red Fort, a minibus screeched to a halt outside and out poured most of the pehlivans with a grinning Guruji in the front who got out slowly, clutching a bag of biscuits.

We were back on the road again with several of the younger pehlivans who were participating that day. We drove through the heart of Old Delhi; a world away from the broad boulevards of New Delhi. Here, it is a hopelessly congested maze of traders, shoppers, vehicles and animals all competing for space, each street specializing in a particular trade – clothes, stationery, motor parts, welded goods or food. The minibus made its way through the predominant three-wheeled cycle-rickshaws – some dragging cargo like twenty-foot-long metal rods, guaranteed to gouge the eyes out of any passing pedestrian or cyclist – bullock-carts, horses, bicycles and auto-rickshaws, noise, smell, heat and people. Eventually we arrived at the ground between the Jami Masjid and the Red Fort, two distinguished landmarks. The Masjid is the largest mosque in India, built by Shah Jahan in the seventeenth century, while opposite it are the red sandstone walls of the Lal

Qila, the Red Fort, which stretch for two kilometres into the smog and polluted haze of the city. In between these great Moghul monuments is a large ragged area of grass, venue to dozens of cricket games. And it was here that the dangal was set.

The ground was surrounded by a high wall, a grassy field with gentle slopes leading down to the soil-covered square in the centre. A drummer stood in the narrow street outside the gate, scowling and beating an old drum to signal the start of the wrestling. An old, bearded Muslim man stood on the gate selling entrance tickets for two rupees. People gradually trickled in and arranged themselves on the grass slopes for a perfect view of the square, with the Red Fort in the dusty sun in the background.

Everyone made a great fuss of Guruji. A large wooden bench was placed at the front where he sat, surrounded by a handful of other wrestling officials from Old Delhi. As always at these events, there was plenty of tea and basketfuls of peanuts and chaat. The wrestling began, rather inconspicuously at first, with the smaller kids, warmly encouraged by the attentive audience (all men). Some of the youngsters had been trained by the older pehlivans at Guruji's akhara.

Any pehlivan who wanted to participate in a fight that afternoon, could – they just waited their turn at the edge of the square, and when it was time for a new couple of fighters, the referee chose two of similar height.

The first fights didn't last very long but were watched with great interest by a knowledgeable crowd. When a fight was over the referee took both boys and threw the arm of the victor in the air in triumph. Then, the young winner ran around the outside of the square in triumph, visiting the audience for donations, coming first to us on the 'VIP' bench presuming that the men sitting there were more important and richer. They handed out a few rupees to reward each winner. Guruji beamed at seeing the young ones and patted them on the head as they came to him for praise.

What was interesting and also unique about this weekly event was that Hindu and Muslim fought together, traditional wrestling having strong roots in both religions and cultures. 'They fight against each other, but together as brothers,' as Mr Mahasingh Rao put it. It is probably the only regular sporting event which makes a conscious effort to bring Hindus and Muslims together.

My bus to Amritsar was leaving that evening, so we made our

farewells and Guruji hustled me through the crowds into the van, beaming at me and plying me with the inevitable biscuits for my long journey.

11

Goatless Polo

This overland Indo-Pak border crossing was livened up by a skinny eighteen-year-old English lad I found sitting, looking petrified, in the small teahouse on the Indian side, waiting for the border to open. I joined him at his table. 'Oh my God – this is my first time out of Europe and I started in Delhi. I couldn't leave my hotel for two days because it was so scary, all those bloody people . . . sodding taxi-driver ripped me off from the airport . . . the Taj Mahal was awful because of every bastard hassling you . . .'

Ben, who had just left school, was suffering the inevitable Delhi Belly (even though he claimed he hadn't eaten anything) and was a wreck. 'And I'm meeting my overland group in Rawalpindi tonight, and I don't know how to get there . . .' He stared forlornly at the milk forming a skin on the surface of his tea, but his misery lifted when I told him that I was also going straight to Rawalpindi and promised to deliver him to his hotel.

The customs and immigration people and I were now the best of pals, after my third crossing in four months. Ben was most impressed by the relative ease with which we got through customs (with the inevitable chat about cricket) and were taken by minibus to the centre of Lahore, where we got straight onto an express coach for Rawalpindi.

The bus rumbled along the Grand Trunk Road, a historical route first built in the fourth century and developed by the Moguls to link the cities of Kabul, Peshawar, Rawalpindi, Lahore and Delhi. For over two thousand years, it has witnessed a constant trail of invaders, traders, pilgrims and travellers. These days, however, it is less romantic than it once was, with inter-city air-con buses, garishly painted lorries with flashing lights and reflective strips and 'Horn OK Please' painted at the back, and slower, passenger buses with vomit stains streaking out of every window.

It was 8 pm when we pulled into Pir Wadai bus station. By then Ben's face was a shade of pale green (probably the undercooked veggieburgers drowned in glowing ketchup we had eaten en route). I dropped him off at his hotel, where he dashed off, doubled up in agony, to the nearest toilet.

This visit to Pakistan was mainly to see traditional polo in the mountains of the north, from Gilgit in the Hunza Valley to Chitral in the north-west. Then, at the beginning of June I would travel to Turkey for the big oil-wrestling and bull-fighting festivals. That gave me five weeks.

Having failed in Bombay to get an Iranian visa in order to travel overland from Pakistan to Turkey – to try to take a couple of weeks' visit to the famous *zurkhanes* (traditional gymnasia) found in every Iranian town and village – I planned to try again in Islamabad. As applying for the visa involves a long bureaucratic struggle I had to apply immediately. Every application is sent to the Ministry of Information in Tehran, who decide whether or not to grant the visa. Besides that, the Iranian Embassy can refuse you without giving a reason, meaning you lose the visa fee which is paid in advance and non-refundable.

The day after I arrived, however, the Embassy was closed for five days because of Ashoura, and I had to wait in Islamabad to get the visa application in before travelling to the northern areas. Ashoura is the tenth day of Moharram, a period of mourning for Shia Muslims for Imam Hussain who was martyred in battle with seventy-three of his family and followers. Most people fast from sunrise to mid-afternoon and it is the saddest day in the Islamic year.

Mr Bukhari, an officer in the main Pakistan Tourist Development Council, had invited me to go with his wife and children to the Ashoura procession in Rawalpindi. That morning, the streets and markets of Rawalpindi were deserted, everything closed and silent. In Mr Bukhari's large house in Islamabad, his family were preparing food to distribute among the fasting people. They had cooked pots of rice with mutton and chickpeas, the traditional dish to break the fast, and were spooning it into parcels.

His brother had married an Irishwoman and their children had been brought up in Birmingham, so there was a curious blend of accents that morning as we sat on the floor. 'My brother has cuts all over his back 'cos he was beating himself with chains yesterday,' said one sister in a strong Brummie accent. I looked aghast at the nine-year-old in a Liverpool T-shirt, slouching across the sofa reading comics. 'Didn't it hurt?' I asked him, as he pulled up his shirt to reveal grazes and scabs across his shoulders. 'It doesn't hurt him,' said another sister proudly. 'When you feel so much emotion, you can't feel pain.' A cousin whispered to me, 'Actually, I think he was just doing it to show off to his friends.'

During the procession many whip and beat themselves with chains and blades, inflicting pain on themselves as a reminder of Imam Hussain and his followers and their brutal slaying. 'Is it permitted for women to beat themselves in the same way?' I asked them. They told me no, instead they go to a women-only mosque the night before. 'We stayed up all night, praying, thinking, listening to the teachings of the Imam. But if it were allowed for women, well . . .' she thought about it. 'Probably I would beat myself. It's such a sad time, I wouldn't care about the pain.'

We drove off in a convoy of vehicles into the increasingly crowded centre of Rawalpindi. Armed police and soldiers stood grimly on the streets and at the many roadblocks. These processions had been the target of many attacks over the years in different parts of the country, mainly by Sunni groups.

We walked on the streets packed with mourners, dressed chiefly in black. Women and men were separated onto opposite pavements and we joined the women, many of them sobbing and wailing. Men paraded down the centre of the street slowly. A group of men dressed in black shalwar kameez made a small circle as they walked, then got out their knives, whips and chains. They removed their shirts, the procession stopped and to the cry of a voice over the loudspeaker, shouting 'Yah Hussain!', they beat their backs with their weapons.

Others beat their chests with their fists in unison. There was an eerie silence broken only by the sound of hollow thumping, clinking of chains and whacking of leather. The men displayed their welts, deep grazes, and cuts across their backs which dripped blood onto the ground. Ambulances attended to the more serious injuries, although many refused treatment. It was emotional and tense. One of the sisters began to speak to me when a wizened old woman suddenly turned and yelled at us, shaking her fist. 'She is angry that we are in such a good mood on such an occasion,' I was told.

When it was time to break the fast, a small van chugged slowly through the thick crowd, collecting the food parcels which individuals had prepared, then distributing them out to those who requested. A few women and children grabbed as many as they could and put them in their bags, whilst the crowds began to disperse and once more the roads were clogged with cars returning home.

After Ashoura, everything reopened and I went to the Iranian Embassy to apply for a visa. The man on the gate treated visa applicants with disdain and denied my request to speak to the cultural attaché. I had to wander down the road in search of a public phone-box to ring the attaché, who immediately invited me inside, which it gave me the utmost pleasure to tell the gate-man.

The attaché produced tea and biscuits and promised to try to push my application through quickly, although this embassy didn't have a particularly good reputation for speed. He was a warm and intelligent man who gave me good information about zurkhanes, even drawing little pictures and diagrams of the interiors, and his enthusiasm was encouraging.

'I really want you to go to Iran. It would be very good for our country, and if it were possible I would give you a visa now, but,' and how heavy that word weighed, 'we have to go through the proper procedure.'

This meant having to fork out for a letter from my embassy and the visa fee, but at last the application was completed and I could set off for the north. I took a minibus to Gilgit – a fourteen-hour ride, but preferable to the slower state-owned large bus. The journey went through the night so we missed seeing the spectacular rise through the mountains. What's more, it rained heavily and continuously throughout the night, the luggage on top of the bus (i.e. my clothes) getting more waterlogged with each passing hour.

The first thing that struck me on our dawn arrival in Gilgit was how much it had grown since I'd last seen it seven years before – more hotels, more traffic, more shops, more restaurants and more people. That afternoon I wandered into the town centre to start my search for polo. Gilgit isn't the most attractive town in the northern areas and is used mainly as a transit point. Since the Karakoram Highway (KKH) opened to foreign tourists in 1984, it's become an increasingly popular route for backpackers travelling between China and Pakistan. Between spring and autumn when the Highway is open, the town is awash with tourists, some of whom use Gilgit as a base to explore the northern areas and cross the Shandur Pass.

My enquiries about local polo matches were fruitful – there was a small tournament starting in Chilas the following day, I was told. This was great news, if correct. 'It's definite,' said one local. 'I saw three friends from Gilgit taking their horses to Chilas. They told me it starts at 3 pm. It's lucky because usually in Moharram there's no tournaments, but you must be careful in Chilas . . .'

Many had warned me about Chilas, a small town three hours south on the KKH. It carries a fearsome reputation as being full of fanatics, underlined by a vernacular greeting that the Chilasis used in the late nineteenth century: 'We kill all infidels.' Gilgitis consider them uncivilized, lazy and violent and told me entertaining tales about locals who frequently open fire on their fellow villagers because they belonged to a different 'group'. James, a student from England, told me, 'A man in Chilas asked me what was my religion. I replied "Christian", and he spat at my feet.'

The next morning I managed, with difficulty and begging and nagging due to the high number of pre-booked Chilas-bound passengers, to board a rusty minibus heading south to the scary town. It took three attempts, but I even succeeded in securing a front seat.

'Hello, madam, I am a student of the English language. Can I practise on you?' An enthusiastic young man poked his head through the open window just as the bus was leaving. He looked at the confusion around him and picked his nose enthusiastically. 'I think,' he decided, 'you are a problem because you travel alone. It is a very bad habit.'

I was nervous as we approached Chilas three hours later, as in addition to the rumour of regular violence, word had also travelled far about the local kids who take great delight in chucking rocks at foreigners. Turning off the main road we climbed slowly up to the bus stand in the centre of Chilas. I asked two bearded men where the polo ground was, and they muttered and mumbled to themselves and replied sternly that there was no polo tournament in Chilas now. It's Moharram, didn't you know?

The old driver asked a few more people who, far from appearing axe-wielding fanatics, looked quite dull and uninterested and grumbled that they didn't know anything about polo. Yet another waste of time, another let-down. I decided to find the ground anyway, and eventually discovered that it was a couple of miles away. The bus driver then said he'd take me there for 1000 rupees which I brought down to a more respectable 50.

On the path to the ground, I was delighted to see ponies ready for action, led by players with polo sticks in hand. The match was obviously due to begin soon, so with a spirited wave, the bus driver dropped me off at the ground and drove off.

I sat with some of the organizers, who were gentle and polite. One told me that this was one of the many regional matches in the build-up to the major polo tournament at Shandur, set for the beginning of July. More horses and riders arrived and a small smattering of spectators, men and boys of all ages, sat patiently.

The only polo match I had seen previously was in Gilgit years earlier for Pakistan Day, with hundreds of noisy fans watching and many musicians. But there were no musicians today. One man said it was because of Moharram, but his friend interrupted and said, 'We never have music here in Chilas. The Mullahs don't like it. A little crazy, you know,' and he illustrated this by jabbing his forefinger to his temple.

There were rolling hills surrounding the ground, a steep grassy slope full of trees to the front, the town in the background away to the left. A few dozen people were perched on the slope and on walls. As the match began, between two teams from the Chilas area, two young boys appointed themselves my guards, flailing around at any of the smaller boys who got too close with sticks. These sticks were actually miniature polo sticks – branches with a small curve or knot at the bottom – carried by most boys there for a number of purposes – as hockey sticks, polo sticks, or for hitting each other with.

Traditional polo in this region, as opposed to its upper-class modern version played in the private clubs in Lahore and Karachi, is a game 'of the people'. Nearly everyone owns, or has access to, a horse, and the young are taught to ride at an early age. It is played with seven horses to each team (as opposed to four in the 'refined' version), the horses are not changed after each chukka, with twenty minutes for each half.

The main difference, however, is that there are no rules. You can charge, leap, drive your horse into your opponent; even hooking – lifting your stick into the air and hooking your opponent's as he's about to swing – is permitted. It is tremendously fast and furious with much dramatic charging and swerving in clouds of dust. The polo ponies of this region are quite small and so are easier to turn than the larger horses used in the version played by Westerners.

In order to avoid unwanted attention, I left shortly before the end and began the uphill walk to the bus stand. I was caught up by a pleasant man wearing a bright blue shalwar kameez.

'Is there any problem here for you?' he said with concern.

'No, everything's fine, thanks. I'm just leaving for Gilgit.'

He spoke in a low voice. 'You shouldn't really have come here, you know. Chilas is a really dangerous place and they are a bit crazy. The locals don't like outsiders. They consider any visitor from outside to be un-Islamic, a threat,' his voice dropped to a conspiratorial whisper, 'especially the British. They are very stupid people. Always having gun fights and killing each other. I'm a trekking guide,' he assured me, 'and not from round here . . .'

He urged me to leave immediately, and we walked down to the main highway where we waited inside a teashop for a bus. Over the door was a large sign: 'PROUD to be a fundamentalist.' No buses came and it was getting dark, so I went to a hotel and with the dire warnings going through my mind, took no chances and heaved a huge table against the door. The staff were friendly and there were no other guests, no intruders in the night and no shoot-outs between rival gangs. It was all a bit of an anticlimax.

Gilgit is one of Pakistan's strongholds of traditional polo and in these northern mountain areas, the polo stick – usually a branch with a bend or kink at one end – takes the place of the cricket bat ubiquitous elsewhere in the country. Small boys are often to be seen galloping along on imaginary horses, whacking small stones on the ground.

The town has an entertaining array of characters associated with the polo scene. I was introduced to Sher Khan, immaculately dressed in white shirt and yellow cravat, a retired brigadier and former star player in the army. Now in his seventies, over tea and biscuits in his garden, he reminisced of the days when he played for the Gilgit team and spoke of its great cultural significance.

I paid a visit to a forlorn band of musicians who were employed to play at polo matches. They lived in a darkened shack on the river-bank, their instruments hanging on the wall, where they lay idly on their tatty beds and moaned that they were paid hardly anything these days. They explained the different tunes to signal different points of the match, and lamented how the tradition of music in polo would soon die.

I also met Gilgit's star player for several years, known as Bulbul, whose house was on the edge of the local polo ground. He had represented Gilgit many times in the famous Shandur tournament, and his living room was adorned with trophies and medals. He was a professional, playing for the Northern Light Infantry A team who paid him a wage, although was employed purely as a polo player.

Apart from a couple of practice matches, there were no tournaments for several weeks in Gilgit, but Bulbul said there was one in Chitral the following week. This was the best opportunity and so I made plans to be there.

12

Hitch-hikers' Guide
to Shandur

Chitral was only a couple of hundred miles from Gilgit and I had a week to get there, but there was a huge mountain range to cross with no proper road.

I had two options. The more sensible, reliable one was the minibus to Rawalpindi, a four-hour bus ride to Peshawar and then a twelve-hour bus journey to Chitral; barring accidents, breakdowns or landslides, this would take a non-stop two days. But it added to the distance, and it was an awfully long time sitting on night buses.

The alternative was to go directly over the Shandur Pass, passing the highest polo ground in the world and venue of the famous festival. There was a track which jeeps could manage, but it was the end of the winter season and the regular service wouldn't start for another month. Hitch-hiking was possible – it was a direct route and infinitely more picturesque, but the journey time was unpredictable.

Ali, who worked at my hotel, helped me ask in the main bazaar but no one knew anything and we were passed from shop to shop like an unwanted parcel. Finally we came to the supposed authority on transport over the Pass, at a stall selling saucepans. He looked up, uninterested, from a pile of small steel frying pans.

'Is there any jeep leaving for Chitral tomorrow?'

'Yes, nine o'clock.'

'Do you have room for me?'

'Yes, no problem.'

'So you're definitely leaving in the morning at nine?'

'Yes, no problem.'

'Do I have to book and buy a ticket now?'

'No, just come tomorrow.'

'What time should I come?'

'Oh, afternoon sometime.'

'But you said you're leaving in the morning?'

'Well, maybe. Better come in afternoon. Maybe he not going if not enough people.'

It sounded dubious and I didn't want to risk wasting another day for nothing. The solution appeared in the form of Yaqoub, a jeep driver who took tourists from Gilgit to Chitral. He was probably thirty but looked around fifty, very skinny and mournful, and usually with a large spliff in his mouth.

He offered to drive me to Chitral but it was expensive and I'd set my heart on an adventurous hitch-hike. 'OK, I drive to Gupis, my home, six hours away. You pay as you like. We leave when you like. From there you will get lift easy, no problem.' We agreed on 500 rupees, and set off at 6 am the next day.

Yaqoub wasn't much of a conversationalist, so I could focus fully on the scenery. Progress was excruciatingly slow and getting slower the further we went, the road deteriorating by the mile. We arrived in Gupis at 1 pm, and I asked his help for an onward lift. His earlier boasts of 'knowing everyone in the whole valley and arranging you a lift' were obviously no more than big talk.

'We have lunch first, then I arrange lift.' He mournfully dumped me on the veranda of his rambling cottage, where I ate a fried egg and spinach while he and the family ate inside. It was probably considered a politeness to the guest, but it made me feel like a leper. His five daughters (probably the reason for his mournfulness, knowing that eventually he would have to pay for five weddings) came out to stare at me and giggle. Then they got a few mates to come over for more staring and giggling, none of them talking to me but all observing me closely.

For Yaqoub the development of the Karakoram Highway and subsequent influx of tourists had meant an improvement in lifestyle. Tourism can have serious consequences in a traditional, simple and religious society like northern Pakistan. The ticket seller in Gilgit's bus stand had complained to me that development, tourism, and satellite TV meant that people were forgetting their traditions. 'Young people are only interested in cricket and Channel V [the Asian music channel] these days.' But the area is becoming more affluent, which some welcome as progress.

After lunch, there was still no news on the vehicle scene, and Yaqoub grumblingly took me to the next intersection. We came to a new hotel built on the edge of a lake, where Yaqoub mumbled I should wait for a lift, and left while I settled myself down to watch for vehicles.

The long wait was compensated for by my surroundings. The lake was a deep turquoise mirror and only the leaping trout disturbed its calm. All around it were fields of the deepest, stillest green with clouds of purple flowers, and folds of mountains were highlighted with just the faintest smattering of snow. It was preferable to waiting for a ride on an English motorway.

Every hour or so a loaded cargo jeep passed, but no one stopped and as night fell, so did my chances. Salahuddin, the hotel manager, popped out to my lookout every few minutes to say, 'Hee hee, jeep not come!' which made me grit my teeth in irritation.

At 10 pm, under a pitch black, cloudless starry sky, I reluctantly decided to take a bed for the night. 'Tomorrow, many vehicles will come by. They start early morning. Maybe.' Salahuddin was vague but promised to wake me at 6 am, ready for the early morning 'rush-hour'.

'I have been up since 4 am to look for a vehicle for you,' Salahuddin said with a martyred look when I got up. Hour by hour, the road remained desolate, save for the occasional bunch of schoolboys walking to their lessons, or a woman carrying bundles of firewood on her head, or a farmer leading a few goats.

Two jeeps came past, with open trailers packed with farm machinery and men sitting high on top. I stopped the drivers. 'Are you going to Chitral? To Shandur? Barsat?' Both times vast sums of money were ignored and they drove off. 'Right, that's it. The next vehicle that comes, I'm on it. Jeep, bullock-cart, motorbike – it's mine.'

Salahuddin laughed. 'You have good attitude. You get your bags on to vehicle, I stop driver and tell him to take you.'

An hour later, looming on the horizon was something which made me bitterly regret my rash promise. Chugging noisily and slowly along the stony track was a tractor dragging an enormous trailer loaded with boulders, with two small boys perched on top. As it approached us, my bags were hoisted on top of the trailer and after some enthusiastic bargaining, the two men in the front re-arranged themselves and I shared the tiny seat behind the driver.

Salahuddin and the four hotel staff came out to wave me off, finding the whole adventure hilarious. No doubt the antics of the mad Englishwoman would be related to everybody who came by for several years.

After three minutes, I bitterly regretted my bravado. My bottom ached, the bumps over each stone caused every muscle to cry, and the noise and smoke made me feel sick. My knees were jammed in front of my nose behind a metal bar which I had to hang on to for dear life or be thrown out with the bumps. At our speed, it would take around six hours to Phandar, another 60 kilometres away.

The track was not just stony and bumpy, it was terrifying. Steep uphill with a deadly drop to our right, every time we turned a sharp corner the front wheels of the tractor rose in the air. On one especially dangerous and steep hairpin bend, we found ourselves actually poised over the edge of the cliff. Everyone – except the driver – leapt out, and I wasn't sure whether it was to lighten the load or to survive.

The driver shrugged and smiled at me, the other passengers stood on the front wheel to weigh it down and after a few hair-raising moments we safely negotiated the corner and were able to breathe again.

Four hours later, I was still there, gritting my teeth as the road deteriorated yet further, when a large jeep began to overtake us with a smug, sprawling European in the back.

I leapt down. 'Please could you give me a lift to the next village – I've been on this for four hours and it'll take another two to get to Phandar.' I gave a pitiful smile which would have melted the heart of Genghis Khan. The thirtysomething Englishman with Proper Hiking Clothes gave a strained smile, indicating his reluctance to pick up extras, but I had already loaded my bags into his jeep. 'OK,' seeing himself forced into a corner, 'we'll take you to Phandar.'

It took just an hour to cover the 20 kilometres to Phandar, a tiny village of several houses and farmland, set spectacularly next to a lake. It was 4 pm, a good time to rest for the night and get a lift the next morning. The Englishman looked self-satisfied as they dumped me off rather unceremoniously at the roadside and roared off.

Phandar didn't have much choice of accommodation, but I found a lodge with bare rooms with no electricity and an outhouse with cold water. The grim-faced owner ludicrously over-charged, and after negotiating for the room and food, I bathed in ice-cold water and removed several layers of dust.

The next morning, I settled down to wait at about six o'clock soon to be surrounded by giggling groups of schoolchildren. I only had an hour to wait before a jeep with trailer arrived. The driver cheerfully put me in the front seat and said he was going as far as Sol Laspur, the first village over the Pass, which created a small dilemma. Since leaving Gilgit two days earlier, I had had an idea formulating in my mind which arose from a casual comment from Ali, who said it was possible to cross the Shandur Pass by foot. When I dismissed this, because of too much heavy baggage, he suggested that I hired a porter, horse, or a donkey.

Never having ridden a horse, I had settled on a donkey. Crossing the Shandur Pass this way would give me the ideal oppor-tunity to see the famous polo ground. Ali had said that I should hire it in Barsat, the final village before the Pass.

Now I was faced with the decision: the jeep was crossing the Pass, I had a comfortable seat and could make quick and easy progress that day, and in theory, could reach Chitral by evening. But the thought of crossing by donkey was too tempting so I asked the driver to let me off at Barsat.

Barsat looked pleasant enough; perched high in the moun-tains, a few stone shacks dotted along the track, animals grazing and no sign of people. Before the jeep left for the Pass, a shop-keeper came to greet us, and I asked if he could help me hire a donkey. 'No problem,' he assured me as we lifted my bags from the jeep. 'I can arrange today and you can leave tomorrow. Porter, guide, whatever.' With that confirmation, I happily waved off the jeep, content with my decision.

The man's small, gloomy store sold dried foods, biscuits, soap and children's rubber boots. He smiled. 'You can have a room and food here, leave next morning. 50 rupees is OK?' The room was tiny, filthy and freezing, the beds covered in goat-hair blankets, black with damp grime. The 'toilet' was the surrounding fields and 'tap' was the river, clogged by the villagers' refuse of plastic bags and paper. But it was the only place to sleep and eat, so I accepted. A bed was a bed and hopefully he would arrange every-thing.

We sat in his shop, his young sons with grimy, snotty faces and filthy clothes staring with wide eyes. 'So you can arrange a porter and donkey to go tomorrow over the Pass?' He looked at me blankly. 'Um . . . it's not easy. You want donkey? If you sit on donkey, you need total two donkeys and guide. This will cost you . . .' he looked at the ceiling, probably to pluck a large sum and add a couple of zeros '. . . 2000 rupees.' It was exorbitant. We haggled for a while and agreed on 900 rupees, for one guide and two donkeys, one for me and one for luggage. He promised to arrange it.

An hour later, he knocked on the door of the damp room and said the guide was here to finalize the trip. The tall, strapping shepherd I had envisaged was actually a gnarled old hunchback, his face lined with dirt-ingrained wrinkles. He eyed me suspiciously. I greeted him and asked, 'So, we can leave tomorrow morning – what time?' Blank. I tried Urdu: '*Kal suba – kitna bajeh?*'

The shop owner laughed. 'He not hear anything, speaks no Urdu, no English.' The old man yelled. 'He wants to know how much you're paying him.' 'Tell him we agreed on 900 rupees for him and two donkeys. He has two donkeys, hasn't he?' They continued a shouted conversation. The guide looked angry. 'No – he says it's too cheap. He wants more. His donkeys are very good.'

A short, shouted argument later, he grumpily agreed to come that night with the donkeys, and we would set off at 7 am for the ten-hour crossing over the Pass of 3500 metres, to the village of Sol Laspur.

Arrangements were finalized by 11 am and the day stretched ahead. The clouds had gathered ominously overhead and the temperature dropped suddenly. The local kids were infuriating, slouched in a large cluster to stare blankly and watch me silently. Several jeeps passed and I was tempted to forgo the donkey and leave, but resisted.

It got even colder, a howling gale drove everyone inside and the rain lashed down. Night fell, but by 8 pm, the donkey-man still hadn't come. At 10 pm, the owner came into my room. 'I think,' he said apologetically, looking at his black nails, 'that the old man will not come now. He is not good man – I think not happy with your price.' Then a commotion outside brought several drunken villagers staggering into my room, shouting loudly. Suddenly they all stopped and rushed out. Just as he was leaving, a smiling man with a Texas Raiders baseball hat said helpfully, 'Barsat people bad people,' and followed that gem by explaining that he was from the next village, and that the old man was bad and always drinking. 'I saw him at five o'clock, he say he is not taking you over the Pass and he was very drunk.'

Furious and miserable, I sulked off to sleep and prepared to wait for a vehicle the next morning. Now that I was desperate to leave Barsat, of course, there were no jeeps to be seen. I sat there the entire day, straining my eyes at the distant road and wishing I wasn't there. The afternoon worsened when the old donkey man turned up (without donkeys) and yelled at me. In rage and frustration I shouted back, which attracted a large amused crowd who appeared from nowhere. The Texan Raiders hat shoved his way to the front and chipped in with another helpful 'He very bad man – too much drink last night' which made the crowd roar with laughter.

After another night in the mouldy cell, I returned to my look-out post. I hadn't waited long the next morning when the dream vision arrived: a jeep laden with men and cargo. Before they had time to refuse me, my bags were in the back and although the driver said he was full, the desperation in my voice won him over. It was glorious to leave.

It was a slow, steep rise towards the Shandur Pass, getting colder and the air thinner. On the roof was a pile of luggage, which included tables, a box of teacups from China, wooden poles, two bicycles, and boxes of fruit, clothes and blankets. On the trailer of the jeep it was standing-room only and everyone surrounding me was a foot taller, limiting my view to chests, beards and backs, but the atmosphere was congenial and the other passengers chatty. After a while they made up a seat for me from someone's baggage. We were now approaching a height of 3,700 metres, the landscape was rough and barren with no vegetation or animals and there was snow on the ground, although the road had been cleared.

I had been looking forward to seeing the polo ground but to my disappointment the jeep sped straight through and I caught barely a glimpse of the ground. It was, however, just enough to recognize that this was the most amazing setting in the world for a sports venue, narrowly beating the world's highest cricket ground in Chail.

Down the other side of the Pass, after an hour's stop at the first village, Sol Laspur, they dropped me in Mastuj, a small town some nine hours from Chitral.

There were the usual 'jeep come, jeep no come' comments in

the local teashop. 'There is a jeep at three o'clock definitely,' said a young man who was going to Sol Laspur. 'It comes every day at same time.' At 3.30, the jeep obviously was not coming but the young man remained optimistic, as he was still waiting for his.

The situation called for urgent action. A local jeep driver said he might go to Buni, five hours in the right direction, and nonchalantly tinkered inside the engine, hoping that I would hire him privately. After some enthusiastic haggling we came to a deal: I hired the jeep and the two front seats, but at a cheaper price if the driver could pick up other passengers in the back. It was the best 300 rupees I'd ever spent.

The journey from Mastuj to Buni was the best of the whole trek, with the rich mustard yellows of the fields, the dramatic drop from the road to the valley, and the flowing trees. The back of the jeep filled up, the most entertaining passenger being Dodo an injured sheep, being taken for her treatment by her owner. Her journey was made more pleasant by the bag of stale chapattis that had been in my bag since Barsat. A grateful sheep spent a couple of hours with her nose inside a pink and white plastic bag, whilst her owner beamed with appreciation. 'Dodo now get better very quickly.'

When I arrived in Buni at 5 pm, I first checked out transport to Chitral, and learned that there were minibuses leaving in the morning. Then I went to look for a hotel. On my way, I was accosted by an inquisitive chap who promised to come round to visit in the evening. And sure enough after I'd settled into a grotty guesthouse (the only one in town), Saddar Hussain arrived armed with a bottle wrapped in newspaper, and a lot of blarney.

'I know everyone, everyone in this valley. You see,' he said discreetly unwrapping the bottle, pouring an innocuous-looking clear substance into two glasses, 'I am a local politician for the PPP.' The PPP is the Pakistan People's Party, founded by Benazir Bhutto's father. He was well dressed, but even so he must have had another means of income, if his tales of owning houses, land and horses were true.

'I own five polo ponies and seventeen acres of land. Then after I came out of prison . . .'

'What were you imprisoned for?'

'Oh,' he gave a smug smile. 'Criticizing the government. I was there for a year in, er . . . well it was either 1982 or 1992.' He dismissed the details with a wave.

'But if you're twenty-eight now, that would have made you twelve years old when you were imprisoned?'

'Yes well, I was a young activist. Have some more wine?'

It was made from distilled mulberries and tasted like lighter fuel. It was difficult to believe anything Saddar Hussain said but it was an entertaining couple of hours.

Eventually he staggered up sending wooden chairs flying, and announced, 'Sister, I will order you a bus at 6 am!' and then he left. At 5 am I was awakened by the clattering of a horse's hoofs, a battering on my door and Saddar Hussain calling out: 'Sister, bus is here!' He then disappeared, confirming my suspicions that he was barking mad. I left on the 6.30 bus and after a few hours on a proper road, arrived in Chitral. The six-day journey was finally, finally over.

It was perfect timing as the week-long polo tournament was due to begin the following afternoon. I was recommended the Chinar Inn, as the owner was Nasir Ahmed, one of the best local players who was pleased to introduce me to all his team.

'The prize money for this is very small, but none of us play for money. The best prize as a polo player is the love of the game and the honour of winning. We love it and feel proud to play for our team. This tournament is important because from these teams we select the best players to represent Chitral to play against Gilgit in the big tournament at Shandur Pass. Everyone wants to play there, it's the greatest honour for a local polo player.'

Nasir Ahmed invited me to the tournament draw at the District Council hall that afternoon, where all eight participating teams were present and the Assistant Commissioner of Chitral was on the stage to pull the names out of a hat. In this assembled gathering of polo players, grooms, helpers and supporters, polo was obviously a great leveller. Princes sat alongside farmers, lawyers and village shopkeepers. There was no hierarchy of professions or background; in the eyes of polo, everyone was equal.

The hall fell silent. The AC came on stage and the first two names were pulled out. This draw was to determine the two groups and the top two of each would enter the semi-finals. It was significant, as the four best teams obviously wanted to be put into different groups. The AC saw me sitting there, and invited me on stage to help: 'The only neutral person in this hall,' he explained to the others, 'so she must help us perform this duty.' The task was almost as prestigious as making the draw for the World Cup, and as I performed my duty of taking out each scrap of paper and handing it to the AC, I could sense the anticipation of the watching players.

After everyone had dispersed, I decided to make enquiries about the possibility of seeing buzkashi in the area, Chitral being so close to the Afghani border. I asked in the Post and Telegraph Office (usually the best information point in any small town), where the assistant manager, with a heavy black beard and huge smile, seemed optimistic. 'I think in Garam Chashma they play, and Gabor, a town on the Afghani border, has a team. I can phone my friends in the Post Office and ask them. Maybe you can go over there to meet them?'

At that point, an imposing figure of a seven-foot-tall Afghani man walked into the Post Office, with acres of cotton material swirled into a turban on his head, an unruly black beard and hooked nose. He carried over his shoulder a large carpet – not an antique, woollen tribal rug or spectacular silk masterpiece, but a nylon printed carpet. I figured that this daunting figure could possibly know something about local buzkashi. 'Could you ask him if he knows anything about buzkashi?' The assistant manager looked, then gave a small gulp. 'I can't ask him. He looks too scary.'

I was excited by the thought that buzkashi might be being played in the vicinity, and already tempted to plan a trip to the Afghan border. And then perhaps into Afghanistan, which has been my dream for years – but many people have told me that since the Taliban have taken control over much of the country, buzkashi has actually been forbidden.

My opportunity to see it came in the form of Machboul Ali, captain of the Mulkow team, a roguish man with a twinkle in his eye. 'I work for the army controlling the Afghan border near Gabor. I can arrange for you to go over the border with my men, and then you can find buzkashi. No problem for you.' Wandering into Afghanistan with 'his men' was not perhaps the most sensible action, but I would have gone to any lengths. Machboul Ali's offer was tempting.

Chitral, a small town with a large Afghani population, most of whom have been there for years and have small businesses in the market, is more attractive than Gilgit and would command more visitors, except it is less accessible. For half the year, all roads to

Chitral are inaccessible and road traffic can only enter from Afghanistan.

The next afternoon was the first day of the tournament. It began at 3 pm with the opening ceremony, which was accompanied by the usual fawning of officials and an array of VIPs. All the players, most of whom were in their team uniform, were introduced to the Chief Guest for the day, the Chief of Police, and as soon as the formalities were over everyone scrambled for tea and cakes in the hall.

'I really do think,' said the District Commissioner through a mouthful of cake and spitting a shower of crumbs around, 'that polo brings together so many great things about our life in the mountains. Look at the different people here today all joining in this celebration.' He waved his hand around the room, sloshing tea in the saucer. Young grooms were chatting earnestly to senior village officials; Machboul Ali was arguing with the Police Chief, and the suave, sophisticated Prince (captain and star of the Chitral team) stood with shabby old jockeys half his height.

The refreshments finished, a slow and ragged procession filed along the muddy, narrow street to the polo ground, led by three musicians, old men from the village who were paid by the council to play on such occasions. The Prince had his jeep and avoided the laborious task of wading through a slow procession.

Half an hour later we arrived at the polo ground at the southwest end of the town, on a small downhill track leading off the main road. At one side of the field I saw a pavilion with microphone and loudspeakers, and the comfortable seats, sheltered from whatever the unpredictable weather chose to throw at them. Opposite the pavilion were the musicians, sitting cross-legged on the wall with instruments on their laps.

The first match began late, so the salesmen had more time with a captive audience. The mountainous Afghani man I'd last seen in the telephone office, still had the nasty acrylic carpet slung over his shoulder which he was trying to interest people in buying, with little success. There were many boys selling cigarettes, peanuts and sweets, and a skinny, nervous man with two ropes slung over his shoulders, a couple of dozen teacups tied to them which clinked as he walked.

It was a small crowd that first afternoon, most preferring to wait until the quarter-finals where the standard would be much higher. They were right, although the 12-0 score-line which would have

Party time in Selçuk, Turkey, where village musicians
play the night before the big camel wrestling festival.

The owner braves teeth and spit to muzzle his camel before a fight.

A tea-house in Sibi, Pakistan, is a daily venue for batir fighting,
where the gambling is more enthusiastic than the fighting.

Half-time at a polo match in Gilgit, Pakistan, with emergency repair work.

Sunday afternoons in the park: practising rhiji, a favourite pastime in Quetta, Pakistan

Bird bath – essential preparation for a cockfight in Quetta.

Won by a head – the finish line at the bull race at
Jindu Shah Pir Mela in Bhawalpur, Pakistan.

Cash handouts to the winning bull-jockey at the races in Pir Batho, Pakistan.

Guru Hanuman, the grand old man who rules the roost at his akhara in Delhi, India.

WORLD HONOURED   PH- 2911188
                         2919693
PADAM SHREE DARUNA CHARYA GURU HANUMAN
PATRON
WRESTLING FEDERATION OF INDIA
DELHI-110007 (INDIA)

INDIAN AWARD WINNER OF   FIRST INDIAN WINNER OF
RASHTRA GURU (HOMEMINISTER 1960)   DIPLOMA OF DE HONOUR (PARIS 1980)
RAJASTHAN SHREE (RAJASTHAN GOVT. 1982)   LORD OF BUDHA (TOKYO - 1981)
PADAM SHREE (PRESIDENT OF INDIA 1983)   MASTER DEGREE BLACK BELT (JAPAN) 1991.
BHISHM PITAMAH (CHIEFMINISTER BIHAR 1989) AMAR SHAHEED UDHAM SINGH (ENGLAND) 1991.
DARUNA CHARYA AWARD (PRESIDENT OF INDIA 1989) MAHARAJA CHHATERPATI SHAHU PURUSKAR 1991.
KUSHTI DEVTA AWARD (AMERICA)

The entrance of Guru Hanuman's akhara in Delhi.

Grinding the almonds for the energy-giving drink that wrestlers consume daily.

Limbering up at Guru Hanuman's akhara.

'Superman' pose from a student of mallekhamb – the sport which shows the balance of mind and body – in Pune, India.

been embarrassing for an English football team, didn't seem to matter and even the losing side, the third team from the police force, enjoyed the occasion hugely.

This tournament typically demonstrated the lack of financial motives for the teams – as with the camel wrestling in Turkey, it is a matter of pride, honour and love of the game rather than financial gain. The prize money here was modest: each player from Chitral received 1000 rupees, with each out-of-town player getting 1300 rupees, and the winning team receiving a small trophy. Even the prestigious tournament at Shandur Pass, which every local player dreams of participating in, offers very little prize money.

I was invited to visit one of Mr Nasir's team-mates, Wali Ur-Rehman, a lawyer, at his mansion, and see his stables and three polo ponies. We lazed on charpois in the shade of blossoming trees in the huge garden, and were served ice-cold drinks. We talked about polo and he was a refreshing change to the grumblings from dusty offices of sports departments elsewhere in the subcontinent.

'People complain that TV is ruining our traditions and young people are going to lose their values. But I don't think it's a bad thing. If a tradition is great, it should be able to withstand the pressure of external attractions.' Throughout India I'd been hearing how satellite TV was the only reason why moral standards were declining and young people were aping the West. I thought of Guru Hanuman, who was stating his wish a few weeks earlier to ban cricket and films on TV.

'Look at our polo, for example, even more popular now than it was fifty years ago. We have survived new fashions and new ideas. Even cricket is no big deal here. Have you seen many people play cricket in northern Pakistan?

'Everyone should be open and receptive to new ideas and cultures and also contribute to them. If the tradition is strong enough, it can survive anything; it shouldn't be kept alive just for its own sake, because then society becomes fossilized. What makes a sport last for ever is its vitality. Polo here has it – you only have to see the enthusiasm of the players and spectators. Players are usually quite poor with low earnings – but most people here would give anything to own a horse.'

Mr Ur-Rehman thought that polo had become more popular in Chitral recently, mainly as a result of increased prosperity in the region stemming from tourism. 'There is definitely more money in the area, especially around Gilgit, and the northern areas are becoming more prosperous. Our people can now enjoy better education and opportunities. There is a higher literacy and employment rate than ever before and most girls are now going to school.'

The Shandur Pass festival has given polo a huge boost over recent years, recently hijacked by the Pakistan Tourist Development Council and turned into a major tourist event. Common to many events organized with enthusiastic bureaucracy, the date was finalized only a few weeks before, depending on the availability of a Chief Guest. This obsession to secure a suitably prominent person to officially open and a different one to close the event – Chief Guest Syndrome, I called it – is the organizers' main headache. It was usually a politician, of no interest to the ordinary man and woman on the street. Even this tournament's organizer, a lovely, kind man who never lost his smile, was worried at the lack of a suitable person to be the Chief Guest for the final, which meant the date for the final couldn't be confirmed.

This played havoc with my schedule, especially when finals have sometimes been delayed by two weeks for this reason. They were hoping to get the [then] Prime Minister Nawaz Sharif, or the Chief Minister of Punjab as a second-best option. I asked why normally sensible sports-loving polo people value the presence of a politician at their match. Nasir made it crystal-clear. 'At a polo final, the whole of Chitral comes to watch. Neither the spectators nor the players care about politics, but the District Commissioner is very clever: he invites a politician to impress him, and say that the people have come only to see him, and not the polo. This flatters the politician and they will favour the region.' So, it was all canny planning and boosting the egos of men in power for the region's own benefit. Not as stupid as I originally thought.

On the second day of the tournament, which were more first-round matches, I was accosted again by Machboul Ali, who used the Buzkashi Factor again to lure me to the Afghan border. 'If you can't go to Afghanistan, we'll play a game after the final, in Gabor.' This presented two problems: the date of the final wasn't yet fixed, and although his intentions were probably genuine, he didn't seem to be very reliable.

The standard of polo wasn't particularly impressive in these early rounds, but the enthusiasm and enjoyment were, as was the encouragement the crowds gave the players.

Most teams had some kind of uniform: Chitral wore smart blue polo shirts, white trousers and long black boots. Some village teams wore coloured vests over their slightly ragged clothes; Gabor had scarlet scarves on their head and looked like pirates, befitting their aggressive play. Some wore proper helmets, some the felt Hunza hat, and some cotton bandannas.

During one of the matches on that second day, all hopes of getting Nawaz Sharif as Chief Guest were well and truly scuppered. In the middle of a match between a Buni village team and the Chitral youth team, an excited announcement was made over the loudspeaker. I asked Machboul Ali what it was about. 'They've just announced that Pakistan have tested again more nuclear weapons. This means that we've now tested more than India.'

'But I didn't hear any reaction from the crowd. Are they pleased?'

Machboul Ali gave a huge chuckle. 'Don't be silly – the people of Chitral are more concerned with polo than nuclear testing!'

Their reaction was very different from that of the rest of the country, where pictures on TV that night showed men dancing in the streets and shooting guns into the air in celebration. It was seen as a victory over India, and only one step beyond similar celebrations when beating them at cricket. Apart from possible escalation into nuclear war between the two countries, it meant that Nawaz Sharif had more important things to do than coming to Chitral, which put the organizers into a frenzy.

The following afternoon saw the start of the quarter-final matches, a distinct step-up in excitement, atmosphere and the quality of the playing. Chitral comfortably beat Buni and looked confident and cool. They were one of the favourites to win the tournament but would be facing Machboul Ali's Mulkow team in the semi-final two days later, the most feared team in the tournament.

In the midst of all this, constant phone calls finally revealed that the Iranian Embassy in Islamabad had refused me a visa, with no reason given. This meant that instead of going by land via Iran to Turkey, I had to book a flight to Istanbul for early June. It was now the final week of May and I was forced to make a quick trip to Islamabad in order to get a plane ticket, as well as extend my Pakistani visa.

The timing was unfortunate, as leaving the following day would mean missing the two semi-finals, returning just in time for the final on the Sunday. Nasir and his Chitral team-mates assured me they would do their best to reach the final for my return.

The next afternoon I took the bus to Peshawar and sat next to a teacher, who began our twelve-hour overnight journey with a little excitement. 'You see the woman sitting behind us?' It wasn't hard, she was the only other woman. 'She's being kidnapped by her lover. He's escaping with her.' This was exciting, but how did he know?

'You can tell – she has her face hidden and she hides when we come to a police checkpoint.' 'But if she's been kidnapped, why doesn't she ask for help?' The teacher looked confused, then he smiled. 'No no, I make mistake. I mean they are lovers and running away from her family to marry.' Eloping was a different kettle of fish and it was good to have some drama on an otherwise tedious journey.

The eloping woman may have had second thoughts because at our first meal break, she was weeping in the restaurant whilst her partner-in-crime looked on helplessly. Halfway to Islamabad in the dead of the night, they got off the bus and disappeared into the night.

I was warned of more tension caused by the nuclear testing – a bad time to apply for a visa extension. In the sweltering queue at the Home Department in Islamabad, the Chinese couple in front of me were having a tough time. The young man yelled through the iron grille to the man on duty. 'This is the third time you tell us to come back – why you not decided our case yet? We have student visa and it runs out next week. Three times you tell us to come back! This is no joke! Are you a joker? I think not!' The irate Chinese man hadn't learned the crucial factor in such situations – that getting angry with an official is counter-productive. The officer grew increasingly stubborn and uncooperative, eventually ordering security guards to remove them. Thankfully, he was more helpful to me and promised I could pick up my visa extension the following day.

There was nothing else to do in Islamabad except collect my airline ticket for Istanbul, so in the late afternoon I took a minibus to Peshawar, to spend one night there before returning to Chitral. It had been four years since my last visit to Peshawar, capital of the North-West Frontier Province, and seven years since the gun-dealer Asad Ullah Khan's memorable marriage proposal. He had promised to drive me over to Afghanistan, along with a boot-load of ammunition, and presented me with armfuls of Afghani clothes so I could pretend to be his deaf and dumb wife. I declined at the last minute, somehow suspicious of any little hidden extras. As I was leaving, he jumped onto the bus, tears running down his face and pleaded, 'Marry me, marry me and you can have all the gun-shops you want in Pakistan.'

Asad Ullah had taken me to his shop in Darra Adam Khel, a Wild West village completely filled with gun-makers who still handmake copies of AK47s and Kalashnikovs in tiny wooden huts. It was also a major centre for drugs, with kilos of high-grade heroin coming over the Afghani border. I wanted to visit the village again because it was so extraordinary, but permits for foreigners had now been forbidden for some months.

I trudged into the Khyber Bazaar, downtown Peshawar, which used to contain a whole string of gun-shops along with more mundane stores selling ice-cream, saucepans and books. But most of the gun-shops had been replaced by dentists, tiny booths on the pavement which replaced teeth. You could window-shop for a tooth, choosing from porcelain, plastic or something resembling Plasticine.

I sat and had tea with one of them, Sikander, in the tiny shop-front with his friends, where the conversation gradually got round to 'Can you help my friend get a visa for England'. Then he asked me what contact I had with trade unions in England, explaining, 'I am a representative for trade union groups here. Apart from helping our workers we also try to encourage families to have fewer children, and teach women to learn literacy skills.' This was a surprising and highly welcome topic of conversation. 'I am also a delegate for the Pakistan-India Federation for Peace and Democracy.' That was a refreshing change to the macho, jingoistic celebrations about the nuclear tests.

He showed me the brochure from their last conference, which had taken place in Calcutta the previous year, and it was uplifting to see a touch of humanity in this small corner of Peshawar. 'Many people are against the nuclear testing,' said Sikander, 'but they get no publicity. The TV would rather show men on the street shooting guns and celebrating, rather than our peaceful protest.'

This sounded rather optimistic, as the newspapers claimed that 90 per cent of people supported the tests, and even the teacher who had sat next to me on the bus the previous night had said,

'India is our enemy and it is worth dying for. This is Jihad, and we will die for Kashmir.'

In the late afternoon, when the sun thankfully decreased its ferocity and people gained a fresh lease of life, I came across Hamid Ullah & Sons Arms and Ammunition owned by Asad Ullah's uncle, one of the only gun-shops still around in the Khyber Bazaar. Seven years before, Asad Ullah's numerous brothers and uncles who ran the business had insisted I should stay in their large fortress which was reserved for their clients.

I went into the shop, and the older brother and uncle were the only ones in the store. 'Hello Emma,' said Saeed, with a warm smile as if we had seen each other only the day before. 'It's been a long time.' And over green tea and fresh dates we caught up on many years and he mentioned casually, his uncle not hiding a grin, that Asad Ullah had just left for Darra. I expressed my disappointment that Darra was now closed to foreigners.

'Why didn't you come earlier? We could have dressed you up and driven you there. No one will stop us, you would have been quite safe. We could drive you over the border into Afghanistan too.' It was tempting to hang around for another adventure with the gun-dealers, but better not to get involved again and, in any case, the polo final was the next day. We said goodbye and I walked up to the bazaar where the bus was leaving for Chitral.

I staggered off the bus in Chitral early in the morning, excited about seeing the much-anticipated final that afternoon. Machboul Ali, driving past on his motorbike, stopped when he saw me. The news wasn't good. 'It rained heavily here the last two days. The ground is still too wet so the final will be held tomorrow. Can you come to Gabor to watch buzkashi on the seventh?' That was only three days later. He had arranged with his Gabor team for a buzkashi game in the border town, but the postponed final now messed up all my plans. I told him that regrettably my flight from Karachi was on the 8th, meaning that yet again I was foiled in an attempt to see the headless goat. Machboul Ali looked annoyed and wordlessly drove off.

I got to my hotel, to be greeted by more gloomy faces. Wali Ur-Rehman welcomed me. 'We have three pieces of bad news: there was bad rain and the final has been postponed for a day; we got beaten by Mulkow in the semi-finals -' then his eyes filled up with tears – 'and my horse died just after our last match – just dropped dead of a heart attack.' He looked away. 'My heart has gone out of the tournament now.' I offered my condolences, and could see his friends and team-mates were also affected.

The delayed final – between Police and Mulkow – posed a problem. If I wanted to watch it, I'd have to delay my journey to Karachi, which meant I would have to travel through the night to reach Peshawar by morning in order to catch a flight to Karachi, and then to Istanbul. But the buses ran only in the daytime, with the last one in the mid-afternoon, and only if there were enough passengers. It would be difficult to see the final and catch the flight.

In recent years, no one ventured over the Lowri Pass between Peshawar and Chitral after dark. Dacoits, or bandits, were rumoured to roam the area, holding up cars and buses at gunpoint. The police told me that although it wasn't officially closed, it was dangerous to travel at night and nearly impossible to hitch a ride. Back at the Post Office, the Assistant Manager scratched his beard thoughtfully.

'You could hire a jeep to Dir and early morning you could try and catch another jeep. But you could be stuck there – it is difficult catching a vehicle at that time.' Another man I had drunk tea with several times (who had first claimed he was studying medicine, then that he worked in the Post Office and then that he'd been sent to Afghanistan to be trained by the Mujaheddin) offered a solution. His friend was travelling back to his village near Peshawar, and perhaps could give me a lift the following evening.

That evening, his friend confirmed that he would take me immediately after the polo final ended, and in return I would pay for the petrol. His name was Imdad Ullah, which translates as 'help from God', and how appropriate. Going over a forbidden mountain pass through the night with an unknown man made me think twice, so I went around Chitral checking him out and telling people exactly who I was going with.

The day of the final was encouraged by a glorious sunny sky. My departure was arranged, with another plan in case Imdad Ullah had second thoughts, and I went to the polo ground two hours before the final began. The whole of Chitral had been buzzing since morning and the organizers were relieved as the Chief Guest (the Chief of Police, who was from Chitral and whom most people knew personally and who had also, rather confusedly, been the Chief Guest for the opening) was coming.

People arrived early, and already all space on the perimeter wall was taken. Chairs were set up in the main stand, children scampered about the field with tiny polo sticks in hand, and a furious game of football was going on among a group of boys on the grass behind the wall. There were several stalls selling blocks of snow from the Lowri Pass, which was scraped into cups and drowned in a sea of luminous syrup. The enormous Afghani carpet seller was there and so was the teacup seller, doubly laden with strings of crockery, clinking his way cautiously around the crowds.

Overlooking the ground was a grassy hill where the women sat, away from the men with only small boys amongst them. Men packed onto the wall and stood five deep behind it, safely away from charging horses. Two groups of musicians sat cross-legged on the wall with instruments on their laps: a couple of zurnas and a type of drum, a little like an Indian tabla but with a rounded bottom, which had to be heated in a small fire to get the parchment top to expand.

An hour before the game began, the goal area was also packed. This was a dangerous place to stand, with no barrier against a stampede of horses galloping at the goal, but it had the greatest atmosphere and excitement. Music began and a slightly crazy old man clambered off the wall onto the pitch and began to dance in slow, deliberate steps, which pleased the other spectators who whistled and cheered him.

Way past the scheduled start time, the most important guests arrived and there was much scuffling and rearranging of seats as most people who were sitting in the VIP enclosure shouldn't have been there and were shoved at the back. Officials and local dignitaries who hadn't previously been there made an appearance. Around twenty local expatriates, mainly European embassy workers with shiny kids and designer trainers, showed up at the last minute to be rewarded with fawning and the best seats.

The two teams were introduced to the crowd, and play began accompanied by music which continued throughout the game. As the musicians in Gilgit had explained to me, a specific tune signalled each different stage of the game. I stood behind the goal posts, now adept at leaping quickly out of the way of an oncoming horse – following the lead of the two officials who were standing behind each goal and waving a flag when the ball went through. When the horses came racing towards the goal and then through the posts, the only way to dodge them was to stand directly behind a post, as if you were hiding behind it.

In just twenty minutes, the favourites Mulkow had quickly raced to a 6-0 lead, which pleased the spectators no end, as perhaps no one wanted to support a police team. Machboul Ali was a star and won my 'Man of the Match' award in the first half, effortlessly covering the whole field, faster than anyone else and the most fearless.

The rest of the team were also strong, except their captain, who according to Mr Nasir was only picked because he was a senior dignitary in the army and was more accustomed to playing polo on the plush lawns of the Lahore Polo Club. At half-time, he looked hotter and sweatier than his team-mates and his breathing was ragged with all the exertion.

After a ten-minute break, the Police made a comeback, to the relief of the organizers who had probably promised the VIPs it would be a close final. The tension increased slightly when the scores got to 8-6, and the cheering grew wilder. But Mulkow were by far the fiercer, superior team and there was no way Police could come back.

It was hard to believe that these same players, looking ferocious and macho, the red scarves on their heads flying behind them in the wind, were the same Afghani men who had a few days earlier uttered to me their fear of a possible nuclear war. 'We have already left our homeland to escape one war,' one had said. 'We only want a peaceful life.' They looked anything but peaceful on the field as they charged, galloped and kicked up dust thickly, crashing into walls and their opponents, hooking with glee and driving their horses relentlessly. When the horn eventually went off, signalling the end, the victorious team leapt off their horses and the crowd invaded the field and lifted the team onto their shoulders. A circle was formed in front of the VIP stand and the musicians played, as spectators and players began to dance. It was pure joy to behold such good-natured celebrations and exuberance, and hard to believe this was a small tournament with no prize money but great honour.

It was in this mêlée that I caught sight of Imdad Ullah, and a feeling of utmost relief came over me as I knew that our plans to leave would be as arranged. The winning teams wore themselves out by dancing, the trophies were presented and all players received a medallion. Long-drawn-out speeches from the guests of honour and VIP and the DC were cheerfully ignored by most people and then suddenly it was all over. Everyone disappeared quickly into a thick cloud of fumes as the jeeps started up and left in a slow trail, while the majority walked in a thick mass into the town centre, in their midst the players trotting home on their horses. Imdad Ullah ushered me away, anxious to get on the road quickly.

13

Proposal of the Month

We escaped the crush, picked up my bags and were waved off by the Prince, Nasir and the rest of the Chitral team. The small jeep had ample room for all our luggage and the seats were far more comfortable than the national bus, and conditions were further improved by playing my favourite Turkish cassette at full volume. At least the first part of the travel arrangements had gone to plan.

We left Chitral as the sun went down and the colours of the mountains and surrounding fields were bathing in a warm glow. I handed Imdad Ullah some fruit from the bag: ripe apricots, apples and pears. He took an apricot and turned to give me a smile. 'I am so happy,' he began simply. 'I am driving in the beautiful mountains. We have the whole night ahead of us. I am being offered fruit from the hand of a beautiful woman and am hearing your sweet voice.'

Oh Lordy. And I thought he was a religious, happily married, trustworthy sort of fellow. This wasn't the best beginning, and with many hours to go. Unfortunately, he seemed to think that by sharing the journey with him, I was making myself available. 'Otherwise, why would two people decide to spend the night together?' he asked. I had already explained, firmness approaching rudeness, that this arrangement was my only chance of catching the flight. And anyway I was engaged to a Turkish wrestler, and wouldn't even look at another man. (The fiancé was an inspired afterthought.)

'So anyway,' I said loudly in a courageous attempt to change the subject, 'how old are your children?' Perhaps a conversation about his family would take his mind off anything else. 'My two daughters are aged two and six.' He looked glum. We drove on further in silence.

His expression was like a love-sick tragic Shakespearean character, mournful and misunderstood. 'But my wife, I don't love her any more. In fact I hate her. I cannot bear to be with her for the rest of my life.' The conversation wasn't going as I hoped.

'How long have you been married?' I asked.

'Eight years. I married when I was thirty-two years old. My wife was twenty-six.'

'But that's quite old for a Pakistani to marry. Why did you marry so late?' There were no taboos about asking such questions here, as nearly everyone I met told me that I was leaving it 'very late to find a husband'.

'I married very late because I had a problem. A serious problem.' There was a long, ominous pause. 'It was a sexual problem.'

Oh, I asked myself, why didn't I get the conversation on to cricket? But please, please spare me the details . . .

'You see, the problem is,' he continued as a cloak of darkness settled on the night and in my heart, 'that I have had this problem since I was fourteen years old. I was completely obsessed with sex and want to do it with anything.'

Anything? Not even any*one* but any*thing*? And this was the beginning of a ten-hour drive over lonely mountains where bandits kept other vehicles away. He continued: 'My only solution was to marry. My religion says it is the best cure of this disease. But now I hate my wife and don't want to be with her. And also, I am still obsessed with sex.' This final statement was weighted heavily with implication. 'Please will you hold my hand?'

Even telling him 'no' failed to have the desired effect. He changed tactic slightly, trying a more permanent solution, rather than a quickie. 'I have decided to take a second wife. Of course, I can marry a woman of any religion or nationality, and probably I will take a foreign woman.' I gave an involuntary inward groan, expecting the worst. 'When I first saw you last night, as you were drinking Pepsi in the shop, I noticed how beautiful you looked in that light.' (It was dark.) 'Would you be my second wife?'

It was neither as romantic nor as dramatic as the Peshawar gun-dealer, who thought that a few Kalashnikovs and AK47s would be the way to my heart. This proposal stank of a convenient way of solving his 'problem'. 'But I'm already engaged – I've told you many times. He's a wrestler. Very big. And strong.'

Imdad Ullah was mercifully silent for half an hour. Night fell quickly and soon the meandering, steep gravel track was lit only by the small beam on his headlights.

'Will you kiss me?'

'Oh shut up and keep your eyes on the road.' Conversation quality had plummeted, and I desperately counted off the miles as if staggering through desert to reach water.

We had planned to drive all night to reach Peshawar, which would at least eliminate the prospect of beds and hotel rooms. I was thirsty, but it was impossible to find a teahouse, which surprised me – on the subcontinent just about any road, whether mountain, desert or through godforsaken villages, has restaurants, shops and cartons of mango Frooti at frequent intervals. But this road had effectively closed at sunset. He refused to stop at the only restaurant that we passed: 'There are many people inside. Maybe someone from my town is there and see me with you. This would not look good for me.'

I stopped making conversation and allowed the silence and stark stillness of the journey to take over. Imdad Ullah suddenly stopped the car, muttered something in Urdu and got out. He disappeared for a few minutes, and returned. 'We have a problem,' he moaned. 'Tyre is flat. I will have to change it, but I need help.' Was this a plot? A ruse to stop for a while and be forced to spend the night somewhere?

There was no one in sight but, there, on the hill, was a tiny lodge with lights glowing warmly, our only saviour. Imdad Ullah ordered me to stay in the jeep and he was joined by two lorry drivers who had stopped for tea at the lodge; together they tried to release the spare tyre from the back of the jeep where it had been firmly screwed in.

Eventually, they gave up trying to unscrew it – the only solution was brute force to bash the wheel off. I stood around being as helpful as possible, holding the paraffin lamp feeling like Florence Nightingale without the apron. Finally, the wheel clanked to the ground and the happy truckers helped to fit it on.

'Where else but Pakistan,' said Imdad Ullah as we continued on our way, 'would passing drivers spend so much time helping and not accept any money in return?' That was true. In England, people would politely drive by pretending they hadn't seen, and in India, passers-by will often lend a hand, but expect a tip. 'More help from God!' he cried, happy and in a better mood, probably because it distracted him from his failure to achieve his sexual desires on this journey.

The hours dragged on and we hadn't met a single other vehicle en route, and I was glad I hadn't risked getting out of Imdad Ullah's jeep to hitch a ride from somebody else, as I had once or twice considered doing. Imdad Ullah made a couple more bleak attempts like: 'I am feeling rather tired. A kiss would revive me.'

He only pounced once. Stopping the jeep suddenly, he turned to me and placed his oily lips on mine. I whacked his balding head with considerable force, and yelled at him: 'Oh for God's sake. You know that I don't like you and don't want to kiss you. Why then do you insist on forcing yourself on me? Your behaviour gives Pakistani men a bad name.' That worked for a while.

Two hours later: 'I am feeling rather tired, and think I need to sleep for a couple of hours. Perhaps we can find a hotel and get a room?' 'Fine,' I replied. 'If you are tired then you must sleep. But I am not setting one foot inside your room. I will stay in the car.'

That was the last conversation we had until four hours later when the sun rose and we mercifully approached the end of our journey. We saw the first signs of life for hours: a smattering of early-morning traffic, delivery carts, groups of schoolchildren clambering on buses and old men ambling gently to the chai house. I assumed, wrongly, that these were the outskirts of Peshawar.

'We are in Nowshera, and I'm going to leave you here. Only thirty miles to Peshawar. There is the bus stand.' Imdad Ullah stopped the jeep at the side of the road, unloaded my bags and dumped them on the street. Wordlessly, he returned to the driver's seat, and before I realized what was happening, he drove off hurriedly, sending a bullock cart scuttling for safety. 'Well,' I said out loud to the disappearing cloud of dust, 'I suppose you've changed your mind about getting married then?'

14

Flying Javelins in Istanbul

The aircraft touched down at Istanbul, to a humid afternoon with clouds hanging heavily like damp sponges. Here, rather than horses galloping in sunny mountains, the sporting event in everyone's mind was the world's largest: the football World Cup, due to kick off a couple of days later. Although Turkey had failed to qualify, it would still be keenly followed here and I looked forward to watching every match in a bar with a large raki in hand.

I was now approaching the halfway point of my year-long trip and although I had seen and enjoyed a great deal in the way of sports and festivals, there was still the small matter of the headless goat: my mission to see the glorious game of buzkashi was still on, although it would have to be postponed until I reached Central Asia, where the date of 31 August, Kyrgyzstan Independence Day, would be my best chance yet to see the game.

Before that, I planned to spend around six weeks in Turkey and in addition to watching the World Cup on television, my priorities were the Kirkpinar oil-wrestling competition near Edirne; the horseback-javelin game of cirit, played mainly in the east of the country; and the annual bull-fighting festival at the Kafkasor festival, near Artvin. I had tentative dates for some of these events, given by the Tourist Office and official organizations which therefore had to be treated with extreme caution and verified before making plans.

But the first, less pleasurable task was to begin planning the trip to Central Asia; this meant applying for visas which would probably take an inordinate amount of time, effort and patience.

This process would be even more complicated if I chose to go overland from Turkey, a plan which had begun to develop in my mind.

My first, rather unsuccessful attempt at getting a visa came courtesy of Mr Osman at the Kazakh consulate in Istanbul, who had worked in Almaty for several years. His promises of advice, contacts and visa assistance for Kazakhstan unfortunately seemed dependent on my visiting his apartment while his wife was away. I rejected his plan and decided to contact the Kazakh Embassy in Ankara at a later date.

Enquiries about traditional Turkish sports were more successful. A couple of sports journalists from the Türkiye newspaper gave me good, reliable information on forthcoming events. After a couple of phone calls they confirmed the dates of the oil-wrestling in Kirkpinar (middle of July) and the bull fighting in Kafkasor (end of June). They also told me of a cirit competition in Istanbul the following Sunday, which was a pleasant surprise as it meant I wouldn't have to go searching for it in eastern Turkey.

The cirit tournament was organized by Geleneksel Spor Dallari Federasyon, or the Traditional Sports Federation and I arranged to visit its president, Mr Alper Yazorğlu. He explained that the Federation originated in 1996, with the aims of giving a higher profile to and encouraging government support for certain significant Turkish sports, especially *yağli güreş*, (oil-wrestling), cirit and *aba güreş*, (another form of traditional wrestling which originated in Central Asia). I was disappointed that he didn't include camel or bull fighting.

The Federation's intention was to advertise these sports both nationally and internationally, to provide social insurance for sportsmen, and to help organize championships at local level through their local branches. Most sports originated, and are still played, in specific regions of the country – cirit, for example, is specifically eastern Turkish. The federation wanted to break down those regional barriers so that the games are played more broadly and awareness increased.

Mr Yazorğlu was a mountain of a man with broad shoulders and a great black moustache which stretched as he smiled. 'I was pehli-van,' he said, using the word known throughout Asia for 'wrestler'. He pointed to photographs on the wall of a man a little trimmer and younger, wearing the *kispet* which all competing oil wrestlers must wear. Kispet are black leather breeches which fasten just below the knee and are covered with oil, like the rest of their body, for fighting. Yağli güreş is the only wrestling in the world in which oil on the body plays a crucial part.

'Here I am Ağa,' he said, as he showed me photographs of him looking noble and dignified. Ağa is pronounced 'aah' and literally means landowner, or elder brother. Traditionally, the Ağa was the landowner in his village area, using his wealth to organize and financially support local competitions and paying a small allowance to the pehlivans. These days, he is usually a wealthy city businessman who pledges a large sum of money for a tournament. In the photograph, Mr Yazorğlu was dressed in a long, coloured shirt and heavy embroidered jacket, a bright tasselled cummerbund tied broadly at the waist with ceremonial dagger tucked in, and a multi-coloured turban tied many times around his head, tassels hanging down like curtains.

'I was Ağa in Kirkpinar for three years, after finishing wrestling,' he said. He pointed to his kispet hanging on the wall, alongside medals and certificates. 'When a pehlivan retires from wrestling, he hangs up his kispet so he can always see and remember them.'

He gave me an invitation to attend the cirit competition a few days later. He explained more about the game, as my knowledge of it was scant and limited to 'a game where men on horses throw wooden sticks at each other in a large field'. Cirit has a noble history: in days when the horse was indispensable to the lives of the Turkish nomads, proverbs, tales and symbols depicted the love and respect they had for their horses. The imagery is still powerful: the Turks entered Anatolia after the battle of Malazgirt, and the symbol of that victory is the rearing horse. The conquest of Istanbul which ended the Middle Ages is symbolized by the silhouette of Mehmet the Conqueror on his horse.

This love of horses naturally influenced their sports, developed from the times when the Sultans held games on horseback whenever they halted their travels. Although the first known horse races in Western Europe were held in 1605, in Anatolia they were much earlier – in 1326. Cirit, a folk game of the Ottoman period, and a symbol of heroism and bravery, was invented by the Turks of Central Asia to maintain the fitness of their horses and soldiers. It was especially popular in Anatolia, where it was played mainly in spring and autumn, during Bayrams (religious festivals) and weddings.

My first sight of this romantic-sounding sport of nomads was not to be in a dramatic setting, like the rolling hills of Central Asia or even a village in eastern Turkey. It was here in the industrial suburb of Kağithane in northern Istanbul at 11 am, an annual event organized by the local Belediye and now supported by the Federation.

I reached the ground at 9.30, early enough to see the preparations watched by a few policemen who were (as usual) slouching around and smoking cigarettes. The ground was approximately the size of a football field, covered with a dry muddy grass around which a man was making slow progress with a bucket of chalk powder, marking out the perimeter line. On one side was a tower with three wooden floors for photographers and TV cameras, and around three sides of the field were temporary seating blocks for spectators.

The final touches were being applied to the VIP stage, which had a smart canvas shelter with flowers and leaves woven into the power cables, several rows of comfortable chairs and a front row of *very* comfortable chairs. Around 10 am the work-rate increased and the first spectators began to trickle in, then the horses arrived from their overnight accommodation in nearby stables, and were tethered to trees at the side of the field.

The riders ranged from young men in their late teens to more experienced horsemen a generation older. Each team wore a uniform: black trousers and a light-coloured long-sleeved shirt, a different colour for each team, with a dark waistcoat buttoned over it. Every player of a team had a number from 1 to 7 painted on his back.

Shortly before eleven o'clock, people started pouring into the stadium, getting seats in the shady areas of the stands. Each team rode out on to the field in formation, the team captains carrying a huge triangular banner with the name of the team. Leading the procession was a single rider bearing the Turkish flag.

The teams were formally introduced to the crowds. They came from Erzurum (the biggest city in eastern Turkey), Bayburt, Erzincan and Uşak, towns mainly in the east. Most of them were farmers, who had doubtless been riding horses since they were young boys. The majority of the spectators originated from eastern Turkey (some of the many millions of migrants who pour into Istanbul every year for better employment) and they gave raucous support to their 'home' team, with especially loud cheers for the

Bayburt team. The inevitable folk musicians emerged from nowhere and struck up folk songs on davul and zurna.

The first game was between Erzincan and Uşak. The commentator, firmly installed behind the microphone, announced their arrival to their respective ends of the field and a cheer filled the air as the referee's whistle signalled the first charge. The first rider from Erzincan ran down the field to the opposite end where the Uşak team were lined up, and as he approached them he threw his cirit, the wooden stick, at one of the Uşak players.

The stick narrowly missed, and the cheers increased as the Uşak player then turned and chased the Erzincan horseman back up the field. As he got closer, he threw his cirit in a 'return' attack, and the Erzincan player managed to lean down elegantly from his galloping horse and catch it deftly in one hand. He held the cirit proudly aloft to the excited announcement from the commentator that he had won that first 'round'; then the second one began immediately as a new pair of players began the chase.

Even though I had read the rules and tried hard to understand it, I still found cirit a confusing game which seemed to consist of guys on horseback racing at each other, chucking wooden spears. Few of the journalists and photographers who were positioned in the tower had seen it before, and hardly anyone was able to enlighten me further.

According to the rules, the ground must measure between 30 and 50 metres wide and 90 and 160 metres long. At either end, an area of five metres acts as the 'Play Station', where the riders can be hit. Behind that, an area of seven metres in width is the 'Forbidden Zone' where opponents are not allowed to enter. Here the horses stand in a line, one team at each end, ready for play. Each player has a cirit – a wooden stick, measuring 110 centimetres with blunted ends, made from dried oak – and the basic object of the game is for a player to throw it, while stationary or riding, and hit his opponent, who must either catch it or dodge it.

Each team lines up in their play station at opposite ends of the field, where they stand and wait before being attacked, and although they can be struck here, opponents cannot ride into this area. One player from side A rides up to side B's play station, and throws the cirit at one of the riders. As soon as he has thrown it (whether successfully or not) he rides back down the field to his play station, hotly pursued by his opponent. The rider from side

B, gets as close as possible, and throws his cirit in return. Once the rider from side A has crossed the line into his own play station, he can't be hit.

That consists of one 'round'; the points are then calculated and the next pair of players begin, and so it goes until all the riders have been on the field. Then, all is reversed so that the team who began the throwing are the ones to be chased. At the end of the two completed rounds, the total points are calculated and the winner announced.

The team whose cirit hits the opponent's rider, either in his play station or on the field, is awarded six points. The player who catches the cirit that's thrown at him, whether in the play station or in the field, receives three points. Sometimes, with the cirit flying towards him, the rider can skilfully hang down to one side of the horse, lower than the saddle. If he does this successfully and avoids the cirit flying towards him, his team scores three points. There were other more complicated scoring systems depending, for instance, on how the cirit lands, but, said the ex-player who was trying to explain the rules to me, 'You don't need to know all of them on your first time.'

There is, however, one very significant rule of which all cirit players (and all Turks) are proud: the rule of 'forgiveness'. If a rider comes very close to his opponent, it's considered unsporting for him to throw the cirit. Therefore, he 'forgives' his opponent, which means that he rides up close, pretends to throw whilst saying to his opponent something like 'You know that I can hit you, but I'll be really sporting and spare you.' For demonstrating such sporting behaviour, the attacker wins three points.

One player said to me, 'This says a lot about our nature, that whether in sport or in war we can show mercy on our opponents.' So cirit is a game which combines not only great horsemanship, honour and glory, and one in which players are formidable warriors showing their might and strength against the enemy, but also, when push comes to shove, that they are man enough to forgive.

Every team played each other once and the two teams with the most points met in the final. I was learning more during every game and knew what to look for and appreciate. Some of the riders were outstanding. My two favourites were from Bayburt who displayed showmanship and skill with great charisma. They enjoyed showing off and joking with their opponents, gesturing to the crowd to encourage their cheers. The younger one's speciality was to hang down the side of his horse while it was running, his head just above the ground, then leaping up and throwing himself over to the other side.

It was 4 pm when eventually Bayburt won the final, after which was another parade of all the teams and flags, then a rousing burst of folk songs. In spite of the heat, some players dismounted, linked arms and kicked up their feet in a hearty dance, while others indulged in a few daredevil horseback tricks, much to the joy of the crowds and the TV cameras.

The after-match ceremony was a delightful end to the afternoon, and a little less chaotic than the polo final in Chitral. Each team was paid a small amount, primarily to cover all their expenses for bringing the horses, and clearly the main incentive for participants was enjoyment and honour. Prizes were awarded to all teams and mementoes to officials, various speeches and votes of thanks were given and then honouring the Aǧa. Spectators began their slow exit home, although many stayed for a hearty display of singing and dancing.

The next morning I took an early bus to Ankara, intending to visit the Ministries of Tourism and Culture, some cirit clubs, and also the Kazakh Embassy. A throbbing headache and bouts of shivering made the journey most unpleasant. By the time we arrived, five hours later, I had difficulty in staying vertical and barely found my way out of the bus station to a hotel.

Assuming this was sunstroke caused by the previous day's exposure, I slouched to the chemist and came back laden with rehydration salts and painkillers and spent the next eighteen hours in bed alternately shivering and sweating, unable to eat. At least watching England's first World Cup victory came as sweet relief even though I was unable to get off my bed to celebrate. Surprising, I thought, that after the baking heat in Pakistan, a mere 30 degrees should cause such problems. Stranger still was it that I, who had never been sick during seven years of living and travelling in countries where hygiene leaves much to be desired, should feel so awful now.

I managed to drag myself off to a couple of meetings and even endured an hour in the Kazakh Embassy (never wanting to repeat the Mr Osman experience again). No one had any idea about their country's traditional sports and they weren't really sure about my visa, other than it would take a long time and it was expensive. But they did give me the interesting news that if I got a Kyrgyz visa (quick and easy in Istanbul) it would enable me to transit through Kazakhstan, Uzbekistan, Tajikistan and Turkmenistan at no extra cost, for seventy-two hours in each country.

On the third morning I felt worse and anything more than standing up was a supreme effort. I managed to get on a bus and, huddled in a seat, made it home to Istanbul.

The next morning I had a series of tests at the local government hospital, enduring lengthy waits in minimal comfort while bloodied bodies were casually being wheeled around in the wrong departments.

A couple of hours later the results came back. Hepatitis, and I must stay in bed for three weeks. 'On your back,' emphasized the doctor, 'and only get up to go to the toilet. Don't eat any protein for a couple of weeks, and no alcohol for six months.' *Six months.* Feeling too flaky to argue with such a long sentence of abstinence, I went home to begin my enforced bed-rest.

Trying to be thankful for something, I was grateful that the illness had struck in Istanbul and not Chitral, where undoubtedly I had picked up the infection through food or drink. So instead of being stuck in a primitive village, at least I was confined to the comforts of my friend's flat and being waited on hand and foot by concerned mates.

15

Black Sea Bull

The Artvin bull fight was fast approaching. Defying doctor's orders, I rose early from my sick-bed in order to attend the annual Kafkas Folk Festival. I caught a flight to Trabzon on the Black Sea coast and then took a four-hour minibus ride into the hills to Artvin, perhaps a bit ambitious as though it was only 5 pm when we arrived I was ready for bed.

Two days before the region's biggest festival meant there weren't many hotel rooms available, so it was a long and tiring trek around the small town. I was joined by a pleasant bunch of college girls, pleased to practise their English, although shocked at some of the unsavoury guesthouses I was forced to try.

In the town centre, I tried yet another guesthouse. 'We, er, don't think you should go to this place. It is, well, not very nice people coming here,' advised the girls. You could tell that from the outside, but I assured them the Kafkas Hotel would be OK and they looked embarrassed and shifted away. It definitely looked sleazy, with an unkempt exterior, narrow entrance on the main road and some broken windows. From the first-floor window, an old unshaven man peered suspiciously at me from behind the net curtains. He had an unwashed appearance.

The reception area didn't look any better but they had a room available, said the old man who worked there. He was short and smelt rather sour. I wasn't keen to stay but there were very few possibilities and I was exhausted. We walked up wooden stairs with piles of rubbish at every corner and the thought of rats came to mind.

But the bedroom and sheets were clean and there was a clear, sweeping view over the mountains. The shared toilet and shower were less clean, but it was adequate for one night and I would look elsewhere in the morning. The old man asked if I was bringing 'a friend' back to the room, tried to double his original price and then offered a few words of advice, in French. 'If you don't want a friend' (he said with heavy implication) 'to visit you in the night, then keep your door locked. If you don't lock it, you can have a friend.'

It could have been some mystic eastern philosophy but I was pretty sure he meant it literally. And judging by the noises that night – heavy footsteps banging up and down the stairs, crashing on doors, men shouting and women laughing – there were a lot of 'friends' in that hotel. The next morning, on my way down the stairs to reception I caught glimpses of the other hotel guests and friends – through open doors. Flabby, balding men with thick waists and drooping nipples wearing baggy white underpants and torn vests, sat on beds smoking cigarettes. Half-naked women sprawled on unmade beds, still in their underwear and last night's make-up, and in most rooms was an intriguing male-female ratio.

I left for the Kaşkar Hotel, which was bigger and more friendly (although with fewer 'friends' likely to drop by); it had one room left. After settling in there, I went to the Tourist Office for a festival programme. A piece of barely legible paper gave the details for the following three days; the bull fighting was on the last day, on the second day was *karakucak* wrestling, another form of traditional wrestling, in which some of the hotel workers were participating.

Later that afternoon was the start of the Kafkasor Kultur ve Sanat Festivali (the Caucasus Culture and Arts Festival) a few kilometres outside the town in the Kafkasor Yaylasi, a beautiful stretch of pasture overlooked by the mountains. Several shacks selling food and drink were being built, and a sound system was being set up for a concert in the amphitheatre scheduled for that night. Groups of people were arriving and putting up large tents in which they would eat and sleep during the festival.

This annual folk festival attracts many people from the Black Sea region, with most interest reserved for the bull fighting on the final day. Traditionally, it was held at the time when farmers moved up to the high summer pastures and people celebrated with music, dancing and wrestling, then brought their bulls up for fighting. Some bulls had arrived on Friday afternoon, with owners and their families settling into their tents on the grassy hills which surrounded the meadow.

Artvin by night brought about a prominent change in ambience. Gone was the gentle buzz of a slow, small town. Most women out on the street were Russian or Georgian prostitutes, indicative of an increase in the profession in the Black Sea region. Over the last few years, many smaller hotels had closed down, making way for the more profitable business of brothels. On the main street, hopeful males peered at every passing woman, muttering something hopeful. Women with very badly dyed blonde hair and brightly painted lips and eyes, walked arm-in-arm in tight skirts, their high heels clicking on the cobbles.

The hotel manager and receptionist were participating in the karakucak competition the next day and invited me to join them in their van, which did not save as much time as I'd hoped – by the time they'd got organized, loaded the van with a whole side of raw meat and the kebab oven, the driver had disappeared with the keys. When he was located it was time for breakfast so we stopped for lentil soup.

An hour later we trundled up the hill to the meadow. The modern stone amphitheatre, looking down to a grassy stage, was filling up with people come to watch the karakucak. Karakucak is one of the oldest forms of traditional wrestling which originated in Turkey, thought to date back some 3000 years. Although not as famous or distinctive as oil-wrestling, it's still popular at local festivals. Mehmet, the hotel manager, changed into the special clothes for his competition: thick canvas trousers in a pale grey, and jacket similar to a judo suit.

The first rounds were the youngest boys, who received great encouragement from the spectators. Several fights went on simultaneously, with four referees on the ground plus three in a raised tower with perfect views over the entire ground. The basic rules of most wrestling applied: having to get your opponent flat on his back twice to win.

Like in the subcontinent and Central Asia, wrestling has great historical importance in Turkey. Although oil-wrestling is the most famous of the traditional forms, with Kirkpinar the best-loved competition, other forms remain popular. The Turks have been more successful than India or Pakistan in retaining their connection with traditional games, celebrated alongside a healthy football fanaticism. At the Kafkasor festival, the noble art of wrestling had an enthralled following of all ages. Historically, the Turks saw sports as a means to beauty and strength, rather than simply competition. Any sport based on war skills, requiring courage, heroism and intelligence, still holds an important place in Turkish life.

The Prophet Muhammad told his people, 'Learn to shoot arrows and ride,' adding, 'He who learns to shoot arrows and forgets is not one of us,' explaining that Muslims must have skills to prepare for war, to protect themselves and be strong materially and morally. This encouraged Turks to maintain their interest in physical fighting, archery, fencing and cirit.

There was a small amount of prize money for the winners, slightly more for the more senior categories. But money is never a motive for these participants. Most said that they would do it if there was no prize money, just to enjoy the occasion. One young man from Trabzon told me, 'My father and grandfather both wrestled at this festival. I want to carry on that tradition even if I never win.'

The lads from my hotel didn't fare well. Mehmet fell in his fight and sprained his shoulder, spending the rest of the day with his arm in a sling, and Hüseyin lost his first-round fight. But both enjoyed the rest of the day running a small kebab stall at the side of the arena, one-armed Mehmet carving slices of sizzling, spitting meat off the whole side of lamb on the grill, expertly shoving a mound into a hunk of bread and filling it with salad.

Sunday was the long-awaited bull fight, and huge crowds arrived early that morning, reflecting the anticipation from many Black Sea residents. 'This is the highlight of our weekend!' many festival-goers told me. Unfortunately, the previous night the heavens opened and a noisy storm swept over the hills, most people in Artvin lying in their beds praying that it would clear by the morning. But it hadn't, and heavy sporadic showers greeted our arrival at the meadow.

I remembered countless rained-off cricket matches I'd endured in England in mid-July and thought of a comment a Turk made about England: 'England would be a lovely country if someone could turn the tap off.' Now the tap was on in Turkey. But apart from dampening the ground underfoot, it didn't threaten people's enjoyment and even the muddy grass caused no problems for the bulls, so the fights began as planned. Bull fighting in Turkey isn't the barbaric man-against-beast bullfighting of Spain, but a variation on the camel wrestling (the Turkish word *boğa-güreş* actually translates as bull wrestling). Two slightly bad-tempered males fight each other, prod around, sniff each other and paw the ground, attempt to lock horns and the winner is declared when one runs away, or topples his opponent.

The spectators don't watch with bloodthirsty glee, like those at cockfights or dog fights, but rather with enjoyment which gives the impression they don't take it very seriously.

As with camel wrestling, the smallest bulls, paired to an opponent of similar size and weight, began the competition and the early fights were about as successful (or not) as most of the camel encounters. The first began when two small bulls were released into the arena to a huge roar of encouragement from the crowd, standing in the morning drizzle with newspapers on their heads or huddled under umbrellas. As they entered, one gave a huge moo and the other looked uninterested. Both pawed the ground for several moments and gave each other a wide berth until their owners, waiting in the wings, tried to prod them together. For a moment it looked promising with a half-hearted charge and a clashing of horns, but it soon disintegrated and they wandered away, bored and pawing the ground again. One of them was so unimpressed that he walked slowly out of the arena, unfortunate for him because it meant he had lost.

The subsequent fights were more exciting but there was never any blood or danger to the animals. Some of them lasted for several minutes, other were over in less than a minute if one bull made a furious charge and the other bolted out of the arena. Sometimes the bolting bull evaded his owner and charged into a crowd of people or into the lads playing football in the car park, when several fearless men with ropes would try to catch the bull by now causing havoc.

I met a family with a medium-weight bull called Ceylan, which translates rather sweetly as 'baby deer'. There was nothing remotely Bambi-like in Ceylan, who lay impatiently in his shelter next to the family.

Most fighting bulls aren't working bulls, so are expensive to the owner who will never make sufficient prize money to pay for his upkeep, unless he is a champion fighter. So those participating in the sport do it for enjoyment, for honour and respect – again, as in camel wrestling. There is a strict feeding regime when training a bull. Every day, from two months before the fight, the owners feed them a mixture of corn flour, egg-yolk and raisins, which gives energy and protein. Unlike camels, two males will instinctively fight each other, and no female is required to rouse them.

Under the rain, families prepared elaborate picnics and barbecues sheltered by plastic sheeting attached to trees, cars and tents. Ozner, who worked in the Tourist Office, invited me for lunch with his family, who came every year for the final day of the festival. From the steep hillside they had a decent view of the bull fights and could watch from the comfort of chairs and hot tea and food. Turks really know how to prepare a good spread wherever they are – we consumed four varieties of cheese, boiled potatoes, freshly barbecued chicken and meat, salads, breads, homemade cakes, fruit and of course endless cups of hot tea.

Next to us, an enormous bull lay (tied up) rather solemnly next to a large family eating a similar spread. 'We now live in Ankara,' said one man whilst offering me a chicken leg, 'but originally we are from Trabzon. Every year we return to this festival – it's one of the few which celebrate the tradition of the Black Sea area. Anyway,' he said patting the bull, 'we came to support this one!'

When it came to the final contest for the title of Baş Boğa, or head bull, it was wetter and colder but that hardly dampened the crowd's enthusiasm for the highlight of the year. With the title and golden belt came the substantial prize money. However it wasn't the money which made people take it more seriously, but the prestige to the owner.

The title fight lasted a long time between two well-trained and experienced beasts who attracted a lot of support. Güneş had won several titles in the past and was expected to win, but it was approaching the time-limit when he eventually engaged in a major tussle with his opponent's horns and using a combination of his weight and some neat footwork, he managed to overbalance the other. Joy and cheers all round, and in the increasingly heavy rain the Mayor made the presentation.

The drizzle meant that there could not be much of a grand exit – the bulls were packed up and tied up onto trailers, tents were hurriedly dismantled and loaded into the back of lorries, and cars and vans revved up and began the slow slippery trail up through the mud and out of the meadow. The most ceremonial exit was that of the newly crowned Baş Boğa, looking content in his trailer, while his owner and supporters tooted their horns, waved the Turkish flag and cheered to the few remaining people there.

With my health improving daily, I left the next morning for Erzurum to look for the best and most authentic cirit. I had no proper information about clubs or dates of matches, but the best thing was to go there and investigate. Travelling the 150 kilometres south to Erzurum, the dolmuş passed through scenery reminiscent of a Scottish highland; very green and hilly, with clusters of purple heather and sometimes the most vivid scarlet of a blanket of poppies. Sunny and clear, the north-east Anatolian Plateau was very different from anywhere else I had seen in Turkey.

Erzurum has plenty of cheap accommodation, and I found a place in a small side-street tucked behind a street market in the north of the city. The city is surprisingly commercial and busy and Cumhurryet Caddesi, its central artery, is lively and even boasts a Wimpy. As usual for a Turkish main street, it contains pastry shops and restaurants, clothes shops and many tea-gardens. The pace of life, even in the city centre, is slower and more relaxed than in other big cities and most people walk slower, spend far more time drinking tea and lazing around in gardens. It was altogether a most pleasant atmosphere, and the comfortable climate added to its calming ambience.

I first tried the Tourist Office in my search for information about Erzurum's cirit. It took a while to find an English-speaking officer (surprising really, in a tourist office) but a few telephone calls led us to Süleyman, who was having the afternoon off but was quite happy to meet me the next morning.

News filtered through to most of the men in the hotel that I was the only non-working woman in the vicinity, which I later discovered was the red-light district. Our small alleyway's plethora of cheap hotels provided colourful clientele arriving and departing at all hours of day and night. Hasan, a travelling salesman, was a regular guest at the hotel. 'Sister here is Azerbaijan. Very ugly woman. You can work here, no? She has big bottom,' and his arms gestured the width of a doorway. Azerbaijan sister soon appeared in slippers and dressing-gown, her bottom justifying its description. She dangled a cigarette out of her mouth, laughed at the other men in the salon and was shooed out.

That night was the much anticipated World Cup quarter-final between England and Argentina, hyped up as a grudge match to avenge the 1986 'hand of God' goal which Maradona stole from England. All other activities in the salon were ignored and attention for the next couple of hours was focused on the TV, which was just a few inches away from my front-row chair. The first thirty minutes was white-knuckle tension as the score went to 2-2, and my language deteriorated quickly, entering into the real spirit by swearing and cursing the referee.

This caused great amusement among the other guests, who watched the match and my antics with equal attention. Violence involving British fans in France during the World Cup was shown repeatedly on Turkish TV and these chaps in this small brothel in eastern Turkey must have considered me a living example of the archetypal 'English hooligan'.

During extra time and then penalties, my language grew worse and more emotional, which luckily no one understood. After those few precious minutes when England missed two penalties and said goodbye to the World Cup, I moaned softly, head in hands and cursed Batty and Ince. The other viewers trooped out slowly, shaking my hand and muttering solemn commiserations and probably quite relieved that I wasn't throwing the TV out of the window.

In low spirits, I met Süleyman the next morning and he offered to drive me around Erzurum to find some of the famous old cirit players. He was having another day off and had planned a drunken picnic with his friend, which he postponed until later in the afternoon in order to help me. 'There are so few visitors who come to Erzurum now. Foreigners are worried about troubles in the East, so they don't come. It's not dangerous at all here, there's no need for people to be so scared. But our economy is losing out here.' He shrugged. 'We go first to the old teahouse in the town; the man I am looking for is always there.'

And sure enough he was; a large man with a comfortable belly and a small woollen hat squeezed onto his white wiry hair, above a thick white beard and a terrific smile. He sat and drank tea with us perched on small wooden stools outside the teahouse, full of old men who looked like they hadn't moved out of their seats for years. He reminisced – through the constant interruptions of his friends who wanted to know who we were – about the good old days of cirit.

'Everyone wanted to play cirit,' he said softly. 'When I played in my village, we all had horses and every young man wanted to be in the team. It was a strong rural tradition. Through it, we remember our ancestors, our Turkish roots when we were nomads. It is important for all Turks to remember that.'

The man was living history, and I only wished that I could have witnessed him in his prime. Erzurum was the principal area for cirit, in the past and still today, and it was clear that the region still clung on to this tradition. 'You had to be brave!' he cried, remembering the skills necessary to be a great player. 'And also noble.' And he took a nibble from the hunk of sugar in his hand. In the east of the country they don't dissolve their sugar in their tea, but bite a piece off which they keep in their mouth, drinking the tea through it. Apparently, this dates back to times when sugar was scarce and one lump had to stretch to many glasses of tea – it lasts longer in your mouth.

The government used to give financial assistance to people who owned and trained cirit horses – a monthly grant, often a sack of feed – which encouraged village people to keep cirit alive. That assistance was stopped, and although the Traditional Sports Association had recently been organizing cirit tournaments, the necessity remains for some kind of monetary, as well as organizational, support to ensure cirit stays alive.

Süleyman also took me to see Nihat Gezder, manager of the Erzurum Sport Institute, who was up to his eyeballs trying to get Erzurumspor's football ground ready for the start of the season. As the abundance of blue-and-white flags, banners and painted fences indicated, Erzurumspor, for years languishing in the lower division of Turkish football, had won promotion to the first league. This meant, apart from pride in the city, that the ground had to be rebuilt to accommodate more fans.

Nihat Gezder was a committed cirit fan, never having played it but appreciating its cultural significance. 'Since I was a small boy I was fascinated with it,' he told me as we watched videos in his office of a cirit match in the snow, a thick blanket of which covers the region for months on end. 'I decided to research its origins and also promote the game. Otherwise, the young generation won't know about it and the game will die out.' He said that every Sunday there are village games, and I promised to return to Erzurum on my way to north-east Turkey, en route to Georgia.

Back in Istanbul, I made more progress on getting a visa for Central Asia. I first visited the Kyrgyz consulate where they confirmed the '72-hour rule', which meant that I could spend up to three days in transit in the other Central Asian republics at no extra cost. The Kyrgyz visa was easy to obtain, requiring neither a letter from my Embassy (frightfully expensive) nor a letter of invitation (even more); and an overland journey would be easy.

The overland route was preferable for three reasons: time, money, interest. The oil-wrestling festival in Edirne ended on 22 July, and after that only revisiting Erzurum was on the agenda. The next big date was 31 August for Kyrgyzstan's Independence Day celebrations, which was said to contain several traditional sports, including *ulak tartish* (buzkashi).

I therefore had one month to get from east Turkey to Bishkek, Kyrgyzstan's capital, and the costly air fare further inspired me to go by land. This meant passing through Georgia and Azerbaijan, from where there was supposedly a boat from Baku (the capital) to Turkmenistan, across the Caspian Sea. I could stay a few days in Georgia and make the journey last around three weeks, infinitely more interesting than a three-hour plane journey from Istanbul to Bishkek.

The Kyrgyz Consul-General was the only consular official in the world who made the effort to help. She had faxed the Ministry of Sports in Bishkek to ask them about sporting events, and confirmed that the Independence Day celebrations were the best opportunity to see ulak tartish. I went to collect my one-month tourist visa four days later and popped in to thank her for her trouble.

Her office was dominated by a deep red sofa, into which I sank. 'I tried to phone you many times to thank you, but you were away,' I said. 'Were you on holiday?'

I shouldn't have asked, as the poor woman had just recovered from an illness and was grateful of the opportunity to talk to sympathetic ears. 'You would not believe how ill I was. It began suddenly with high fever, and then my whole throat swelled up.' With her hands she indicated the width of an elephant. 'Then I couldn't breathe.' She made the noise of a cat about to cough up fur balls. 'And I thought I would die. I tried everything. The Turkish doctors here didn't know what to do and it continued for weeks. It was so miserable.' I tut-tutted in sympathy, casting a sneaky look at the clock.

'I went to four hospitals and I didn't get better. Then, my friend in Bishkek said I should try spiritual healing, so a woman telephoned me and gave me healing.' 'What, do you mean she was in Istanbul?' I asked her, confused. 'No, she gave me healing over the telephone from Bishkek!' she announced triumphantly. 'And I got better! Well,' she added after a minute's thought, 'it could have been the antibiotics they gave me but I am sure it was the healing.'

After twenty minutes of marvelling at the benefits of telephonic healing, I thanked her again, propelled myself out of the sofa and decided that since she was the only Embassy official to give any constructive help, I would forgive her lengthy descriptions of her health problems.

16

Black Leather Thighs in an Olive Oil Dressing

The Kirkpinar yağli-güreş festival was two weeks later in mid-July but there were regular small village competitions every weekend during the summer, in different villages. Mr Yazorğlu had told me of a festival in Isparta, about 100 kilometres north of Antalya, the following Sunday.

The last thing I wanted to hear after a sleepless fourteen-hour bus journey was that the festival wasn't in Isparta at all but in the village of Ulüborlü; but it was only another hour away on the local bus and I was able to see something of the region around Isparta, which, with its sandy soil is famous for its roses. Every imaginable type of rose product – beauty creams, jam, sweets and especially oil – are sold and exported.

I arrived in Ulüborlü at 9 am, two hours before the wrestling began. A man who'd been on the bus noticed my dazed confusion and introducing himself as Vali, brought me to a teahouse where our companionable silence was pleasantly interrupted by six musicians playing to 'advertise' the festival. We followed them when they moved off, up a stony path to a meadow.

The small field was surrounded on all sides by tiered wooden seating with basic shelter. I had read that oil-wrestling is always performed in a grassy meadow, to emphasize being 'at one with nature', and the grass here was thick, bright green and brushed softly against the ankles. The finishing touches were being put to the VIP stand at one end, with soft armchairs being positioned for special guests.

There were cherries everywhere – large bowls scattered about including a display made of cherries in the shape of '75', marking the seventy-fifth year of the Turkish republic – as this was the climax to Ulüborlü's three-day cherry festival. Such festivals are common throughout Turkey, especially in the summer months, held to celebrate the harvesting or season of the speciality fruit of the region. It is a fabulous reason for a festival and is a strong tradition throughout the country.

Many pehlivans were preparing themselves for their fights, and they made a magnificent sight. I had only seen photographs of oil-wrestling in leaflets in the tourist office, and it looked far more impressive in the flesh (literally). It wasn't their appearance or even their bodies, but the colours and textures of the whole scene: the glistening flesh tones and black leather on green.

Every part of flesh and leather was being drenched in olive oil, poured from cans. Men and boys from the age of eight prepared their bodies for the assault to come. They lay on the grass in groups in casual bonhomie, massaging their legs and each other's shoulders, collecting oil from the attendants to smear all over their skin, helping each other to ensure their entire body and kispet was covered.

The stands were filling up, the musicians were already playing and next to them was the *casgir*, the announcer, dressed in formal traditional costume. His role is clearly defined and his presence as important as the pehlivans'. He gives information on the action, announces the fights and introduces each pehlivan, often with anecdotes, poems and stories to create the atmosphere, and recites the prayers before each fight.

Before it began, they performed the *kurban*, the slaughtering of an animal in the halal way, with blessings offered to Allah. This was my first experience of this and for a squeamish vegetarian not easy. The sheep (I named her Dolly) was brought in frisking and kicking, led on a rope by two men. I wondered if she had any inkling as to her fate, but she was quickly despatched and prayers were offered up.

The sacrifice carried out, the tournament could commence, beginning with the youngest boys. In oil-wrestling, there are specific classes depending on size, and most begin around the age of eight or nine. This was the smallest class, with no specific title but created if there is sufficient interest from younger boys. The first official class is called *teşvik boyu* or the encouragement class, for twelve- to fifteen-year-olds, and, at the other end, the *baş* (head) is the biggest, strongest and most experienced – the elite of all pehlivans.

The first group were ready to begin, their kispet and bodies glistening, and then began the *peşrev* (prelude) which takes place before every fight. The casgir announced each boy and where he came from, then launched into the prayer in a deep and dramatic manner, which signalled the start of the ritual as old as the sport itself.

> Allah, Allah, Illallah,
> Hayirlar gele inshallah . . .

The prayer translates as:

> Allah, Allah, Illallah
> May we prosper
> Our patron is Hamza the wrestler
> Our ancestors were wrestlers
> Two valiant men take the field
> One is blond, one dark
> Both are keen to win the prize
> Do not despair when down
> Do not boast when up
> When above, do not loosen your grip
> Meet leg trip with leg trip
> Offer a prayer to Muhammad
> I hastened to the spring
> May Allah be with you both.

As these significant words were recited, the young wrestlers stood in a line facing towards Mecca, took three steps back and then three steps forward. They knelt down on one knee, touched their right hand to the ground, then touched their knees, lips and head three times. While doing this, they say to themselves: 'Wrestler, don't feel pride at your strength, intelligence, wealth and position. You came from the soil and will return to the soil. You were absent, and you will be absent. You will account for the power which you have in the next world, to Allah. Use your power for right and justice, to prevent oppression and not to torment.'

The crowd cheered as they walked the length of the field, striding purposefully and masterfully, slapping their hands on their leather-clad thighs with each step. On their return, on passing another pehlivan, they shook hands as they did so. As they passed the second time, they touched each other's belt, and then their own right lower leg and heel – a mark of respect and honour to the opponent – finishing off with wishing each other success and asking for forgiveness if any wrong or incorrect moves which cause injury were made unintentionally.

When that was completed, the pehlivans paired off and spread over the whole arena. Several referees were on the ground, and three more in a tower overlooking the entire field, linked by walkie-talkie. According to modern rules, there is a time limit of twenty minutes for junior classes, and forty minutes for senior. To win, a pehlivan must lift his opponent at waist level and take three steps, or get him flat on the ground; if this cannot be done within the allotted time, the winner is decided on points.

Some of the fights finished after only a few minutes, the referee consulting those in the tower for confirmation, before raising the hand of the winner. Those fights taking longer stayed on the field until the finish. Their oiled skins meant that, unlike ordinary wrestling, gripping each other was impossible. The only way to throw an opponent was to get a hand into the waist of his kispet, or inside the bottom of his trousers, and carry or overbalance him.

The thick green grass brimmed with pure colour. Against that were the striking contrasting shapes and solid colours of shiny black glistening in the sunlight, and assorted tones of skin, equally shiny. Faces were contorted with concentration, as the wrestlers writhed and wriggled, gripping the other's legs, hands grasping the waistband of the kispet, legs trying to overbalance. Throughout all this, the cheers from the crowd gave these young pehlivans great support.

After each fight, the two competitors embraced and lifted each other off the ground, which is taken as a sign of forgiveness. The younger one kisses the elder's hand, the elder kisses the younger's forehead. The winners progressed to the next round, until the final two would fight for the title in his class. When all the fights in this smallest class were completed, it was the first round of the next class. The procedure recommenced with the Peşrev, the casgir's announcement, and the prayer and march up and down the field.

As the afternoon progressed the men grew bigger, their shoulders broader, their thighs firmer and the fights more aggressive and longer. Yet each still displayed unfailing courtesy towards his opponent and the combination of enthralling procedure of the prayers, the striding up and down the field and the music accompanying the fights, turned wrestling into performance.

It illustrated perfectly an old poem which an ex-wrestler translated for me, demonstrating the importance that the pehlivan used to hold in society not just as a sportsman, but as a respected and dignified man of strength.

> This is a page of epic poems,
> Not just a chest
> And the gold medals are not just ornaments on it.
> The place we wrestle is not just the wrestling ring,
> It is the world.
> This is a memorial to pehlivans all over the world.
> Pride of divine light emerging from your majestic
>   forehead,
> The nation will honour you endlessly.
> Your achievements have given your people a place of
>   honour,
> Now our country celebrates with great happiness, like on
>   National Day.
> All the neighbours
> Are waiting on the roadside for your arrival.
> They want to see your huge arms which defeated the giant,
> For you have put our nation on a pedestal
> With your courage in the arena.

After the first round of the başpehlivans, it reverted to the second round of the youngest, and on it progressed until each round then had the grand final between the unbeaten two of each class. The climax to the afternoon was the final of the başpehlivans, two hulking figures weighing over 100 kilos. The small stadium had reached capacity, as all the locals were especially interested in this match and had slowly filtered into the wooden stands. The Mayor, now proudly seated on the leather sofa at the front of the VIP section, munched from the huge bowls of cherries with his guests.

The finalists emerged to the casgir's announcement; his tales and poems had been growing longer and more eloquent throughout the day. The two performed their march up and down the meadow, each one encouraging the crowd to give them vocal support. By this stage of the late afternoon, as the sun was beginning to sink behind the mountain and casting an orange glow on their glistening skin, much of the grass was flattened and had big oily patches on it.

The duel began in the centre of the field, watched at close quarters by the referee, with every move and hold greeted with appreciative murmurs from the audience. Every few minutes the pehlivans stopped, pausing to wipe the sweat from their eyes and get their breath. The fight had a maximum time of forty minutes, the longest time for any class, and this one looked as if it would go the entire distance as neither wrestler appeared likely to tumble. (As in boxing, a 'knockout' can be achieved, but if neither man falls to the ground on his back, the fight is judged on a points system.)

As the two heavyweights continued, the crowd and casgir grew more excited, with spectators and other pehlivans coming onto the field and forming a large circle around them. It was an equal fight; first one seemed to get the upper hand and nearly overbalanced his opponent as he deftly hooked his fingers inside the other's waistband. Then the other would retort with stout defensive moves to retain his balance, and use his legs to try and knock the other over.

Eventually, at the end of forty minutes, it had to be decided on points, and when the referee raised the victor's arm, the newly crowned başpehlivan was picked up by friends and carried around on their shoulders. He was presented with his medal and his picture taken for the next day's sports page, and immediately the Mayor hijacked the microphone and gave a speech to an already emptying stadium. It was astonishing how quickly the arena emptied, while the pehlivans moved en masse to the small stone buildings to shower and change. As the spectators were leaving to get buses home, the wrestlers emerged transformed back into young Turkish men.

Vali and I joined the tail end of the crowds to the free bus-service back to Isparta; conversation on the bus was an excited happy chatter about the competitions. The day had given me a taste of the great Turkish tradition of oil-wrestling, and this small village festival had helped whet my appetite for the grand show at Kirkpinar beginning just a few days later.

*

After returning north to Istanbul and extracting a visa for Georgia from an extremely reluctant and surly consular officer, I set off to Edirne for the Kirkpinar festival, which lasted three days and engulfed the whole city. This was the Cup Final of oil-wrestling, the world's oldest and most prestigious traditional wrestling tournament.

There are many legends and theories about the origins of Kirkpinar, which gives it an almost romantic status. The most widely accepted dates back to 1360 when Süleyman, son of Orhan Gazi (son of Osman Gazi, founder of the Ottoman Empire) and forty of his troops were returning from a successful battle to capture Rumelia. They rode for many days and rested overnight at a camp in Samona (now in Greece), wrestling each other to pass the time.

They wrestled in pairs, the winners staying on until the best one remained. But the final two continued to fight each other for hours and then days, neither able to win, and each aware that to give up is as shameful as surrendering in war. Their bodies continued but their hearts couldn't take the strain of several days' fighting, and eventually, shortly after midnight the two men were found in a deathly embrace. Because wrestling is considered as the perfect preparation for battle, it is therefore thought of as a prayer and worship of Allah, and as they died simultaneously whilst preparing for war, they were acknowledged as martyrs.

Their friends buried them on the spot where they died (the preferred practice when a person dies as a martyr) and continued their journey. A year later they returned to the spot to visit their graves, and were astonished to find a lush meadow had appeared with forty springs where the graves should have been. They named the place Kirkpinar, Turkish for 'forty springs'. (Forty is said to be one of the sacred numbers in Islam, which adds significance.)

After Edirne was conquered in 1361, the wrestling was performed annually to honour the two wrestlers, a few kilometres from the city. Over the centuries it has evolved into a major festival and the most prestigious traditional wrestling competition of the year, where all the best pehlivans gather to participate. In recent years it has developed into a highly profitable tourist and commercial event. Not that the true spirit of its origins has ever died. Many would say that Kirkpinar is the best example of a true Turkish sport, as it celebrates not only the beauty of the sport but also the spirit of the Ottomans. Oil-wrestling is an expression of being strong materially and morally; individually and as a nation.

Even today, the competitors are still honouring the two martyrs and are present-day examples of such heroes. Each wrestler is seen as a living representative of the *alperen*, the most significant concept of Kirkpinar: *alp* means someone who possesses strength and courage, is self-sacrificing and unsurpassable; *eren* is a person who has died, but who in his life sought to follow the words of Islam, living for peace and giving up his own desires. The alperen, therefore, is said to be a 'light' which continues to enlighten spirits both alive and dead.

The arena where the competitions take place is a significant venue. Sarayiçi, an area of meadow several kilometres from Edirne, was used as a prison-camp for Turkish soldiers captured by the Bulgarians, and many thousands died there from cold and hunger. The Turks believe that if they aren't physically and morally strong enough, they will again suffer at the hands of enemies.

The wrestlers approach the arena to the call of 'Allah, Allah . . .' and their salutes to the holy prophet Muhammad symbolize how Turkish soldiers were sent to fight. The wrestling at Kirkpinar has many parallels with war: there was an elite military band which sent the armies into battle by playing marches to induce a spirit of excitement – today the folk musicians play heroic folk songs to encourage wrestlers with drum and zurna. The drum is only played on three occasions in Turkish life: war, weddings and wrestling.

Edirne is a historical town in the far north of the country, close to the Greek and Bulgarian borders. It was the capital of the Ottoman Empire for ninety-one years after being captured in 1363. For almost a century, the Ottoman Sultan used Edirne (then called Adrianople) to set out on battle to Europe and Asia. When eventually Constantinople (Istanbul) was captured and became the Ottoman capital, Edirne still played a major part in life and society and was an important staging post en route to Europe.

These days the city isn't a prominent place of tourist interest, although the festival attracts thousands of Turkish visitors and surprisingly few foreigners. Edirne has retained its very Turkish characteristics, more so than many of the other cities which are swamped by tourism, and holds great interest to the visitor.

Soon after arriving in the city, I went to the Tourist Office for a festival programme and was pleasantly surprised to see an organized and friendly office, having been so accustomed to chaotic and uncoordinated organizers on the eve of major events. Extra English-speaking staff were brought in from other regional offices and were well-prepared to cater for foreign photographers, film-crews and local journalists, most of whom were pretty demanding.

'A few years ago, it was only the wrestling that people came to see. But recently there has been a massive growth in the commercial value of this festival. Many companies now hire stalls around the outside of the arena to trade and advertise. More people set up restaurants and entertainment here every night, and the local Belediye has promoted the event to attract more tourists.' The Tourist Office was in the throes of arranging Press Passes for many visiting journalists and there were, according to Mehmet Ali, far more foreign media coming every year.

'For the last few years we have had TV crews from Japan, Germany and France. They always think it is a really unique event.' It was obviously a great novelty for foreign media, apart from being a tremendously photogenic sport. And here in Kirkpinar with hundreds of wrestlers from throughout Turkey, it promised to be quite a gathering.

The festival programme announced that the first four days would consist mainly of music, dancing and art displays, with the wrestling due to begin on the fifth day, Friday. I had two free days and ample time to track down a kispet maker in Turkey. After seeing this unique and most famous item of sports attire, I was intrigued as to how and where they are made, especially because there were very few makers left. Two years earlier I had visited the workshops in Indian and Pakistani villages where cricket balls, bats and stumps are handmade; small dusty workshops where old men worked by the light of an oil lamp spending many laborious hours on their craft, and I imagined a similar scene here.

The Tourist Office helped me locate Irfan Şahin who owned a workshop in Biğa, near Çanakkale and I made a quick trip there from Edirne before returning for the first day's wrestling. I arrived in the afternoon on market day, and hoped that Mr Şahin was expecting me. I found his shop with no difficulty, a big sign announcing 'Kispet Ustadi' and a picture of kispet above the door, and he was indeed expecting me. It wasn't the dusty workshop with an old man working by candlelight that I had imagined. His shop was well equipped, if small, and filled with kispet in various stages of completion. In one corner was a man cutting out shapes from a huge sheet of black leather. In another was a pair of kispet nearly fully made up, one corner wedged under the needle of a sewing-machine to give it its characteristic stitching.

The interior of his small shop was covered in photographs, newspaper articles, some faded with age, and a certificate from the Biğa Belediye in appreciation of his services. In pride of place was a picture of Ahmed Taşçi, the current heavyweight champion of Kirkpinar: 'My hero,' Mr Şahin beamed. 'All these pehlivans get their kispet from me,' he said. 'They phone me with their waist measurement, leg length and height, and it takes me three days to complete. Then I send them by post.'

I asked him how he began in this trade. 'My father and grandfather had this business and I learned from them. For thirty years I have been making these, but I don't think there is anyone else left in Turkey who makes them. When I retire what will happen? People aren't interested in this trade because it isn't very glamorous. My son went to university and he doesn't want to carry on my business.'

I was reminded of the man I met who makes havut for the wrestling camels – essential equipment for the sport but a tradition not associated with glamour or wealth. One day, it is feared, these crafts will die out. 'We used to use buffalo skin, a hundred years ago, but that was too thick and heavy. These days cow hide is used.' The phone shrilled in the corner of the room and another order came through. He wrote down a couple of measurements and promised that their kispet would be completed in a few days.

'I get plenty of work in because there is no one else in the country – maybe in the world – who does this. Each pair costs about $200 [about £130], more if the wrestler is bigger.' Some pehlivans want their names to be written in shiny metal studs on the back of the waistband, and some of the top pehlivans have sponsors, usually banks and big companies and their names are also written.

Mr Şahin knew at least that he would have work for as long as he wanted, but clearly his skill and the trade couldn't really be guaranteed of survival. Would kispet last as long as the sport I wondered, whilst on the bus back to Edirne.

On Thursday, the night before the wrestling, the town centre filled up with hundreds of young men in casual tracksuits, walking around in small groups, eating and meeting up with old friends. All the restaurants were full, anticipating several days' soaring profits from the constant streams of extra people with very large appetites, while in the public squares folk-dance groups performed to much applause.

On Friday morning, the formalities began with a procession to officially greet the arriving Ağa as he entered the city. (In fact, it was purely a symbolic gesture as he was already in the city, but he drove to the gates and then walked in.) He emerged from a large car and was greeted by the Mayor and a few dozen officials, who then all returned to the Mayor's office in a large parade, which also included several prominent wrestlers.

The Ağa didn't look comfortable in all his regalia of embroidered shirt, turban and heavy trousers. He was short and pale and looked uneasy, probably because he was in fact taking over the duties of his elder brother, unable to attend because of serious illness.

There were over forty drummers who actually drowned out the music from the zurnas. They stood on the street and played while the parade moved to the Attaturk monument to lay a wreath and observe a minute's silence. The police band played the national anthem and we moved slowly down the street to the Wrestlers' Graveyard, a tiny area with just a dozen graves, to lay a wreath and recite prayers in memory of the dead wrestlers. This was the first time I had ever come across such a practice, where deceased sportsmen are given a status close to that of the original Kirkpinar martyrs.

After the Friday midday prayer at the Selimiye Mosque where there was a special service for deceased wrestlers, the pehlivans enjoyed some impromptu dancing. It began with three of them dancing to a folk tune played by one man with a zurna, soon to be joined by others until there was a line of a dozen pehlivans in tracksuits and foam slippers, arms linked on shoulders and swaying, kicking and dancing in unison to a group of five musicians.

The opening ceremony at the Sarayiçi stadium, a purpose-built stadium set in a few acres of grass a few miles out of the city, was at three that afternoon. The stadium was about half full for the first hour of the competitions. There was a parade of all the pehlivans, a couple of hundred of them in all shapes and sizes, led by the stocky başpehlivans (the 'heavyweights'), the Turkish flag being held high by the previous year's winner, Ahmed Taşçi. The flag was hoisted which signalled the fanfare from forty zurnas, this time giving a very reedy rendition of the national anthem. It was followed by yet another minute's silence for deceased wrestlers and a brief round of speeches by the officials, including a very sweaty Ağa. Then at last the action got under way.

The scene was like the Ulüborlü arena multiplied by ten. The arena was massive, enclosed on all sides by a high spectator stand of wood and concrete (which, some argue, makes it look like a football stadium and loses the atmosphere of 'being at one with nature'). On one side, behind fencing, was a special area for the pehlivans to watch from, while journalists were given a large space on the third floor which presented a commanding view of the arena.

Outside the arena among the stalls, photographers from Turkey and abroad were crouched on the grass, balancing zoom lenses and tripods. The security which surrounded the event bordered on the paranoid, and all photographers were given numbered bibs corresponding to names on the list and woe betide if anyone should take the wrong number.

If the Ulüborlü event was a small and cosy affair, this was anything but. The sheer scale of the event made it magnificent. It was obvious that its noble and distinguished past meant that it transcended its purpose of an annual sporting event – there was a sense of sacredness to its rituals which gave it a near-religious aspect.

Everything was on a larger scale: instead of one casgir, there were four; instead of four musicians, there were forty. And instead of the one medical officer who sat on the edge at Ulüborlü field, there was a team of ten doctors in a well-organized 'surgery' under the main stand.

The smallest boys sprawled out on the grass and massaged each other's shoulders, then queued up and faced the organizer's administrative nightmare of trying to identify them from his sheaf of papers. The gnarled old oil-man was yelling at a bunch of small boys who wriggled under his arms to get more oil.

It began punctually. The smallest pehlivans were oiled and ready and the casgir, even more eloquent and charismatic than before, began the prelude which officially opened the annual Kirkpinar Festival, 1998.

'Allah, Allah, Ilallah! . . .'

And the young boys bent low, touched the ground, touched their mouth and head and stood, striding and slapping their legs, embracing their opponents and gesturing towards the crowd. Some were muttering prayers under their breath. Some looked terrified, other swaggered with confidence.

The first wrestling bouts began and it broke the tension that was building amongst the young wrestlers, together with great mounting excitement from the spectators. There were over twenty pairs of boys engaged in fights, dotted around the magnificent green arena, and it was well co-ordinated with the referees in the tower in good communication with those on the ground. It all ran smoothly, one bout ending and the winner's arm being lifted, the others running through until the time limit was reached, others decided on points. When all the fights in that round were finished, the next level up began. That afternoon there were only two hours of fighting, but everyone left in anticipation of two full days starting the next morning at 9 am.

That evening I was invited, along with Mehmet Ali from the Tourist Office, to a pehlivan's house for dinner. His name was Emrah, a huge hulking giant in his early twenties and competing in the başaltı level, one below baş. He obviously possessed great power and strength on the field, proved by the medals and trophies displayed in the living-room, and by his hands the size of plates and shoulders the width of a door. Yet he was very shy and said little, looking embarrassed when he spoke to me, glancing bashfully across the room.

His mother sat us down at the circular dinner table and served bowls of soup, rice, börek and chicken. Emrah took about five pieces of chicken and ate them with his fingers, whilst his mother complained that she had to feed him so much even when he was a small boy. 'Even when he was twelve years old, he was so big for his age. He always ate more than everyone else.' His father came in with a sheaf of newspaper articles and showed them round, brimming with pride, much to Emrah's obvious pleasure.

'When he was only seven years old he wanted to be a pehlivan like his grandfather, so we had a tiny pair of kispet made for him. He won his first prize that year for the smallest boys.' The photograph showed him in confident pose as a small boy.

'Emrah!' yelled his mother and he shrank back with rueful sheepishness, his hands dripping with chicken grease. She gave him a wad of napkins and scolded him for putting his dirty hands on the table. It was obvious that this short, squat woman ruled the roost at this household.

Typical of many high standard pehlivans, Emrah had a sponsor, Loin, a fashion chain selling jeans. Their name was written in bronze studs on the top of his kispet and they gave him a monthly allowance which probably contributed to paying for the vast quantities of food he demolished. He did a little modelling on the side which meant that he could afford to have a mobile phone and other modern fads that his grandfather could never have dreamed of. He told us that he was hoping, if he performed well enough this year, he would be promoted to the başpehlivan class and that in order to do that he had to eat lots of carbohydrates, which his mother provided in loving abundance.

Eating with us was one of his friends, another Mehmet Ali, who was also beginning his fight in the same class the next morning. 'Have you noticed that most of the pehlivans come from the south?' he asked, which I had in fact seen from the list of competitors, which also gave each person's home town. 'We have a better climate there, and can fight all year round. I don't earn much money from being pehlivan, I'm not as good as Emrah here, but if I can get my expenses paid it is enough to do it just for enjoyment.' Mehmet was a farmer near Antalya and earned a comfortable living on his land – typical of most 'average' pehlivans, for it was only the very best in the country who received great amounts of prize money and sponsorship deals.

Despite all the anticipation surrounding Emrah's fight it didn't last very long, however. Quietly confident of reaching the fourth round, he was demolished after just three minutes in the first round and came off in tears, limping on his left leg and implying that he had sustained a serious injury. Hopes of becoming a başpehlivan dashed for another year, he spent the rest of the time sulking and behaving like a very bad loser. His sponsor, who ran the Loin shop in the city, was furious. 'Why do I bother giving him all that support when he loses so badly?' I asked him if he was going to end the sponsorship deal. 'Well, we'll have to talk about it,' he said grimly.

Through the rest of the day, hopes were fulfilled and dashed. Each class progressed, round after round. The afternoon ended when the başpehlivans completed their first round. There was a tremendous ovation for Ahmed Taşçi, winner of the grand title for seven years. His greatest rival was Cengiz Elbiye, with whom he had had a bitter tussle in 1994's final and eventually lost. But he had won every other year since 1990, and this year he was going for a record eighth title. There was an almost identical ovation for Cengiz Elbiye and it was amazing to see such superstar status placed on these two wrestlers. The two big-shots predictably won through to their next round, at which stage the day's wrestling ended until the next morning and the climax.

That night, the Sarayiçi field was transformed: all around the stadium were restaurants and shops, plastic tables and chairs on the grass and young men sitting round drinking beer. Everywhere there were people out to have a good time, down to young children on their fathers' backs. There was a fun-fair, and while in the crush for the big wheel I saw Emrah, attempting to forget his disappointment of the morning and enjoy himself.

Back in the city, the folk festival which accompanies the wrestling every year was in full swing. Groups from Macedonia, Hungary, Croatia, Bulgaria, Romania and Georgia performed nightly, in front of the glowing Sarayiçi mosque and Selimiye Park. It was there that I met Givi, a slightly drunken young Georgian who was studying in Edirne University, and helping translate for the Georgian folk-dance group.

I told him of my forthcoming trip to Georgia and did he know of any traditional sports that were still played there? He pondered. 'Actually,' he mumbled, swaying slightly on his feet, 'I'm rather drunk right now but I'll think about it and see you tomorrow.' I told him about my rather unpleasant experience in the Georgian consulate when the young visa officer treated my application with rudeness and an icy expression, and asked him if this was typical of Georgians. 'Look at me,' he laughed. 'I'm not rude like that, am I?' which was reassuring enough.

Sunday was the big day, the climax to the festival and the day which would decide all the titles. The town had filled up even more. My hotel was completely full with many wrestlers, and there was an increasing problem trying to get hot water in the morning. The restaurants started their day early with pehlivans tucking into bowls of chicken soup and mounds of bread for breakfast.

In the press box that morning was a Turkish doctor who had

been living in Holland for twenty years. He was explaining his plans to get some of the best pehlivans over to Holland for a competition. 'There are so many Turks who live there, it would be great for them to come and see oil-wrestling. I also want the Dutch people to learn something about our traditions. Unfortunately Turks don't have such a great reputation; people look down on them and don't give them much respect. They tend to be portrayed in a negative light through the media. This is a way that we can give a positive impression of ourselves through our culture.'

The stadium was completely full as each class went through their different elimination rounds, the afternoon ending with the finals of the two heaviest classes. At 3 pm, the preparations for the following year's festival began with the auctioning of a ram to decide next year's Ağa.

The ram is symbolic of the money which the Ağa would donate for the following year. A struggling, frisky ram was decorated with tinsel and ribbons, with pink painted on its white wool. It was paraded around the field to great cheers, and then brought to the VIP enclosure where all the dignitaries were sitting.

The five hopefuls, all businessmen from different parts of the country, were put at a table on the edge of the grass. The voice over the microphone gave us a brief introduction to each one, and then the bidding began. Each man looked slightly worried, obviously having his own vague limit as to the maximum he could promise and as they went around the table, the figures were leaping up. It went to billions of lira (the inflation rate of the Turkish currency is outrageous) and when one man knew he was being out-bid, he would give a grim shake of his head and opt out to a round of applause.

It was left to the final two and then eventually one was left, promising the equivalent of about £65,000 for next year. It was announced to the crowd who stood up and applauded, then he was handed the ram and they made another lap of honour around the arena.

With all the other rounds finished, the finals of all the other classes determined, it was left to the semi-final and final of the başpehlivans. Ahmed Taşçi and Cengiz Elbiye won their semis and set the scene for the final that everyone hoped for. They didn't let the thousands of fans down. Many wanted to see Taşçi win a record-breaking eighth belt. But his younger, taller and fitter-looking rival looked fresher and perhaps this was his year and he would take over and Taşçi would retire.

The casgir found fresh impetus to recite long-drawn-out poems about the heroic başpehlivans and their role in Turkish society, for a sufficient build-up to the grand final. This was the bout that the three-day competition had been awaiting, and the crowds had packed into the stadium especially for this.

The two men in question appeared grim and avoided looking at each other, fuelling the stories that there was no love lost between them. They both spent a long time preparing their bodies, pouring on more and more oil, massaging their shoulders. Taşçi's semi-final had taken a draining forty minutes and it was thought that this might disadvantage him.

At last they began the peşrev, the final one for Kirkpinar 1998. They marched up the field in line with each other, though several metres apart and as each one neared the crowd, the audience screamed and rose with delight. They then swaggered to the centre of the field and, eyeing each other, began the long-awaited final bout. As everyone anticipated, it was a hard-fought battle. It began with aggression and to a huge roar from the crowds, but after only a few minutes it was clear that defensive tactics were preferred, with both wrestlers avoiding further attacking moves which would leave them at risk. There was a lot of watching, waiting, both approaching the other tentatively and both trying for the all-important grasping of the belt, and trying to lift the other.

As time crept on, they frequently stopped, as the rules permit, to wash the sweat from their faces and apply more oil. Tasçi looked to be tiring and everyone sensed that his strength was beginning to sap. And then, when the forty-minute limit was approaching, Cengiz made a move and had Taşçi down, whilst the crowd went wild. The younger man punched the air victoriously with Taşçi still on the ground, motionless, eyes closed.

Medics came to his rescue and revived him. He looked to be in great pain, and it took a long time until he was able to be carried off. The cynics amongst us wondered if he was making a great show of being injured to detract from the fact that he was being beaten. His last chance at heroics, perhaps.

While this mini-drama was unfolding at one end of the arena, the crowd went wild. Cries of 'Cengiz, Cengiz!' filled the stadium. Some of the pehlivans, as well as spectators who had been watching from their own stand, ran onto the field and lifted the new champion on to their shoulders and did several laps of honour, mobbed by more fans.

The prize-giving was the last formality of the day before everyone packed up and went home. Süleyman Demirel, President of Turkey, and known as 'Ağa of Ağas' presented Cengiz the prize of the Golden Belt, and thereafter it was a confusing mob of people running in different directions. Taşçi's heroism during most of the 1990s was temporarily forgotten and some journalists were wondering if he would now retire, as I left the stadium quickly and went straight to the bus station for the bus to Istanbul.

Kirkpinar alone was worth every minute of being in Turkey (even with hepatitis and England crashing out of the World Cup) but there was still the cirit left to enjoy in Erzurum, the last event which could be enjoyed on my way to Georgia. All my visas were now in place, except for the Azerbaijani transit visa which I could get in Tbilisi.

So, saying a reluctant goodbye to Istanbul until perhaps the winter, I set out on the journey of over 1000 kilometres back east to Erzurum, where the cirit was happening every Sunday. This time, I didn't have to endure a big-bottomed Azerbaijani sister or chain-smoking football nights, as Nihat Gezder had arranged for me to stay in the guest-rooms of the sports complex.

On Sunday morning we drove out to the farming village outside Erzurum. The setting for this cirit was in contrast to the industrial sprawl of outer Istanbul. It was exactly what I had envisaged, and I was grateful for this opportunity to see cirit as it is meant to be enjoyed. The distant greens of farmland, grey, stony hills and greyer clouds threatening an approaching storm, made it the most perfect site.

The local cirit committee welcomed us, brought us into their office for tea and just as we moved outside, the clouds burst and heavy rain fell. But it didn't deter the players and the game began; a few people squatted on the mud and stone slopes to watch. The scene satisfied my romantic notions: hoofs thundering on wet mud, cirits flying through the air and the whoops and calls of riders. The standard wasn't quite as high as the matches I saw in Istanbul but they were played with more fervour and aggression, and the riders, all of whom were farmers, clearly enjoyed their weekly games.

Most people in rural areas own a horse, so training and keeping them isn't a great additional cost to them. Watching it here made it easier to grasp the relevance of cirit. I asked one old man who used to play and now comes out every Sunday, come rain or shine, to watch the matches, why he still thought cirit has a part to play in everyday Turkish life. He looked at me as if I was quite stupid. 'Why, to prepare for war, of course.'

Today's game was certainly more warlike than the match in Kağithane, rougher, tougher and a little wilder. The shrieks were louder, the spectators fewer by far but more knowledgeable. Even the cold rain didn't stop the game. It really was a step back in time, reminding me of the furious warrior-like acts of the Pakistani polo players, reliving their history.

At last I could understand some of the literature and poems which illustrate the importance and drama of the horse to every man, which as one folk song explains, 'Horse is mine, woman is mine, gun is mine.' A poem written by prominent nationalist Turkish poet, Yahya Kemal Beyatli shortly after Independence, is famous for expressing the nobility of man and horse, and could well be applied to the cirit games of the past.

> On a thousand galloping steeds, we pranced as spirited
>   children when attacking.
> That day, a thousand mounted heroes vanquished a giant
>   army.
> Victory beckoned from our chieftains' gleaming helmets,
> As our group surged across the Danube that glorious
>   summer's day
>
> Like lightning on the horizon, our warriors routed ranks,
> With speedy Turkish horses turning the road to dust.
> One day, astride our lathered steeds, we left this earthly life
> And ascended to the seven levels of Heaven.
>
> This was the day that red roses bloomed in Heaven
> A shimmering dream intact before our very eyes.
> On a thousand galloping steeds, we pranced as spirited
>   children.
> That day, a thousand mounted heroes vanquished a mighty
>   army.

I departed the city of shady tea-gardens and wild horsemen to leave Turkey and face the unknown, travelling towards the north-

east border to enter Georgia, and spend a few days there before
the long, long journey into Central Asia, a region of dramatic
horseback games which could make cirit look a placid pastime.

17

Into the Unknown

O n the bus journey over the Georgian border, it occurred to me many times that I knew little about the Republic of Georgia. In fact, the scant information with which I entered the country could be listed on the fingers of one hand:

1 The capital is Tbilisi
2 England beat them (twice) in the qualifiers of the 1998 World Cup
3 They don't play cricket
4 Neither 'Georgia on My Mind' nor 'Midnight Train to Georgia' is about the Republic of G.

The windows of the battered green minibus were darkened so it was impossible to catch more than a glimpse of the Georgian scenery. The impression I did get was of damp hills, deep green; not unlike the rolling Yorkshire Dales on an October afternoon after a storm.

At Kutaisi, the country's second-largest city, I got down at the bus station and stood there in the middle; in a strange country, unable to understand or read a word of their language, with no map, guidebook, or clue how to get out. A foreigner with a large rucksack wandering aimlessly around a bus station usually attracts a swarm of taxi drivers, hotel owners, money changers, drug dealers and everyone else ready to take their money. But maybe that was just Asia. Now, of course, just when I really needed them to show up, they didn't.

It was sweltering and humid, and two huge bags arranged on

my front and back gave me an uncanny resemblance to a Siamese-twin turtle. I didn't know the Georgian word for 'hotel', but tried saying it in a variety of accents whilst miming, smiling, putting my head on sleeping hands and looking desperate, which provoked impatient looks or apathy. I approached money changers, bus drivers, wretched-looking old ladies selling grey bread from plastic bags. Even the taxi drivers swatted me away like an irritating mosquito.

I tried saying 'city centre' in many languages and someone waved me onto a stifling half-full bus, where people fanned themselves miserably and then trooped off after half an hour. Gloomy sellers swarmed on, selling greasy pastries, unlabelled pharmaceuticals and bottles of vodka but they lacked the panache of Indian hawkers.

One hour later, a driver arrived unwillingly and started the engine with a crank until it clunked into life and we moved off. An old man with greasy hair and bad halitosis squeezed next to me, cackled at my baggage and chatted away. Any goodwill and harmony I had left were diminishing rapidly; I tried saying 'England' in many dialects, languages and accents so he would quit talking and laughing like a hyena.

In the distraction, I realized too late that we were speeding along a scenic country road and nothing like a city. I got off the bus in the middle of a forest and tried to hitch-hike back to town, and after I'd been ignored by many vehicles, a Tbilisi-bound minibus came and took me to a public bus and told the bus driver that I needed a hotel. He brought me to Kutaisi's main square, smiled and directed me to a hotel and wouldn't even charge me. Maybe Georgia wasn't so bad after all.

It was a short walk to the hotel along bright, clean streets that were devoid of people. Only a couple of shops were open, several bars and small carts selling cold drinks. Most shops and buildings were closed down and derelict.

The Hotel Kutaisi was a gracious stone building with an air of faded decadence, an elegant interior dominated by a large spiral staircase and rich, dark wood panelling. The rooms had grand wooden dressers and french windows, large baths and high ceilings but they all needed urgent repair and redecoration. None of the bathrooms had running water, the carpets were worn through and the walls were dirty. I took the cheapest room, and the manager's wife said she would bring me a bucket of hot water.

There was a noisy buzz of activity on every floor. Through the wide-open door of the neighbouring room, I could see a family of eight cooking a meal on a Primus stove on the table, and clothes hanging up to dry. The hotel, I learned, used to be private but was now government-owned, and gave the majority of its rooms free of charge to refugees fleeing their homes in Abkhazia, in the north-west of Georgia. Since 1989, the Muslim Abkhazians have been fighting for independence from Christian Georgia and after capturing Sukhumi in 1993, they have a de facto border just west of Zugdidi. For over a decade, most non-Muslim residents of the area have been fleeing their homes in terror. Fighting has died down recently but the area is still dangerously volatile.

I phoned Mr Amaglobelli, the father of Givi whom I met in Edirne, and he came to take me for dinner downstairs in the restaurant, but was most disturbed when I refused a drink. 'But how can I toast a welcome to you to my country without alcohol?' He commented throughout our meal that it was the first time he had entertained a guest ('and a young lady at that') without a bottle of vodka.

The food was ample compensation, as he persuaded the woman in charge to prepare some traditional Georgian dishes. The only other customers were a few old drunks who clattered in, sucked on a bottle of booze, then staggered out noisily. It was a large, cavernous dining-room with large windows which over-looked the main square, now dark and silent.

Mr Amaglobelli promised to check his contacts in Tbilisi about the possibility of seeing any of Georgia's traditional games. I planned to spend around ten days in the country before going to Azerbaijan, and intended to spend it mainly in the capital. He agreed that nothing would happen in Kutaisi, especially during summer.

There were two Georgian games I was anxious to see. *Zkhenborti* is a type of horseback lacrosse, possibly related to the Argentinian game of *pato* whose origins lay with catching a duck in a net and throwing it between your team-mates. (They now use a ball.) *Leloborti* is a free-for-all rugby on a mammoth scale, where a game consists of two teams from neighbouring villages, each team often the size of an entire village, who have to take the ball and return it to their village. Unfortunately, it being August, when the whole of Georgia migrates to Batumi, the seaside town just over the

Turkish border, meant that it was impossible to see these games. Everyday life, business and organizations grind to a halt.

After our large and pleasant dinner we strolled around the square, deserted at 10 pm with just a few black-clad old ladies sitting on the monument's stone steps selling sunflower seeds. I found it quite depressing, although Mr Amaglobelli was cheerful and optimistic. 'This city was desperate just after Independence in 1991. There was rioting on the streets and people were afraid to go out. We rarely had electricity, there were food and water shortages, little heating in the freezing winters and nearly total unemployment. Now,' he waved a hand around proudly, 'everything is so much better.' Kutaisi was certainly an attractive town but my first few hours showed little evidence of happiness, prosperity or optimism. 'But it will take a few more years,' he said. 'The economy is slowly, slowly picking up.'

Mr Amaglobelli had arranged for his colleague at the university to take me for a tour of Kutaisi and the next morning Irakly, a pale, gaunt young man, arrived at 10 am. Our first stop was the Museum of Sports near the main square and with the shabby, gloomy façade of most other buildings. The tiny office held three friendly staff in a cramped chaotic work-space with dust-gathering files and papers.

The museum, totally deserted, contained old photographs of wrestling stars, Olympic competitors from Georgia when it was part of the USSR, footballers, weight-lifters and basketball-players. My favourite exhibit was an Ireland football shirt which once belonged to George Best. The curator Mr Balavadze remembered the occasion when they acquired it. 'His team came to play a match against Kutaisi. He was very well-known but he didn't play very well probably because he enjoyed our hospitality the night before.' Which probably meant he had a raging hangover. (Georgian hospitality is famous for its emphasis on alcohol.)

Wonderful black-and-white photographs, from the early 1900s, depicted zkhenborti and leloborti and the old curator's eyes lit up when I asked him about them. Both originated in the west of Georgia and used to be wildly popular, although he thought it unlikely that they were played today. 'Maybe only on special occasions.' 'What, like a wedding?' I suggested. 'I doubt it,' murmured Irakly. 'Everyone gets so drunk at weddings they can hardly stand up, let alone play anything.'

Leloborti, the anarchic rugby, still takes place once a year for a special festival but he wasn't sure when. I would have given my eye-teeth to see it. He described another game, sounding suspiciously like cirit, which had now completely died out, but he wasn't sure of its origins. I suggested that it could have come from Turkey.

His reaction was one I learned is typical of Georgians: an emphatic insistence that it must have originated in Georgia and therefore other countries had 'stolen' it. 'Even the name,' he declared, 'is from our language. The word "jireed" translates as "horse running quickly".' And with that triumphant proof it was difficult to suggest otherwise.

Irakly and I ventured into a dimly lit bar occupied by men sitting in small groups at Formica tables, drinking their lunch-hour away, I presumed. But Irakly told me otherwise. 'No one here has a job so they can only drink with their friends. Most have no money but tell the manager they will pay when they get a job. The manager has to agree to this, otherwise the customer will move to a different bar. Maybe one day they will get their money.'

Irakly was highly intelligent and nationalistic, immensely proud of his country and its heritage. He often made comments like, 'These foreigners working here may have lots of money, but we have our history and our culture and that is better than anything.' Jews were OK though. 'They work hard, and are good at business. We don't have any problem with them.' There are still many Jews in Kutaisi, forming the core of most trade. He said that many of them emigrated to Israel after Independence (forbidden when Georgia was part of the USSR) but a significant number returned when they realized they were better off in their home town.

Kutaisi seemed to have closed for the summer and the sports organizations were inactive. Their offices were inside a dishevelled building which looked as though it had been disused for years, with concrete and plaster flaking off the walls and the wooden stairs broken. As I took the bus to Tbilisi, I hoped that the organizations there would be more active.

In Artvin I had met a French couple who had just come from Georgia and they had given me their map of Tbilisi, so at least I was able to find my way about. As they had told me that accommodation was very expensive, I hoped that the Hotel Iveria, which now housed refugees, would have cheap rooms.

I took a minibus to Freedom Square, a grand cobbled square next to the river. On one corner was the main post and telegraph office, along one side was a large casino (with a sign at the entrance saying 'please leave your guns outside'), in the middle was a large fountain where children were paddling, and along another side was the Hotel Iveria. The few vehicles that were there were driven at a terrifying speed.

The hotel was visible from everywhere: a great skulking tower block – a decayed and depressing shadow of its former self. The main entrance looked like that of a neglected apartment block, its gloomy interior lit by yellow fluorescent strips. A couple of dowdy shops sold vodka and bread, and several people loitered around looking as if they had been there for hours.

As I looked for a reception desk, a voice behind me said, 'Hello, can I help you?' A weary woman lugging heavy shopping bags introduced herself as Gulya and invited me up to her room for coffee. She knew nothing of hotels in the area and all the rooms in the Iveria were occupied, apart from one floor now privately owned and charging over £25 a night.

Her minute seventh-floor room was dominated by a large double bed, and a table piled high with books. All her clothes and belongings were in boxes on the balcony, and the tiny bathroom was the only place to wash dishes and prepare food. A Primus stove sat on the balcony with some potatoes and rotting onions, and she heated a tiny electric water heater for our coffee. It was dark inside, mainly because she kept the sun out with a heavy grey blanket across the window.

Gulya was a teacher, and had had to leave her home in Sukhumi two years ago at the height of the civil war in Abkhazia and was now trying to earn a living giving private French, German and English lessons in her tiny room. Eccentric and given to rambling though she was, she was extraordinarily helpful and generous, insisting I stayed with her that night and promising to help find me a place to stay. She knew most people in the area and put the word out that I needed a room to rent cheaply.

Later that afternoon we walked south over the Kura River, towards the recently restored Old Town. It was peaceful and quaint, with the magnificent Metehki Church, old dungeon-like bakeries, cobbled streets with red-roofed houses and wooden-fronted tiny terraces.

We turned onto Prospekt Rustaveli, Tbilisi's main boulevard known ironically by foreigners and locals as The Champs Elysées of Tbilisi. It was hard to believe that in this same city desperate old ladies sell their household goods on the pavement, and men drink shooters of vodka instead of buying bread. Rustaveli is lined with churches, hotels, shiny marble government buildings and the Opera House, dating back to 1896. The glossy designer clothes and foreign labels lie dormant in boutiques, where sleek snooty assistants look bored inside empty stores.

Several bars had sprung up recently, catering mainly for the foreign companies constructing the oil pipeline from the Caspian Sea. Heineken and Guinness signs dazzled the doorways, mirrored walls and tall, wooden bar stools attracted foreigners who bought imported beers and liquors with dollar prices.

That evening we ate bread and hard, smoked cheese and drank coffee. Gulya only had one cup so I drank mine out of the milk jug. Realizing this put severe strain on her food rations, I invited her for dinner but she refused. Her one-room home, given free by the government to refugees, was being 'sub-let' to her by a Russian couple (earning a healthy income in Moscow) for 50 lari (about £16) a month, but as it was her only opportunity of an affordable home she had to pay.

As we listened to a cassette of Italian opera, a pale, gaunt girl slid in through the door and wordlessly plonked herself in front of the soundless TV. 'That's Katarina. Her mother works in the market till 10 pm and they don't have a TV. She comes here every evening.' The young girl's arrival was neatly timed for *Dallas*, and for fifty minutes they watched with dropped jaws, drinking in the escapades of diamond-dripping oil tycoons. I knew that every other room in the Iveria was also watching.

Outside the Dynamo Stadium, banners announced the first league match of the season and I arranged to watch Dynamo Tbilisi (the best team in the country) with people I had met from a local newspaper. It was a six o'clock kick-off on a Wednesday night, and when I suggested we should leave early for decent seats, they laughed. 'You'll see when we get there.'

At the ground there were hundreds of soldiers on duty, yet when we sauntered in three minutes before kick-off, the huge stadium contained only a sprinkling of spectators. There were fewer than 4000 people at the match, including soldiers, all bunched into the same block.

When the teams entered the field there was barely a sound and during the game the crowd sat silently, solemnly, studiously.

Dynamo won 6-3, yet each goal provoked nothing more than a slight wave of applause, with no cheering, shouting or abuse. It was a far cry from the last football match I had seen, in February in Istanbul.

The fans aren't segregated in Georgia, astounding to someone coming from a country of football hooligans. My companions here were immensely proud of such good behaviour. 'Even when English fans came here for the World Cup qualifier, they sat together in the same stand as Georgians.' Natalie remembered the game and laughed. 'They really behaved themselves though – probably so shocked at the passive atmosphere that they were too stunned to do anything. Anyway, there were a couple of thousand of them compared to over 30,000 of us.'

My room suited me perfectly and I grew accustomed to life on the eighteenth and top floor of the Iveria, which Gulya had helped me acquire (it belonged to a friend of a friend who was on holiday) after only one day of looking. At least the lift never broke down. In a block which housed a few thousand people, where unemployment was around 80 per cent and a bottle of vodka was most people's entertainment, there were never any incidents of aggression or signs of vandalism.

The Olympic Committee confirmed a *tchidawoba* (traditional Georgian wrestling) competition for the following Sunday, the day before I was leaving for Azerbaijan. I met committee members and wrestling officials outside the Ministry of Culture and we crammed into the back of a battered white Skoda. It started to rain as the road turned from main paved highway to cart-track, and the city was soon behind us as we approached Mtzkheta, Georgia's old capital.

By the time we arrived, however, it was sunny. The small wrestling arena was picturesquely set in the grounds of an old church, typical of Georgian villages where sporting events were traditionally connected with religious festivals. On the ground was sawdust and the tiered wooden benches circling the arena were full, with a surprising number of women – a pleasant change from the male-only audiences in the subcontinent.

Two musicians sat on the front row with an accordion and drum, and many more spectators were perched on the surrounding high wall. A wooden table at the edge of the arena had the prizes for the different age-groups, from pairs of ceramic vases, to the major prize of a trophy. The judges sat at the table with a microphone and announced the start of the afternoon's competitions.

This festival had been organized by a local wrestler on the anniversary of his father's death. Tchidawoba has enjoyed good status in the country and before Georgia became independent, it was a common local event especially popular in the villages, where festivals are still held at weekends and holidays. Common to traditional wrestling elsewhere in the world, it retains exemplary sportsmanship and spirit.

The rules of tchidawoba are very similar to those of other forms of wrestling: when a wrestler touches the ground with both shoulder blades simultaneously, his opponent gains absolute victory. There are points for technical advantages: one point if a wrestler throws his opponent face down on his knees and hands, two points given if he lands face down and his whole body touches the ground on his side, and three points if his whole body is on the ground with one shoulder blade.

All competitors must wear the *chokha*, a costume made from a hard cloth, like a heavy cotton sleeveless judo jacket, with cotton shorts underneath and soft canvas pumps or socks. Some of the prohibitions include seizing the edge of the chokha with both hands, fighting your opponent when he is lying on the ground, grabbing the chokha or shorts below the belt, twisting the head with one or both hands (one of my favourites), and throwing your opponent head-first onto the ground. Each bout lasts for a maximum of five minutes, and if there isn't an overall victory, then penalty points are calculated to decide the winner.

The competitions began with the youngest, boys only around seven years old and showing great skill. They were the ones who received most encouragement especially from the women in the crowd, particularly one small boy, wearing only a tiny pair of underpants under his chokha, who fought ferociously. He won the first two rounds but got beaten in the final for his age group, and sat at his father's feet in tears.

The most impressive aspect of this afternoon's entertainment was its atmosphere and at last I saw Georgian people animated, relaxed, humorous, vocal and emotional. They called out, shouting encouragement, laughing and joking and made more festive by the folk music. It was a great contrast to the deathly atmosphere of the football match with a few thousand spectators.

The finals for all rounds were held over till the end, and after each final (as in Kirkpinar, decided on weight – except these wrestlers are much slimmer than the Turks) the trophies were presented, all recorded on official video and photographs. As the sun began to sink over the church, the last, most senior final was fought out between two local men, both aged eighteen. When the last and biggest trophy was presented, people rose from their benches, those who had been sitting on the ground shook the sawdust off their clothes and people drifted home.

'Now,' said David, the teenage son of one of the officials, who had volunteered to spend the day with us and translate for me, 'this is where the real competition starts: the banquet and drinking,' and we joined the other members of the committee to go to the organizer's house for the traditional after-tournament feed. They all promised it would be alcohol-flowing traditional Georgian hospitality.

We drove out of the village and into farmland, eventually pulling up outside a huge farmhouse, and joined the crowds ascending the staircase to the first-floor patio. Acres of agricultural farmland were slowly disappearing in the sunset and we were brought to a long wooden table on the balcony which seated over twenty people, with several more tables inside the house.

Our table filled up mainly with old men, and it was already laden with plates of bread, cheese and wonderful local tomatoes, and many glasses in various shapes and sizes. David sat next to me, giving me a constant, and hilarious, translation of the conversations around us. 'I just saw two big wrestlers standing on the balcony. One said to his friend, "I want to get so completely drunk tonight I can't stand up."' He rolled his eyes. 'Sometimes Georgians drink far too much.'

Colossal tankards were filled with a wonderful golden home-made wine that had, for the last few years, been buried underground to brew. It was extremely tempting to forget the hepatitis and enjoy a few sips but it would probably taste too good to stop there. So I had to be content with lemonade.

Just as we began to tuck in with a comfortable murmuring and clattering, it was the time for the *tomada*, or toast-maker, to start. This is the most sacred ritual at the Georgian dinner table, where one man performs a series of toasts to the guests. It is performed with dignity and solemnity which hardly relates to the English 'well cheers then' crash of glasses.

The tomada was a heavy-set, serious-looking man who stood, raised his glass and began a speech, which David explained to be a toast of thanks to the hosts, always the first people to be addressed. After his long speech he drew to a close, then the whole table stood, raised their glasses and repeated a few words in unison. Then they drank.

The clattering and eating resumed but no sooner had the first tankard gone down than the tomada was back on his feet and ordered glasses to be refilled. His next toast was to the host's late father, the ex-wrestler in whose memory the tournament was held. When he finished an even longer speech, others around the table then stood up and chipped in. Then the host, already so drunk he could barely stand up, came over and made an emotional contribution about how proud his father would have been to see his friends gathered in his home, promoting the glory of the wrestling.

David was getting increasingly cynical and amusing, obviously not impressed with the traditions of a Georgian dinner party. 'When you have a party, what do you do? Do you make long boring speeches like this?' he asked. I said we usually spend more time on the eating and drinking than the formalities. He looked around at the others and snorted with irritation.

'These old guys look so miserable! Do you think they're actually having a good time?' I looked around. The atmosphere wasn't particularly festive, though probably typical for the occasion. In fact, the assembled troops were getting more maudlin as the booze went down, and we were up and down constantly as the tomada continued with his increasingly longer toasts.

Emotions ran higher when one old wrestler, who many years earlier had won Olympic medals, embarked on a bitter attack on the government for their lack of interest in the sport. Even after he'd competed at international level, he claimed, the government awarded him a pension of just 7 lari a month (about £2.20). The men around the table all rose in unison, angry at such injustice and full of respect and sympathy for the old man.

The man next to me, also drinking lemonade rather to my surprise, broke his silence to tell me of his visit to London. He worked for the Bank of Georgia and had had to visit the Bank of England either to learn or to teach about forgery. (I couldn't quite grasp which.)

'The taxi driver at Heathrow airport asked where I was from. I told him Georgia, but he didn't know it. I told him "Shevardnadze?" He didn't know. I told him "Tbilisi?". He never heard. I told him "Kitzbaia" [a great Georgian footballer who

The action gets close to the spectators at a polo match in Chitral, Pakistan.

Musicians always accompany polo matches in Pakistan, with specific tunes played at different points of the game.

An enthusiastic throw at a mallakhara competition at the Pir Batho Mela in Pakistan.

The unique sport of cirit – throwing a javelin at your opponent on horseback – in a tournament in Istanbul, Turkey.

Offering Ceylan the bull something tempting before his fight in Artvin, Turkey.

Head-to-head bull fighting during the Kafkasor festival in Artvin, Turkey.

Musicians playing davul and zurna during oil-wrestling competitions in Ülüborlu, Turkey.

A helping hand to smear olive oil over the back of an
oil wrestler before his fight at Kirkpinar, Turkey.

Above and below: Oil wrestlers enjoy liquid refreshment
between bouts at Kirkpinar, Turkey.

Young wrestlers take a shady break at the Kirkpinar festival.

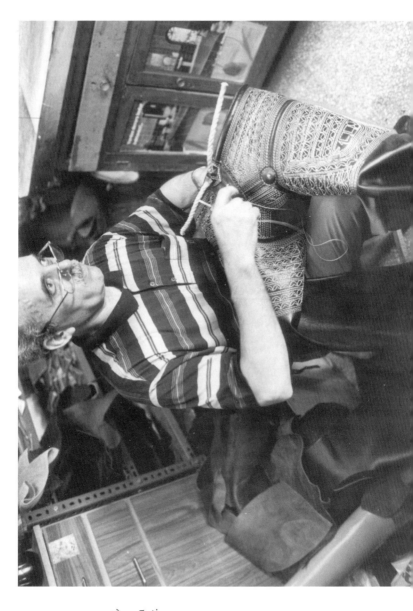

A dying craft: Irfan Sahin hand-makes the kispet, the leather breeches for oil-wrestlers, in his workshop in Biga, Turkey.

played for Newcastle United], he said, "Oh *Georgia*! Why didn't you say?" '

More food, more bottles and still more speeches from an increasingly slurring tomada followed, and David stopped translating for me as he was getting bored. 'When I get married and have my friends round for dinner,' he said, 'we'll be happy and not like this lot. Sometimes our traditions are really boring and useless.'

A couple of hours later most of the table was comatosed and our group was planning to leave, at which point the tomada rose again and began a long, laborious speech about 'our foreign visitor', and how they all appreciated my interest in their sporting tradition. David had no longer the patience to give an exact translation: 'Oh my God,' he rolled his eyes up to heaven, 'he's just going on and on about how you've honoured our table by being here. He's never going to stop . . .'

An old man struggled to his feet to contribute: 'And let's not forget she comes from the great cultured land of Shakespeare, Keats and Byron,' and everyone nodded furiously in agreement. 'And of course, the Queen!' It provoked such excitement that I could hardly admit to being an anti-royalist. The host returned, propped up by a couple of equally drunk wrestlers, enthused that I was now part of his family and always would be welcome. Finally the ex-Olympic wrestler rose and added his contribution.

'Let's not forget that apart from Shakespeare, Byron and of course the Queen,' a pause and his voice rose to a crescendo, 'that she also comes from that great country of the dead Princess Diana!' And with that dramatic finale, the old boys around the table were practically weeping into their plates.

It was time for some drastic measures to lift the gloom, so I dragged a reluctant David to his feet to translate my speech to a now growing audience. Perhaps, inspired by Shakespeare and the Queen, they expected a memorable speech because a small spotlight was switched on in the gloomy night and guests from other tables came over to hear. What could I say as a representative of my country, culture and people?

'I begin with a formal apology from my country.' They hung on every word as David translated. 'I have to apologize for England beating Georgia in the World Cup qualifiers this year. I've assured Kinkladze and Kitzbaia that it won't happen again.' That provoked gales of laughter all around, at least enough to stem the tears. It was then more appropriate to finish on a more serious note, so I thanked them for their gracious hospitality and spoke of my appreciation of their rich traditions and pride in their history.

18

Night Train from Georgia

Gulya came to the station to see me off to Baku, brought me to my train, and waved me off from the platform while I settled back into my compartment. There were few passengers in the carriage, and a tiny old lady nearly bent double was the only other person sharing my four-berth compartment. The windows didn't open, so most people stood out in the corridor to get fresh air.

We rattled though unspectacular scenery and my mind drifted towards Azerbaijan, where I would spend just a couple of days on the way to Central Asia. The staff at the Azerbaijani Consulate in Istanbul had found it difficult dealing with relatively simple questions like: 'I am visiting your country. Where do you suggest I should visit? Do you have a map? Is it possible to get a visa in Tbilisi?'

Their response was a bewildered, 'Why are you going to Azerbaijan?' Someone eventually rustled up a booklet entitled 'Azerbaijan in Figures, 1997' which told me that in a population of 7.6 million, there were 1359 cases of hooliganism, 696 cinemas, 47000 marriages and 270 newspapers. There were no guidebooks, and the only other information was from the United States Information Service website which implied the country was dangerous, crime-ridden, corrupt, don't go.

After many stops, the train crawled over the border into Azerbaijan and the first thing to strike me was the Arabic music emerging from a teahouse – the first teahouse I'd seen since leaving Turkey. Unlike Georgia, my first impression of Azerbaijan was favourable.

The entry procedures took place in the first station, and immediately a policeman glared at my documents and called me into an empty compartment, talking quickly in Russian until I suggested speaking slowly in Turkish. He tried to charge me £6 to stamp my passport but I informed him that £25 for a two-day visa was quite enough thank you. This was the first time I had ever been asked for a bribe.

He looked angry and then sneered, gave a parting 'Big problem' and disappeared into the dark platform with my passport. Giorgi, a good-looking Georgian I'd met on the train, appeared looking white. 'He told me my visa wasn't valid unless I pay $50 [about £30], or I have to return now to Tbilisi.' This was far more serious than my £6 threat, because Giorgi couldn't afford it. 'I've refused to pay and insisted on seeing his superior, the man with the hat.' Luckily The Man With The Hat was a senior and slightly less corrupt official who agreed to stamp our passports without any extras.

In the morning we drew into Baku station; hot, crowded and lively, it felt more like Asia. Heaving my bags off I began the long search for a cheap hotel which had been recommended. Accommodation is a major problem for visitors to Baku, as there are few affordable places and even the expensive hotels are lousy value for money. With the oil-pipeline going through Azerbaijan and bringing in money and foreign workers, hotel prices had rocketed over the previous few years because rich foreign companies could afford them. Several foreign workers I had met who came on business trips to Baku, complained of filthy hotel rooms which cost £65. 'I used up a whole bottle of disinfectant just to clean the bath so I could use it,' an Englishwoman told me in Tbilisi, talking about the government-owned Hotel Azerbaijan.

I eventually found an old Russian hotel with an indecipherable name, and with a spot of bargaining secured a room with a bathroom and huge fan which clanked and roared like an old bus. Later that morning I went to the ferry port to enquire about the ferry to Turkmenbashi. This was the next stage of my journey to Central Asia, taking me to Turkmenistan and nearer to the ultimate goal of Kyrgyzstan, and in particular the 31 August buzkashi match – now ten days away.

At the ferry ticket office, the waiting hall was huge and echoed with desertion. My conversation with the ticket officers, in basic Turkish, went something like this:

'Is there a boat to Turkmenbashi tomorrow?'

'Yes, every day.'

'What time does it leave?'

'Around 4 pm. Well, sometimes 1 pm.'

'Can I buy a ticket now?'

'No, come tomorrow morning. Maybe the boat is not going.'

'Why won't it go?'

'Oh, sometimes it doesn't go.'

'How many hours does it take?'

'Maybe twelve. Or sometimes twenty-four.'

'So I can buy a ticket tomorrow?'

'Maybe. Come early.'

The price for foreigners was listed in dollars and was higher than the local-currency price. Five categories ranged from push-back seats in an open lounge, to the luxury single-berth cabin with shower. I opted for the fourth-class, a four-berth cabin costing a pricey $60 (roughly £38).

I spent the afternoon sitting idly in a tea-garden watching the world go by. Baku is the perfect place for that, with a vast expanse of grassy and shady space on the waterfront and many tea-gardens. The centre of Baku came as a great surprise: the main square was the meeting point of several shopping streets, all of them modern, with supermarkets, restaurants, pizza parlours, international banks in modern tower blocks and smart clothes shops. The streets were bright, clean and busy, a great contrast to the mostly-empty streets with a few weary plodders in downtown Tbilisi.

In the evening I sat in a terrace bar watching the bright young things of Baku cruise by: men and women mainly in their late teens, most of them dressed for a night on the tiles, although they didn't seem to be going anywhere. Some women were dressed in gold lamé to match their teeth, teetering on high heels, many had long sleek hair and low-cut, tight tops. Young, old, tarty, gay, straight – all were talking and laughing loudly and parading around in small groups.

The next morning I returned to the ferry port for a ticket, although no one could confirm a departure time and still said 'Come back at 1 pm and we will say if the boat is going.' There was no one else waiting, which wasn't a good sign as I expected queues of people with bags and children sitting in the burning heat.

I returned at 1 pm with all my bags and waited over two hours in an empty hall, until a ticket officer told me to go to the other port, which was rather shabby and consisted of a few sheds and a couple of offices. There was a boat in dock and a few hundred people sat with bags and children, waiting like refugees, uncertain if they would leave that day.

Every half-hour I pestered the immigration and customs officials, asking what time we were leaving; the reply was always 'in half an hour', but it seemed certain that we would leave that day. At 4 pm, we were beckoned to join the scramble for immigration and customs control, and board the boat.

The *Professor Gül* was similar to a European car-ferry and I figured would be pretty certainly overloaded. I found my cabin which was clean and quite comfortable with four bunk beds, two-by-two, and lockers. The drawback was its stuffiness, with no ventilation or window. The two women with the keys tried to offer me a deluxe Class 'A' cabin with private bathroom, for a crisp $10 in their hand, which I declined. Until I saw the public toilets off the main lounge.

Their condition persuaded me to seek out the two women and take the luxury cabin: one bed, a smart wooden desk and chair, a large porthole and a bathroom with toilet and a shower, which alone was worth the ten dollars. I moved in and inspected the cabin. The walls were covered with posters of lingerie-clad models, eight long-haired beauties gazing down at me which was a trifle intimidating. One was a black-haired woman in red undies and red very high heels with Chinese characters down the side and 'Fengzi fengzi fengzi' at the top; I wished I understood what it meant.

By 6 pm the boat hadn't left dock and there were hardly any passengers or vehicles. The two women returned and invited me into their lounge where they cooked and served the food for the captains, and we stood on deck where no one seemed overly worried at the inactivity except me. Thick smoke curled out of one funnel, and none from the other, supporting the rumours of engine trouble.

Back in my cabin and leafing through some papers, I made the disastrous discovery that my visa was probably not adequate for Turkmenistan. I thought it allowed me to transit through Turkmenistan, or so they told me in the Kyrgyz Embassy. But I now suspected that this information was wrong and my guidebook confirmed that it wasn't enough, which could mean a major fine and being sent straight back to Azerbaijan. There was little I could do but worry during the entire journey – obviously far longer than twelve hours, as we hadn't moved for the last six.

At nightfall the boat was still surprisingly empty. Even the large seating lounge, the cheapest section, was only half-full and the deck was empty with a few benches, a small counter selling tea and empty tables. There was a restaurant run by a friendly cook who invited me into the kitchen to check out the chicken stew and soup. Women with flashing gold teeth looked weary as they gave food to their families, and older children scampered amongst the deck and life-boats.

The only other person out on deck at midnight (when we were still docked) was a fat, bald Georgian man wearing slippers and tight white shorts revealing flabby thighs. He was a truck driver going to Aktau, in Kazakhstan, which is stuck between the Caspian and the desert and wildly inaccessible. But he could be my solution. He offered to drive me up the narrow strip of land from Turkmenbashi to Aktau, through endless hours of sand and bleakness. If I hid inside whilst he cleared the immigration procedure, I could enter Kazakhstan and Kyrgyzstan, avoiding the Uzbek border which was said to be rife with bribe-hungry officials. If I could get through Kazakhstan within three days (the maximum time allowed to transit) I could then get to Bishkek and out of trouble. But the journey from Aktau to Almaty in Kazakhstan, as the crow flies a distance of around 1500 kilometres, would be a problem. Trains are infrequent, horrendously slow and over-crowded and tickets difficult to acquire: it would take around five days, over the limit for transit time on my visa. To reach Bishkek unscathed would depend on my getting into Turkmenistan, crossing Uzbekistan and travelling through Kazakhstan by train or bus.

At midnight the boat still hadn't left, so I settled down for a worrying sleep dreaming of being locked up by police in various uniforms, and woke at 2 am to the unmistakable motion of sea-travel and the lights of Baku in the distance.

Even when the journey should have been over, the ferry remained stationary for ten frustrating hours just short of the Turkmenbashi docks. It was 10 pm when we docked and then I got nervous. It was impossible to hide in a truck to go through immigration, as the drivers were queuing up with other passengers clutching their passports, including the Georgian trucker. We queued at the customs yard, and there I made the decision to brazen my way through, take the first bus to Ashkebad the capital, and take a train or bus through Uzbekistan to Bishkek and deal with police when necessary.

The immigration police looked at my passport and asked the dreaded, 'Where is your Turkmenistan visa?' After a long and heated discussion they told me, quite emphatically, that my Kyrgyz visa was inadequate, and turned to the next person in the queue.

When there was no one left, they let me into the customs hall where lots of men in uniform cast cursory checks over mountains of baggage, while someone consulted a higher authority. The message came back that I needed a separate Turkmen transit visa, and the consular chief was on his way. It was now 11 pm, and I was relieved not to be sent back to Azerbaijan.

He turned up half an hour later and gave me a six-day transit visa for $41 (roughly £26). It was after midnight when he helped me change money, and then walked with me the two miles to the only hotel in town, as there were no taxis. Turkmenbashi, once called Krasnovodsk, is Central Asia's only port and link by sea to the Black Sea and Mediterranean and deals mainly in oil. But the town doesn't have the metropolitan buzz of other Asia port cities like Karachi or Bombay.

At the Hotel Khazar, the receptionist was woken up and, obviously annoyed by this late arrival, shoved a registration form in Russian at me and barked something which I assumed meant 'Fill this in, thick wench'. My Consular Man gently took it from me and filled it in, showed me the room – clean and air-conditioned, with a tiny bathroom full of leaking pipes, for $8 – shook my hand and walked back home, at 1.30 am.

I had imagined that getting a bus to Ashkebad would involve a fist-fight for a ticket, a scramble on to old bangers, insane drivers and endless delays. So it was a shock the next morning to see two smart Turkish buses waiting in the main square, which the driver said left at noon. He told me I could buy my ticket from him, which even had a seat number. I was relieved that Turkish was understood here, being very similar to Turkmen, which made up for my complete lack of Russian.

In the bus, which left miraculously on time, I chatted in Turkish to the woman sitting behind me, another Gulya, who invited me to stay with her in Ashkebad for a night so that I could look for a hotel the following morning.

The scenery was dull; desert but not the undulating glow of golden dunes, simply a grey, flat scrub with a straight row of electricity pylons lining the road. I would doze off for an hour and wake to find the same scene out of the window. We made the occasional stop at a wind-swept cluster of concrete shacks huddled in bleak blinding surroundings, where a clump of people would shuffle out of nowhere to stand and gape at the bus, probably the highlight of their day. The women wore long, tailored, brightly coloured dresses with matching turbans, and long trousers in bright pink, their luminous colours dazzling in a drab landscape.

After seven hours, we reached Ashkebad, and Gulya and I took a taxi to her home, during which she explained her marital situation: divorced and living with her ex-husband and their two children but also remarried with her second husband working in Turkmenbashi. Arriving at her home – in one of many grey, identical concrete blocks – we entered the living-room, which contained an old black-and-white TV and several sofas – and, on the wall opposite, a familiar poster of a black-haired beauty in red undies and red stilettos, under the words 'Fengzi fengzi fengzi'.

19

Introduction to Islam

We went next door to her neighbours' for dinner and were greeted by Katarina, a brunette in her thirties wearing only a skirt, with the elasticated waist pulled up to her armpits. Gulya wore hers in identical style and I felt over-dressed in shorts and T-shirt.

Five people sat on the living-room floor around a small wooden table covered in food and bottles. Natalya, younger and blonde, wearing a bra and denim hot-pants, was next to a skinny man with a concave stomach wearing trousers and no shirt, who staggered up and grinned a mouthful of gold teeth.

He shook my hand. 'I am Islam,' he said solemnly and poured me a large tumbler of vodka. This was Gulya's ex-husband and father of her children. Natalya's younger brother Viktor was cele-brating his twenty-seventh birthday and this was his party.

I tried to explain in Turkish what 'hepatitis' was, whilst refusing the vodka, and also 'vegetarian', turning down roast chicken. There was a cassette of Russian 1970s disco hits, and we all danced around the living-room, Islam gyrating his body so it nearly snapped, and Natalya writhing and undulating her body around him. We made an unusual dance troupe.

They got plastered knocking back neat shots of vodka, and I left. Gulya was crying softly in the kitchen. 'My husband rang me,' she said. 'I miss him and he wants me to return to Turkmenbashi. But I can't afford it.'

I offered her the $40 she needed for transport and food, if I could sleep and eat in her house for four nights. It solved our problems and she gave me a huge hug. I wouldn't have to search for a hotel and living with a family, however dysfunctional, would be far more interesting.

I tried to sleep in the stuffy room (door and windows closed) and soon after drifting off, was awakened by Islam groaning noisily. Then there was the unmistakable sound of vomiting.

The next morning, already regretting my decision to stay but unable at this late stage to ask for the money back, I went into the kitchen. Islam sat on the kitchen floor at the low wooden table, nursing a large black coffee and hangover. I gave him two painkillers for his headache, and he offered to take me into town to the Olympic Committee offices, where I imagined there to be some information about the sports of Central Asia and a useful starting point.

We went by bus into the city centre, an array of neat boulevards and shiny marble government buildings with little to attract the eye. On every street corner, far larger than life, was the omnipresent figure of President Saparmuradi Niyazov, a man whose huge ego was matched by the enormous pictures displayed on every building façade. As head of the Democratic Party of Turkmenistan, his statue is prominent in most towns and villages.

I went first to the Ministry of Culture, to see if there were any sporting activities taking place in the near future. Some friendly members of the Olympic Committee told me, like in Georgia, that I was 'here at the wrong time'. The best time to come, they said, was for Turkmenistan Independence Day. 'Come back in October and you can see buzkashi at the Hippodrome!' It was difficult to return, as I only planned to spend six weeks in Central Asia. 'We have a massive race that day – cars and TVs as prizes.'

At the Hippodrome on the edge of the city, I met the president of the Equestrian Association, who waxed lyrical about 'horse culture' which is prevalent throughout Central Asia. 'It used to be allowed that people ate horsemeat in this country. But I encouraged a decree from the government that it is now illegal. We must respect horse culture!' Primarily used for horse races, the Hippodrome was occasionally the venue for buzkashi matches, but these were mainly for special events. The president told me proudly about a herculean horse race he had organized fifteen years before – from Ashkebad to Moscow. 'People must learn to ride horses for long distances,' he said, finger wagging. 'Our Ahalteke horses [the local breed] are made for these long rides, but never used.'

I managed to find a bus to take me back. The man sitting next to me talked to me in Russian. I shrugged and said 'Anglia.' He looked delighted. 'Anglia?' he said unable to believe his luck, and prodding his son next to him. 'Anglia,' he repeated to him, and turned back to me. I wondered what this was leading to. 'Anglia? Michael Owen!' he announced proudly.

His son, around twelve years old, looked embarrassed and muttered something to his father. Dad beamed in undisguised delight. 'Michael Owen, Alan Shearer, Paul Ince, Paul Gascoigne . . . Ah, Paul Gascoigne *nyet*!' He remembered that Gascoigne had been dropped for the World Cup. 'David Batty, David Beckham . . .'

Then he recited the England champions of 1966, and their local clubs. 'Bobby Charlton, Jimmy Grieves, Stanley Matthews, Alf Ramsey . . .' and his son cringed even more. As an encore, he rattled through the France '98 winning team, at which point I got off.

I spent three days in Ashkebad before setting off for Charjou, a large town on the border of Uzbekistan from where I would go to Tashkent. The eight-hour journey, on yet another old Turkish bus with broken air-conditioning, rarely stopping for food or toilet, got me to Charjou at 5 pm. A town with no charm or interesting features, described in my guidebook as 'an unsightly, industrial sprawl', it had only one hotel, which was old and shabby and cost over $100 (approximately £64) a night, and I was anxious to leave immediately.

I had struggled with a basic conversation with a woman sitting near me, an attractive and vivacious middle-aged Kazakh woman who was returning to Shimkent, and passing through Tashkent. She offered to help me get as far as Zhambyl, just a few hours from Bishkek.

She tried to buy two tickets to Tashkent at the ticket-counter, to be told by the woman there to board the train and pay the ticket collector. This arrangement, although probably the norm for the citizens of Central Asia, worried me, as there was a rule in Turkmenistan that foreigners had to pay three times the local price. Boarding a train illegally would surely make me an easy target for demands for a large bribe. But all I could do was to rely on the patience and assistance of my new friend, Galina.

As Galina knew two women who worked on the trains, we were

allowed to sit in a stationary carriage for a couple of hours and make tea. Two Uzbek men, one called Zak who was also going to Tashkent, told me that on Uzbekistan Independence Day, 1 September, there would be ram fighting in Mustakillik Maydoni, Tashkent's main square where the celebrations would be held. I'd never heard of ram fighting before, but the way they described and mimed it, it resembled Turkish bull fighting, two animals head-butting each other until one ran away. So 1 September was now well and truly marked in my diary, and worth coming to Tashkent for.

After some five hours a train approached with a shriek and a roar. There was an urgent scramble as people tried to wedge boxes and bags and themselves into it long before it came to a standstill.

Our plan of action was more relaxed: Zak boarded the sleeper compartment to arrange three berths for us and a few minutes later he gave us the signal to board. Having no tickets wasn't a drawback – just part of the unofficial system.

Half an hour later at the Uzbek border, I was worried but Zak and Galina were emphatic that I should remain silent in front of any official – ticket inspector, police officer, customs or immigration – which would lessen chances of paying a bribe for not having a ticket. Zak took my passport and returned quickly, grinning, and said, 'All is OK. They asked for a fine but I told them you had no money, so they said OK.' We were soon assigned a four-berth first-class compartment, and we paid the ticket-collector and settled down for the night.

When the train drew in to Tashkent, Zak carried my rucksack and I his baskets to lessen attention from station police, renowned for picking on tourists and extracting money for no apparent reason. Galina and I went across town to the bus station where she bought two tickets for Zhambyl in Kazakhstan, and we boarded without having to show the police our documents, which by law every passenger has to do before leaving the city. It was a huge relief not to be questioned and we giggled quietly at a minor victory over officialdom.

When we arrived in Zhambyl many hours later at 10 pm, Galina insisted I should stay with her and continue to Bishkek the next day. The next morning, I packed, gazing out of the window at a truly miserable public square. It was a concrete 'lawn' in the middle of half a dozen blocks, with a couple of rusted slides and swings and a broken bench. The whole area was deserted, except for a couple of wretched dogs wandering around.

I compared it to India, having lived in a similar housing block in Bombay, where there were always children playing cricket and men sitting around chatting, hawkers selling vegetables and fruit and newspapers; the hiss of several pressure-cookers steaming with dhal, and the buzz and business of life which, for all the poverty, made it a happy place.

We went to the bus station where Galina bought my ticket to Bishkek and I repaid her for everything in dollars. I got on the bus still not speaking, in case Kazakh police wanted to check my documents. Galina ran onto the bus as we were leaving and handed me a large piece of flat bread and a hard-boiled egg, and kissed me goodbye.

The crossing into Kyrgyzstan was uneventful – no border rituals, no guards or barbed wire, which I would have expected, given the difficulty in getting a visa. The bus stopped briefly to get the entry recorded, and only a Russian sign announcing 'Welcome to Kyrgyzstan', indicated we were in another country, for no one even checked our papers.

So, where were all the police checks? What about the rumours about money-grabbing officials and constant passport scrutiny to ensure no one had overstayed their visa by a couple of minutes? It made a mockery of the visa panic, and I stored for future use the knowledge that I could cross the border without undue worry.

20

'Everyone at Heart Plays Ulak'

It was 22 August when I arrived in Bishkek, with ample time to prepare for ulak tartish (buzkashi). I planned to spend around six weeks in Central Asia before another massive overland trip, this time to try to reach India by mid-October. Although I had experienced numerous cancellations or wrong information about events, I figured that the Independence Day celebrations on 31 August would hardly be postponed, especially to a newly independent country.

I headed straight for the recommended Business School Hotel, a fifteen-minute taxi ride from the bus station along quiet tree-lined boulevards with no traffic, shops or people. It had the atmosphere of a suburban residential area when everyone's out at work – lifeless and sleepy.

The hotel's name, and its inclusion in several guidebooks, had led me to suppose it would be an English-language oasis in a Russian-speaking desert. But the trio of ferocious-looking women in reception looked as if they neither cared nor enjoyed their job, and only spoke Russian. The price wasn't displayed and they looked insulted when I asked them to write down the price. Above the desk was an ominous notice: 'All foreigners must register with OVIR (the Government Department for Immigration) within two days of arrival otherwise you will be evicted out of the hotel.' Thank you for your welcome.

I went to the Ministry of Culture and Information down the lifeless road to ask about Bishkek's Traditional Sports Federation.

The office was on the second floor of a large old stone building inside the Spartak stadium, and contained a couple of hard wooden chairs, a laden table, four telephones and an over-painted, pouting young secretary who filed her nails whilst chatting on the phone.

Reluctantly she put down the phone when I requested assistance to make appointments with the relevant people. Pursing her deep scarlet lips with concentration, she preened herself in the mirror and smoothed down her micro-short skirt over her thighs.

'Who are you working for? I want to see all your papers before I arrange anything.' Indira (named after Indira Gandhi who visited Bishkek just before she was born) made a couple of calls and said that the head of her department, Bolotbek Shamshiev, was a 'very busy man and probably will not have time to see you'.

I insisted she make an appointment for me, which didn't please her. After a couple more calls, she looked up. 'Come back tomorrow at 10 o'clock to see him.' She preened again in front of the mirror which I took as a cue to leave.

That evening I ventured out for food and entertainment, which didn't result in much. My hotel was in the north of Bishkek, opposite Panfilov Park, but even walking through the main street of Frunze didn't answer the million-dollar question: where were the people? Perhaps, as in Georgia, everyone goes away for the summer.

Panfilov Park was very green with an assortment of trees and low deep green hedges, dotted about with a pleasant selection of sculptures, statues and a few empty benches. It was well-maintained, and in the centre were several outdoor cafés, with umbrellas emblazoned with the logos of Marlboro', Coca-Cola and Camel sheltering the empty white plastic tables and chairs from the evening sun.

Several other foreigners were staying in the International Business School and judging by their hale and hearty appearance and designer walking boots, they had come predominantly for trekking. Since independence, Kyrgyzstan has begun to open its doors to tourists, most coming for the spectacular mountain ranges that cover 94 per cent of the country, far more challenging and deserted than the overcrowded mountains in Nepal swarming with backpackers.

At the Ministry of Sports and Tourism the next morning, Indira with a vividly painted smile informed me that: 'Mr Bolotbek

Shamshiev is very busy today, but perhaps you could come back this afternoon? There is a Press Conference at 4 pm and all the people you want to see will be there. Please come.'

That afternoon the conference room filled up with sportsmen, members of the Sports Ministry and journalists. TV cameras began to roll, and the invited guests (national swimmers who were medal winners from a recent tournament) looked uncomfortable in suits and ties. The elusive Mr Shamshiev, whom it was still impossible to meet, sat at the head of the table and chaired the meeting. Indira looked harassed and introduced me to Selima, a large smiling woman who offered to translate for me.

'I am a teacher but now out of a job. My husband left me and I look after my two children so really need the work. Life is very hard.' Her English wasn't good but I was touched by her honesty and knew that she might represent my only chance of understanding anything, as there was very little English seen or heard in the country.

Selima and I went into the conference room and sat at the edge of the room. She whispered in her stilted English what was happening, as each sportsman was presented with a bouquet of flowers to a sprinkling of applause, and then Mr Shamshiev spoke at great length.

'He used to be a movie star,' she explained, adding that many years later he left his wife, married an actress half his age and went into politics. As she was launching into more details, a matronly woman with a shelf-like bust came over and barked at us in Russian. Selima looked puzzled and answered, and the woman turned to me. 'Why you are here? This is not for you. No other foreigners here. Who said you come?' 'Indira invited me to meet journalists and officials.' 'Well you cannot be here. Please leave.'

In India or Pakistan, they welcome visitors and would never dream of throwing a foreign journalist out of a press conference. I was incensed. 'But I was invited, and Bolotbek Shamshiev is expecting me.'

Her lips disappeared in a grimace and we had no choice but to leave, both of us seething. Indira shrugged and failed to back us up. We rebelliously smoked cigarettes in the corridor and dropped ash on the floor. A grim-faced man glared at us as he walked into another office. Selima asked him if he knew anything about the Federation of Traditional Sports and he glared again, but reluctantly brought us into a tiny room and pointed to a chart.

The chart was the national league table of *kyz kumay*, the traditional Kyrgyz game of 'kiss the girl', and listed all the teams in the country. This game is traditionally seen at festivals and weddings but it appeared that there are now regular competitions. The game, which I had read about, sounds fascinating: a horseback contest between a man and woman where the man chases the woman and if he succeeds in catching her, he kisses her. But if after a certain time he can't reach her, she takes a horsewhip and thrashes him. I was delighted to see evidence of it and desperately hoped I could see some of their league matches.

We tried asking him – are there games now, are they in Bishkek, or all over the country? But he was unenthusiastic, shrugged and replied, 'Come on 31 August for the game at the Hippodrome.' That was all we could get out of him.

Selima and I continued to wait in the corridor until Indira eventually emerged, nervously informing us: 'They are going to be a long time now. Perhaps you can come back tomorrow?' Selima nudged me after Indira had left. 'She means they are going to start drinking, and she cannot disturb them.' As we were about to go, however, someone helpful actually came along – Kabil Makeshov, a sports writer and member of the elusive Federation of Traditional Sports. He arranged to meet us the next afternoon, and promised to introduce me to the best-known and most respected buzkash in town, which was the most encouraging news I'd had for days.

The next day we went to his newspaper's office and were introduced to Murat and Emil. 'Murat is one of the greatest players of ulak tartish in the country. Now he is a coach and he organizes one of the teams.' My first glimpse of this famous Central Asian ulak tartish player slightly shattered my illusions. Far from the dramatic and exotic riders of Baluchistan, Murat was a short, slightly plump chap in his late thirties, wearing smart trousers, shiny shoes, a freshly ironed shirt and carrying a mobile phone.

Murat told us that these days he doesn't play competitively but he coaches, and visits surrounding villages to hunt potential players. 'These last few years since independence, private companies have more money and are looking for ways to get publicity. Some of them are sponsoring ulak tartish teams, paying the riders and buying the horses. Now the country has more money and we can afford to finance our traditional sports, which we could not do as well when part of USSR. The Kyrgyz people are able to respect their own games now. Dordoi is a communications company, they employ me and sponsor a team. And this is Emil, one of the best players today.'

Emil was young, very tall and shy, smiling down into his shoes. I asked him what made ulak so special and he smiled more, looked at the ground and just said simply, 'When I am on that horse and playing, I forget about everything else in life. I can be a hero.' Emil worked as a security guard for Dordoi for a small wage but his main income – about $100 a month – came from playing for their team. It was like the club cricketers in India and Pakistan who are 'employed' by companies but in reality are professional sportsmen for the company's team.

Murat explained the game's appeal to a Kyrgyz man. 'This game is all about our past, our background, history and also future. These days there is more commercial activity, which has made it more popular. Since independence, we are more proud of ways we can show people our true identity. Every man and boy wants to play ulak tartish. It is the sign of someone who is skilful, brave and strong. A hero.

'At heart, every Kyrgyz man is an ulak tartish player.'

As in Turkey, the horse has a great romantic status in Kyrgyz history. 'The horse is a man's wings,' goes the folk saying, handed down through the generations for centuries. Poets and story-tellers praised a winged, gold-maned, fleet-footed animal in their stories and songs. The horse made it possible for the cattle-breeders to journey to and from the mountain pastures, carry loads, guard the cattle and maintain communication with populated areas. Warriors used horses in warfare and, later, horses were an essential part of the development of farming technology. Then the horse became a feature of sports and games.

A lasting and distinguished bond between man and horse is elaborated in the heroic epic *Manas*, the ancient folkloric verses which are a prominent part of Central Asian culture, Manas being the superhero, a brave, fearless warrior as described in the verse: 'The mighty Manas, resembling a silver tower, rode his snow-white steed Ak-Kula over the mountain tops. The steed looked like a bird hovering over the sharp peaks.'

The Kyrgyz horse is still cherished and is said to possess qualities of lightness and good co-ordination in the mountains, to be exceptionally hardy and unfussy about food, able to acclimatize to rapid changes in altitude and temperature and endure long distances carrying a rider.

Ulak tartish is one of several horseback sports that the Kyrgyz have played 'for centuries' and in recent years are keen to develop further. In June 1996, a journalist, Pavel Ilusanov, wrote in the *Kyrgyzstan Chronicle*:

The Kyrgyz, scattered all over the mountains and gorges in nomad camps have not historically had the opportunity to hold frequent and regular mass sporting events. Therefore each event – wedding, funeral feast, call to war or its triumphant finish – was accompanied by such events. Equestrian contests – horse races and trick riding – have always been at the culmination of festive occasions.

From the *Manas* epos and from old experts of national contests and games, we know about the special diet and regime of traditional Kyrgyz sportsmen, or 'baatyrs'. The menu of men preparing for a duel included lamb meat and koumiss [fermented horsemilk] and avoided drinking boso [a revolting substance I once inadvertently drank, which I thought tasted like a mixture of vomit and beer]. The epos immortalizes the images of legendary Manas, his son Semetei, his grandson Seitek and their companions, who were endowed with athletic strength, physical perfection and great bravery. Courageous and hardened people, capable of overcoming any difficulties, were held in respect among the Kyrgyz people since the beginning of time, and continue to be respected today.

Murat and Kabil told me about the origins of ulak tartish, which by different names is also popular in Kazakhstan, Tajikistan, Uzbekistan and of course Afghanistan. (Like 'buzkashi', 'ulak tartish' translates as 'goat dragging'.) It is also known here as *kok boru*, which means 'grey wolf', and most believe its origins lie in ancient times when herds of cattle grazed on the steppes and mountains throughout the year without shelter, exposed to attacking wolves. With no weapons, it was hard for shepherds to defend themselves or their flock, but the braver ones chased the wolves away, and tried to catch them and beat them with sticks. This, the Kyrgyz say, is the main origin of ulak tartish.

The Afghans claim that the game dates back to the time of Alexander the Great, and it is also associated with Genghis Khan. It is likely that the game emerged from the aggressive manoeuvres of the Mongol horsemen warriors who made swift, fierce raids on enemy encampments, often snatching sheep, goats and other possessions (and perhaps even women) without dismounting. In retaliation, the Afghans made mounted defence against these raids. Several Afghanis have told me that since the Taliban took control of most of their country, buzkashi has been banned, but there used to be huge games in Kabul lasting for days during *Nauruz* (Afghan and Persian New Year on 21 March), with dozens of riders in a stadium half a mile long with little regard for rules and safety.

Kyrgyzstan, on the other hand has, with independence, enjoyed a recent revival of its traditional games and in particular during the celebrations of the Manas in 1995, a year that UNESCO picked out to commemorate '1000th Anniversary of the Manas Epos'. People said that these celebrations gave the games exposure and encouraged their popularity.

According to Murat, the games are a little smaller now, with better organization and more respect for the rules, and sponsored competitions. The playing area for ulak tartish is now 200-300 metres long, and 100-150 metres wide. Its ends are marked with flags, called gates, and in the centre of the field is the *mara*, a circle of 6 metres in diameter where the goat's carcass is placed to start the game.

The rules state that the players can pick up the carcass from any place within the field, take it from their opponents, pass or fling it to their team-mates, hold it by the leg, carry it closely pressed to the side of the horse or over the front of the saddle. It is also permitted to cover your team-mate while he is carrying the goat, preventing attackers from snatching it. It is forbidden to make your horse rear or collide with an opponent's at high speed; to seize your rival's horse by the bridle, take its reins off, or hit it with your whip.

As I listened to him, I could hear the ferocious cry of warrior horsemen and the roaring crowd, and smell the flying dust. Murat might have looked like just another businessman clutching a mobile phone, but inside was the heart of a fearless warrior, a hero. 'On Thursday we are having a festival in the village nearby. It is a big sports day and we will be playing ulak. Would you like to come?' Would I? Would I *not*.

21

Dead Goat Day

We set off late. Kabil's car broke down just outside Bishkek, we lost sight of Murat's car on the way and then stopped for petrol, which was much cheaper outside the city. Out of Bishkek we drove, along winding grey tracks with no other traffic visible and the mountains glowing in the distance, looking so close you could touch them, yellow cornfields and small stone houses dotting on the horizon. It was topped by the clearest, deepest blue sky.

About 50 kilometres further we came off the main road and drove to the edge of a field, from where we could see four men on horses having a tug-of-war with something rather goat-like. On seeing this, I realized the extent of my joy at seeing this game and it even made me alter my unfavourable thoughts on the city so far, for at least Bishkek had given me this opportunity.

The Alatau mountains ringed the huge meadow of bright green, and a small stream rolled down towards the road. Some of the surrounding fields were yellow, others a patchwork of different shades of green. We walked through the field towards the action, narrowly avoiding an oncoming horse, and I feasted my eyes. The four riders were galloping in a cluster, with two of them frenziedly stretching and pulling a medium-sized goat as they rode. A little more force and it would have been ripped apart.

Selima looked scared and we went to stand near the other spectators, who were unique in that most were mounted – a couple of hundred men and boys on their horses in a wide semi-circle watching the match, which was a practical system as when the action moved from one side of the field to the other, so did they.

There was also a large trailer on the back of a truck which served as the VIP gallery for about thirty people, sitting in slightly more comfort and sheltered from the overhead sun. Also loaded up in the trailer were cardboard boxes with the prizes to be handed out later.

Most of the spectators – especially the older ones – wore a *kalpak*, the traditional Kyrgyz hat, which is a vague triangular shape, made from white felt with black embroidery at the edges and a small black tassel at the bottom. Many wore long black coats and black boots, and their weatherbeaten leathery faces bore witness to years spent in fields sitting on horses.

Most ulak tartish in Kyrgyzstan, Kabil told us, has teams of four players. In Afghanistan, as in Baluchistan, the norm is for dozens of players to compete on an individual basis. Today, there were only two men on each team, and the action was extremely fast. There was one goal area at the end of the field nearest the spectators, marked rather casually with a couple of old sacks flung on the ground.

The spectators watched with mild enjoyment, trotting casually from side to side to follow the action. It was obviously a tremendous effort to lift the goat: its head had been removed, and the stump of the neck was tied up and stuffed with sand, the legs cut off around the knees, providing four stumps which acted as handles to pick it up from the ground.

With only two horses per team, each rider had to be fast and when his team-mate was in possession of the goat, either draped over the front of the saddle or held to the side, he had to ride alongside to prevent the opposition from snatching it. It was hardly like a rugby ball which can be passed between players until they are in the perfect position to score, and even flinging the goat on to the ground in the correct spot took effort and strength.

I was mesmerized during this match, especially pleased that after all my searching, my first experience of the game was in a rural setting like this – perhaps a little more authentic than the forthcoming matches in the Hippodrome.

Selima in the meantime was complaining about wearing the wrong clothes. She was in her best suit and high-heeled shoes, perfectly unsuitable for a long-grassed meadow in the hot sun with no shelter and nowhere to sit, which she blamed me for. 'But you knew it would be in a village and not as comfortable as a modern stadium,' I told her. 'But I have never been to a village before,' she moaned and asked when we were leaving. I said that, having waited several years for this opportunity, I intended to stay until it ended, but as Kabil and Murat were leaving very shortly, she could leave with them. Or she could stay with me.

She grew angry. 'These people here are dangerous! It is not safe for us to stay alone. They are drinking and we are miles from anywhere. They will probably rape or kidnap us.' Looking around at the spectators, it was difficult to imagine any of them over-powering two strong women, as most of the younger ones had been drinking and showed no interest in us, or were so old they could probably hardly get off their horses.

I advised her to return with the other two, assured her that I would find my way back to Bishkek, and tried to get closer to the goal area for the next game. This could be dangerous – the great advantage of being on a horse, I thought grimly, was that when the action got too close and fierce it was easy to trot away.

Two riders were practically falling out of their saddles, hanging off their horses trying to grab the goat off each other in a tug-of-war, each grasping a stump of a leg and pulling at it. Eventually the goat, which wouldn't give way, slipped out of both their hands and fell to the ground, immediately to become the target of another tussle between the other two riders. The referee, also on horseback, kept close to the action, mainly to judge whether the goal was valid or not.

The only sign of the goat's previous existence was a large patch of blood near the goal area, where it had been beheaded shortly before the games, which made me wonder what happened to its head and legs. Murat said that the goat is taken by the winning team at the end of the day, cooked and eaten at a big feast. At least it would be nicely tenderized.

Horses clashed with alarming regularity and it was amazing there were no injuries. Riders cared little for space and fragility and barged in front of their opponents to block them, or rammed into their horses to seize the goat. Most players chose to throw the goat in front of their saddle for greater control and if that wasn't possible, they held it to the side, just above the ground. This, of course, made it easier for your opponent to get it, although it was also easier for your team-mate to protect you by riding alongside.

During a break between games, I tried to lift the goat with one hand, the action which every player does countless times a game. This goat was quite small, weighing around 25 kilograms, but it was still hard to lift and the stump wasn't an easy handle to grip so I could appreciate even more their skill in doing it so effortlessly whilst riding.

Each game lasted 50 minutes and the winners were applauded enthusiastically. Emil captained his team to reach the final, and as he rode off the field his small son was up on the saddle in front of him, possibly being trained to follow in his father's hoof-steps. During the final, Selima again grumbled about not having taken a lift with Kabil and her feet were killing her.

Emil's team predictably won the final and he scored a hat-trick, and rode off to the applause and cheers of the spectators, who gathered around the winning team. They were presented with their prizes: television sets, teasets and kettles, which seemed remarkably pedestrian for such a wild, barbarous sport.

The next event was *at-chobish*, long-distance horse racing, which was held in the next field. Everyone walked over to the meadow, some people driving and parking their cars in the field above, and those on horseback trotted over. It was a huge field, with waist-high yellow corn with a track cut around the edge, around a kilometre in circumference.

At-chobish is another ancient sport, with the emphasis on longevity, races traditionally covering up to 30 kilometres – outside Central Asia it is uncommon to have races which are so long. These endurance races are apparently one of the most ancient and widespread types of competition and according to legend, epic heroes raced up to 100 kilometres. Very few of them could finish this and the winner was given great respect.

In a race held by Shabdan Jantai-bei in 1913, 172 horsemen participated in a 40-kilometre race along the bottom of a gorge. The winner broke the record with a time of 1.5 minutes per kilometre. These races are usually held during a holiday or commemorative feast, with the winner given jewellery and cattle as a reward, and usually the riders are young boys.

Soon it was time for the start of the first race, the youngest class, with boys looking as young as eight or nine who were to ride 10 kilometres, all bareback. At the starting line, forty horses had their riders wearing numbered bibs, their names and details announced one by one by a commentator.

The whistle blew and they began, each boy riding like a professional with perfect balance and poise; even more remarkable when considering that they rode bareback and used only simple reins to keep their balance. They circled the field, soon spreading out in a long line and at the end of each lap, the last few riders were eliminated so there were fewer riders as the race progressed.

I was amazed at the skill and confidence of these young boys but locals told me that this was to be expected, as children are still 'born on a horse' and know intuitively how to ride. The original purpose of this type of long-distance race was to test a horse for its strength and stamina, and a potential buyer would take it out over several miles to judge its skill. It was important in Central Asia that a horse should show ability in mountainous terrain as well as on the plains, and above all show great endurance. These tests were then converted into competitive sports.

When the first race ended and the prize was awarded to the delighted winning jockey, the next one began, which was over 35 kilometres. Most of these jockeys were village farmers, older and more experienced. While watching the races and the audience's appreciation of them, I found out what happened to the goat's head and legs. Circling the yellow field, calmly watching the races, were an old man and his son sitting together on a horse. Tied onto his horse with string was a goat's head and four legs, each secured with firm knots so that they hung in an even line slung over the horse's back. This man wasn't a player and I wondered why he earned the right to take the goat remains home, but hoped he would enjoy a good soup that night.

Independence Day was on Monday and the main attraction of the celebrations was the regional ulak tartish final. Two days before, I went to the Hippodrome, mainly to locate it and to see if there were any interesting preparations. This is the place where regular horse races (the more conventional kind) are held and is also the location of national parades, festivals and major ulak tartish matches. Inside the stadium, one side of which is a high concrete grandstand, a scattering of people were making repairs, alterations and sprucing it up for the year's biggest event.

I wandered around the outside by the offices and peered inside a couple of windows. In one room were four men sitting around a table eating. I went in. They looked up, astonished, and immediately invited me to sit with them.

It wasn't yet midday and they were quite clearly drunk, and as soon as I sat down they filled up their vodka glasses, plus one for me. Laughing and joking, they delved messy fingers into slices of watermelon and roast chicken. I had obviously found the right people as they were committee members of the stadium and organizers, so I asked them, in Turkish, for details of the ulak tartish. I was delighted to hear that as well as Monday's final, there were also the two semi-finals the next day.

One man took out his business card, sat thoughtfully for a while and then wrote, 'Augustos 30 31. Com in pliss', which I took to be my personal invitation. It was difficult getting any more information out of them because no one spoke English and they were all drunk. But they were good-natured and hospitable and it was useful to meet the committee people involved in the organization, in case of any trouble getting in.

The next morning I made my way to the Hippodrome, to arrive just after the first semi-final had begun. In contrast to the game a couple of days earlier in the field, this one was played in a proper marked playing area, approximately 300 metres long, and the two 'goal' areas at either end of the field were actually large rings resembling giant doughnuts, thick walls about five feet high encircling a pit in the centre.

This meant that it required effort not just to pick up the goat, take it to the other side, ward off four opposing riders and get it to the goal area, but also to hoist it high enough to drop it inside the goal.

As is the norm in these competitions, each team had four players and one of the semi-finalists was the Dordoi team with Emil. The small crowd cheered loudly for a goal or a fine tackle, the loudest fan being a woman who was nearly bent double with age, cackling and yelling with her mouth wide open and pointing at the men standing behind her.

The atmosphere was completely different from that of the village game; being in a conventional stadium lent it an element of ordinariness and the crowd were higher up which not only gave everyone a better view, but concentrated the cheers so it was much noisier. It also had the advantage that no one had to go trotting round on a horse for a better view. There was a commentator linked up to a microphone, who sat in the commentary box high up inside the grandstand.

Before the next semi-final began, there was an important task to fulfil which I was determined to witness, and having seen Dolly's demise at the oil-wrestling in Turkey, decided wouldn't be too difficult. Two young men led out a frisky goat, an announcement was made and the crowds fell silent. In the middle of the field, right by the central circle, with the two teams lined up behind it, the goat was held down and one of the men put a knife to the goat's throat and the prayers began.

The knife went through the neck, cutting through the jugular vein and a gushing stream of scarlet soaked into the grass. The head was finally cut off, with the goat giving a few kicks and then falling still. The crowd, watching intently, repeated the blessings which were part of this ritual slaughter, cupping their hands to their eyes then bringing them down their face and holding their palms up to the sky. Then, after the legs had been chopped off, the goat was removed to be brought back shortly afterwards with the neck sealed.

In spite of the fact that an animal had to die for this sport to take place, at no time did it seem a cruel or bloodthirsty waste of life to me. Perhaps it was because the goat was slaughtered in a painless way; perhaps because at no time did anyone glorify the death of the animal, rather they offered prayers for it. The goat was killed in the same manner as those which are eaten, which this would also be, the main difference being that between its death and being someone else's dinner it would also be pummelled around a field for an hour.

The following morning – Independence Day – I joined thousands of others in Al-Atau Square, which had two diametrically opposed icons. In the centre was a hulking statue of Lenin, which was due to be pulled down in the near future. Opposite that was a leather shop of an Italian designer, with handbags on sale for over $200 which made me wonder, when the average wages were around $20 a month, who on earth would be buying them.

The square was full and the streets leading to them were busy, with families dressed in their best clothes. There was a special stand for invited guests, with most of the people crammed behind a perimeter fence which went two sides around the square. There was also an awful lot of police control and restrictions.

In the streets running off from the square, I came across a game which had been described to me: *ordo*, a game a little like bowls except instead of a smooth, round spherical object, they played with the knee-bone of a sheep or goat, polished and smoothed. The basic objective is to throw your *alchik* (bone) as close to the opponent's alchik, and it has a number of variations and complications. It originates from long summer evenings in the mountains, using sheep bones left after a meal, for hours of family entertainment.

Here, it was a little more organized, with a large circle painted on the road. The circle was marked into sections, and in each one was an alchik weighing down a 20- (about 65p) or 50-som note. A player paid 5 som to throw his alchik and tried to hit those on the notes – a variation on the basic fairground game except the winner gets money instead of a goldfish.

In the main square, the ceremony began and was predictably military, with marches, bands and pompous displays. The forthcoming celebration in the stadium that afternoon was obviously going to be much more fun. By 1 pm the crowds were flocking there and it was a struggle to get through the gate, past people who were pushing to show their tickets.

The stand was nearly full, with most people dashing for the shady areas, and I headed out to the centre of the track reserved for media, officials and participants. There I met Askar Salymbekov, another member of the Federation of Traditional Sports and one of the main people involved in the Dordoi team.

'Come in, come into our tent!' and he invited me into the hospitality tent, which was a traditional yurt set out with a table, laden with food and tea, which circled around the interior. The players were preparing their horses for the final or just lying casually on the grass. One team wore the strangest head-gear: a kind of riding helmet of battered leather, with ridged padding fitting snugly over the entire head.

'These were from the Russian invasion of Afghanistan,' Mr Salymbekov told me. 'The men in tanks wore these, and now our boys are wearing them for another war, no?' He roared with laughter. I picked one up which was lying on the ground, tempted to put it on. But the young man who it belonged to shouted something and grabbed it from me. It turned out that for some reason, whether culturally, superstitiously or just fear, women aren't permitted to touch these helmets and I could have brought about bad luck on the whole team.

This time I watched the match from inside the perimeter wall, which at the start of the game looked to be a safe place. It gave me an 'on the ground' thrill, as the horses galloped close by me; I could feel the ground trembling and hear clearly the riders' shouts and the whistling and thwack of the whips; I could feel the skin of the goat being torn and stretched.

Clinging to the wall I was relatively safe in the knowledge that the horses couldn't trample me down, as they had to stop short of it. But my heart nearly stopped when I saw three horses pushed up against the wall in a furious struggle as the riders were tangled and fighting over the goat, being pulled three ways. They were trampling the ground, throwing clumps of grass and mud and even crushing down some small bushes, in the exact spot where I had put down my camera bag. After they had cantered back up the field again, I nervously edged my way to it, expecting to see my photographic equipment fragmented and crushed. To my huge relief the bag lay intact, about a metre away from the spot where they had been.

After the final of the ulak, I had my first opportunity to see three other horseback sports. First came the zany-sounding *kyz kumay*, 'kiss the girl'. Originally, this game was part of the wedding ritual, the participants being the bride, groom, sister-in-law and other friends. The bride would try to ride away from her soon-to-be husband, given a small lead and assisted by her sister-in-law, on the fastest horse. The groom would set out to chase her, having to catch her up in order to prove his love and his right to marry her. Being at a disadvantage meant he sometimes failed to catch her, but she never rejected him and the wedding continued and presumably they lived happily ever after.

The traditional game is still carried out especially in the green meadows of high-mountain pastures, and in more modern times on race-courses. Several pairs of players, each a man and a woman dressed in national costume, complete the game over a length of not more than 1000 metres. The woman has a lead of 20 metres and the man must chase her and then kiss her whilst galloping, or at least touch her with his head-dress.

Galloping back, the woman must chase him, and when she catches him she removes his head-dress, which is regarded as the sign of her victory. But if he fails to catch up with her within the allotted distance, she takes out a horse-whip and beats him. When I first heard about this game, I envisaged wild mountain games with the groom getting humiliated in front of the wedding guests and the bride beating him senseless, putting her mark of authority on their future life together.

What I saw was much more benign. Four pairs of riders went up to the starting line, all dressed in very elaborate Kyrgyz dress, the women painted and doll-like looking most unlike whip-wielding horsewomen. Women in Kyrgyzstan have always been extremely competent riders and girls learn to ride from a young age. In the highlands with severe winters, deep snow and for driving sheep up and down steep mountains or across turbulent rivers, a horse is a necessity and women play their full part in farming life. The popularity of women's participation in equestrian games like *kyz djurysh* and *kelin djurish* (both types of horse races) is growing and now included in many national competitions and celebrations.

Here, I got the impression that kyz kumay is seen more as a showpiece rather than a serious sport. The first horsewoman thundered down the track grinning, and hot on her trail was the young man, also in elaborate costume. Eventually he caught up with her, to the disappointment of the crowd – as most people wanted to see the whip. But the difficulty came when he had to kiss her with both of them on galloping horses, and she still trying to escape him.

Riding alongside her, he finally managed to kiss her cheek, which denoted victory for his team. The next pair also resulted in victory for the man's team, but the third woman managed to avoid her man and then on the return gallop, she took out her whip and hit him – though not too viciously.

Before the end of the afternoon, there were a couple of rounds of *oodarysh*, the horseback wrestling which seems to exist only in Central Asia. Two riders try to pull each other off their horses; it is also permitted to knock the horse over. According to the rules, there are four weight categories for competition and a wrestler must be at least nineteen years old to compete.

They wrestle bare-chested, and it is permitted to grab one's opponent's torso, arms or the sash round his waist, or even to press one's knee or feet against one's rival's horse. Overall victory comes with one wrestler throwing the other off his horse, or by gaining on a point system as judged by the referee.

Another sport which was demonstrated briefly was *tyin enmei*, which involves picking up coins from the ground while on horseback. It bears a slight similarity to nezabazi, in that it requires not only accuracy and steady riding, but the rider has to bend right down the side of his horse whilst on the gallop to achieve his objective, in this case to pick up coins.

The coins are placed in a line on the ground, usually on a small pile of sawdust or marked with coloured ribbon, about 50 metres apart. When the whistle goes, the rider must gallop along the line, bend down to pick up a coin and continue down the line to collect as many as possible on his first go. There is no fixed distance for the course, but there is usually a time limit, so he will return to the beginning within his time for a second attempt.

What these different horseback games acknowledge above all is the steadfast rapport that the Kyrgyz people still have with their horses, even though most people living in Bishkek have no day-to-day contact with them.

Sports writers maintain that these traditional sports have been a springboard for the success of Kyrgyz athletes in the international arena, especially in wrestling. As Pavel Luzanov wrote, 'The sports and games of our people have proved their right to exist. They give us not only athletic passion, strength and skill, but also a sense of victory over ourselves and an opportunity to touch history.'

The day's events were winding down to a close when I left the stadium and headed for the night bus to Tashkent. At last I had seen the wonderful game of ulak, and what's more, in two very different environments. It had been well worth the worries and difficulties of that mammoth overland journey.

22

Ram Searches in Tashkent

From Kyrgyzstan's Independence Day celebrations, I was on my way to Uzbekistan's Independence Day celebrations. Remembering Zak and his friends' description of ram fighting in Mustakillik Maydoni which had intrigued me and I was happy to undertake another long bus journey – and face possible problems because I didn't have an Uzbek visa – to see it and other traditional sports of Uzbekistan.

It seemed ludicrous that while acquiring a visa was expensive, bureaucratic and complicated, crossing borders was a doddle. The Turkmenistan-to-Kyrgyzstan journey had passed through no monitored international borders or controls of any sort, so perhaps I could get in and out of Tashkent for two days with the police none the wiser. There was, however, always the danger of being caught and shelling out vast sums of money in return for freedom. We skimmed out of Kyrgyzstan and into Uzbekistan without so much as a uniform on our bus checking anyone's ID. Just after the border at about 3 am, two money-changers got on the bus but at that hour, feeling groggy and unfamiliar with the currency, financial transactions seemed too risky. The Uzbek *sum* is a controlled currency so Uzbekistan is the only Central Asian country with a thriving black market, where the street rate is at least double the bank rate; but of course there is the threat of imprisonment if caught.

We entered Tashkent as the sun was rising. The bus station looked to be well-organized and clean with neat signs on each platform. I changed $10 with a group of taxi drivers hanging around, and left quickly before the police could fling me in jail for changing money illegally *and* being without a visa.

217

My first stop was most definitely breakfast. The walk to the main road passed through a market selling fruit, vegetables and cassettes, and a small arcade with several food stalls selling all sorts of tasty treats. This was far more promising than the food situation in Kyrgyzstan, and enough to cast the country in a favourable light. Being a public holiday, most of the tables were busy even at that early hour, with people tucking into hearty breakfasts. Old men sat alone drinking tea, some of them wearing the colourful *tapan*, resembling a brightly coloured, long, belted dressing-gown, and *doppe*, a black four-sided green skull-cap with white embroidery. The buzz of chatter and warmth was especially welcome after the cold silence of the Bishkek streets. I headed for the *plov* stall and bought a steaming plate of the staple food of the country – rice cooked with carrots, chickpeas and onions. A pot of green tea, a circle of flat bread and a small salad completed the feast after which I felt so devoted towards the Uzbek people I would probably have accepted nationality.

Tashkent is an easy city to get around, mainly due to the underground which I took to go north to Mustakillik Maydoni. It contained only a fraction of the passengers on the London Underground, the Hong Kong MTR or similar systems in major cities. It was clean, well sign-posted, in both Uzbek and Russian, with clear announcements at each station. The entire network, opened in 1978, contains only two lines and twenty-two stations.

The stations' decor is stunning: enormous chandeliers hanging from platform ceilings and the interior of each station in a different style and theme, usually decorated with mosaics, Russian-style reliefs and murals. The trains and stations were clean and graffiti-free.

I eventually found a hotel which didn't demand to see my visa (which all the state hotels would do) and began an unusual bargaining process conducted in Turkish (very similar to Uzbek) with the receptionist. The agreeable price of $4 (£2.50) came with the unusual condition that I had to check out at 7 am. 'Police are coming,' he said. 'Every morning at seven. Big problem for me if you are here. You must leave.'

If the police really did come every morning, it would be a big problem for all of us. Dumping my bags in the room I set off for Mustakillik Maydoni, quite close to the hotel.

Mustakillik Maydoni – Independence Square (formerly Lenin Square) – was where the celebrations of Uzbekistan's seventh year of independence were being held, and clearly most of the country's 23 million people were there. To say it was crowded was an understatement. Still, in the midst of the throng I caught a glimpse of a circus act, with a man performing skilful tricks on a tightrope. And there was a stage with a band performing a funky mix of Arabic and Western music which had the tightly-packed audience jiggling about. On the other side of the square, a large stadium was preparing for a military march and seats were starting to fill, most people putting the cushions on their heads to shield themselves from the sun. But I was still no nearer finding rams.

Ram fighting is a sport which seems peculiar to Central Asia, although there was evidence of it in rural India. I had seen TV footage of a wedding party in the ancient town of Khiva in northern Uzbekistan, where guests were treated to food, drink, traditional wrestling and finally ram fighting. Zak and his friends had assured me that there *was* ram fighting every year in this square, so I scoured every inch and enquired by miming a ram and asking for *koç gureş* (Turkish for 'ram wrestling') but people said no, not here. An ice-cream seller said I should try the Hippodrome where horse races took place, which was a logical suggestion as perhaps there were sporting events similar to Bishkek's the previous day. I made my way there but the Hippodrome was now just a market selling plastic kitchenware and nylon clothes and hadn't seen horse racing for years. Back to the Maydoni.

The afternoon afforded me nothing more than the opportunity to observe the Uzbek people, who were a much jollier lot than the Kyrgyz, more gregarious and chatty. However, it was a letdown that having been promised rams and come all this way, there were none to be found. The number of people swelled even more by the evening, and with little else for me to stay for, I walked back for food and my hotel. Tashkent struck me as a pleasant city, where it's possible to see evidence of Uzbek culture which hadn't been whitewashed by Russian. The Uzbeks were able to resist Russian influence more successfully than other Central Asian countries, and entered Independence still retaining most of their identity, cultural heritage and religion.

This was visible in the many mosques, traditional dress, architecture, teahouses and music. Where in Bishkek the most common sound in shops, bars, and buses was the soundtrack to *Titanic*, Tashkent had more Uzbek folk music and contemporary singers like Yildiz Usmanov, who sings haunting, stirring melodies in Uzbek based on traditional folk songs.

The hotel was deserted when I got back. I was awoken by a loud, continuous knocking on my door which made me remember the police. It was 6.30 am, so I took the sensible option and stayed in bed but the banging continued and someone was calling out, walking down the corridor to thump on every other door. I dozed and hoped that they would soon lose interest and go away.

My eye flew to the window to be struck with the alarming sight of a man climbing onto my balcony and peering in. He could only have got there by a precarious scramble from the balcony around the corner with a three-storey drop to contend with, and such a risky effort indicated that he was pretty keen.

'Bugger off!' I yelled to him, not worrying about translations. He didn't look particularly threatening, but peered in the window: 'Good morning!' he smiled – one of the hotel staff, demonstrating a most unusual wake-up call. He waved politely and disappeared, either over the edge or to the next room. This must have been his way of ensuring that everyone kept their 7 am check-out time, and it must have been him banging on every door.

I got up unhurriedly and checked out at exactly 7 o'clock. Leaving the hotel with me were women, children and old men trooping out with all their belongings, rather like refugees trudging out in a little line; I wondered if this was their daily procedure and if so, why not bribe the police to stay away?

I spent the day trying to track down ram fighting, even dog fighting which was reputed to be a major spectator sport here. Going on the good advice of the head of the British Council, I went down to Chorsu bazaar, rather than look for a national sports council or the Olympic Committee.

Chorsu is an enticing area of the city, the thriving old part of Tashkent with a crumbling but still existing old city and market. The bazaar is a farmers' market, one of seventeen in the city, selling everything from fresh produce to clothes, electrical goods and fabrics. The watermelon section alone is a square mile, and the quality, quantity and selection of fruits was astounding. For instance, grapes, now in season, came in every size, shape and colour from dusky pinks to dark green to purple; the size of huge golf-balls and bursting with sweetness.

A huge circular monstrosity in the centre acts as the 'indoor' market, with everything radiating from it. There was an area for fabrics, electrical goods, kitchenware, pirated cassettes, shoes and of course there is the ubiquitous food alleyway with a dozen small stalls cooking up and serving an unsurprising selection of plov and *shashlik*.

The area of my interest was at the edge of the bazaar. Two rows of cages were on the ground and beside each one stood a man who discussed the contents of the cage with passers-by. This was the live birds section, selling chickens, hens, roosters of all sizes, conditions and purposes.

Most chickens were being sold for food, judging by the plump housewives who picked them out, gave them an expert prod and squeeze, casting experienced eyes into their mouths. Most of the roosters were sold for fighting, the most obvious sign being the red combs on their head: if they looked ragged, torn and bitten away, then the rooster was a fighter. If it was in perfect shape and untouched, then it was yet to enter the ring (or the cooking pot).

These were the men 'in the know', the people who could inform me where and when was the best cockfighting in town. Beginning with a pretence at buying a rooster and asking basic questions about their fighting abilities, I soon had a group of sellers around me demonstrating which was the best rooster and which chicken would make the best soup. They passed on the information that every Saturday and Sunday was a major cockfight, near an out-of-town bazaar, beginning at 10 am. I would have to save it for my next visit.

Leaving Tashkent posed a problem, as I didn't have a visa or hotel registration so was illegally in the country. I had planned to register at the appropriate office the previous day, but it was closed for Independence Day. This wouldn't have been much of a problem, except that leaving Tashkent by bus meant getting a note of permission from the police booth, who required to see passport and papers.

An attempt to buy a ticket for the 7 pm bus to Bishkek was futile and the woman shrugged and told me to go to the police booth in the bus station, which would have got me in trouble as they would clearly have seen no entry stamp or registration. I asked a group of bus drivers if they would let me on without a ticket, explaining 'passport problem', which they understood perfectly. Giving me a knowing smile, they told me to get on the bus and pay the driver, which suited them because the money stayed in his pocket.

Twenty minutes before the bus departed, I hopped onto the bus and took a back seat just as a policeman got on and began checking everyone's papers. I hurriedly hopped off again, waited until he got off and as the bus was reversing out of the platform, the smiling driver beckoned me on and pointed to the back again. It was easy, but could have been nasty.

Bishkek had failed to make any favourable impression on me, and the days I was spending in the city (luckily out of the hotel and staying with a friend who was working there) were dragging. There were no more events to see after the first days, so I wasted some time trying to find something lively in the city.

The sole area of interest in the centre of Bishkek is the only shopping street, which is amazing not for its goods on sale, but for the fact that there are many people there. Near Victory Square is the nucleus of consumerism, of which the focal point was the TSUM department store, apparently drastically improved with its selection and quality of goods, with one floor even boasting an Italian man importing fake-fur coats selling for over £65 and wildly popular.

I went shopping with Selima one afternoon and I was tempted to have my fortune told by one of the many old women who set up on the pavement outside. We went first to Baba Lena, a Russian grandmother with white hair topped by a scarf, woolly socks and slippers and layers of warm clothes covering her plump frame.

She took out a deck of playing cards and said that yes, I was happily married with two children and everything was good and I would have a long life, and would I like to have a cup of tea with her? The next woman wasn't as charitable. Her method was with small grey pebbles, shaking them whilst holding my hand then scattering them on a flat piece of wood.

After giving me the usual good news, her face darkened. 'You have enemies. There is a woman who hates you and is going to try to harm you,' Selima translated for me. I treated it with cheerful cynicism, not believing for a minute that there was anyone out to 'ruin' me. 'If you pay a bit extra, I can put a curse on her and you will be all right,' the woman continued. When I told her that I wasn't interested in paying for any curses, she glared at me and packed up the pebbles, annoyed that she wouldn't get any more money out of me.

That afternoon in Bishkek I had to apply for my Iranian visa and I dressed in my headscarf and long skirt, essential just to enter an Iranian embassy, and brought my passport to an increasingly friendly Mr Abbas for our third meeting. He agreed to my request for a seven-day transit visa, costing $60 (roughly £38). 'Normally it takes three days to process, but if you wait ten minutes I will do it now.' And he went into his office, only to emerge a second later.

'Would you like a tourist visa? I will give you a ten-day tourist visa for $70.' Yes please, I said gratefully, wondering why he had changed his attitude. He came out with the appropriate visa stamped in and then asked, 'Would you like a job here? I think you are a clever woman. Will you teach English to our Iranian girls here?'

I told him thanks, but I really didn't want to live in Bishkek. 'But why? Are you married?' When I told him no, he got quite excited. 'Do you want to marry? I have a nice friend from Maashad. You could marry him for a couple of months or so.' And he laughed, so I was never really sure if he was serious or not. But I didn't really care, I now had the Iranian visa as well as an Uzbek visa, and could leave Bishkek and go to Uzbekistan legally.

23

Last Trip to Uzbekistan

The Chinese visa (for the transit trip to India) had taken five days; the Uzbek visa took ten days plus a letter of recommendation; the Iranian visa had taken one day: I should have gained a degree in Visa Studies. My current Kyrgyz visa couldn't be extended again, although I had serious doubts whether the first extension was actually legal, or whether they had a convenient way of getting money out of me. It was still impossible to confirm if I required a Kazakh transit visa in order to cross into China. So far I hadn't been stopped for an illegal or improper visa, and I didn't want to see a first time.

Holding a proper Uzbek visa meant that I could stay in a 'normal' hotel, a legal one which wouldn't turf me out at seven in the morning. Tashkent's Turon Hotel, close to my previous hotel of the 'Man on the Balcony' fame, was a real bargain and complete with the exceptionally unhomely feeling of a Russian hotel, though now state-owned.

I returned to the Chorsu bird-men, who greeted me warmly and produced a vast selection of birds for me to choose from and even a baby hedgehog, assuring me that for ten dollars, it would make a tasty meal. They confirmed a cockfight the next morning and gave me directions to the venue.

These directions led me to the edge of a field the following morning, which I entered passing a disused office, an old railway track, and to one side, I went down a steep track to a large shed. A car came screeching past and pulled up by the shed, which had many cars outside. (And, unlike at the cockfight in Pakistan, these were big, expensive cars.)

Now I could hear the unmistakable sounds of a cockfight: the occasional shout of encouragement, the crowing of cockerels awaiting their turn, flapping and squawking. This was it, so taking a deep breath and wondering what sort of blood-bath would await me, I stepped inside.

It was a large wooden shed with no walls but with a roof over a sawdust-covered floor. Men were sitting in a ring around the outside on wooden crates, boxes and the type of folding chairs you might see on an English lawn, all watching a cockfight in the middle. Several men clutched their roosters, preparing them, perhaps, for the next fight. Here, in contrast to Pakistan and Turkey, the owners definitely took a more 'hands-on' approach. During the fights they were in the ring right next to their birds, constantly blowing water on them, picking them up, replacing them, washing them again and smoothing down their feathers.

The men noticed me there and made polite, friendly gestures to sit with them, and I ended up sitting on a piece of cardboard with three men involved in some pretty heavy gambling.

The atmosphere was more relaxed than in Turkey, and friendlier than in Pakistan. Cockfighting here is a weekend affair, every Saturday and Sunday for several hours and of course all-male. The only other women present were selling cigarettes and sunflower seeds, all looking bored. Behind the fighting area was a small stone building with a kitchen where food was being cooked, and several long wooden tables where a constant stream of diners took a break from the action. Next to that was an old ceramic bath, containing dozens of bottles of soft drinks lying in cold water. I joined one group of men for tea and they insisted on opening the bottle of vodka in my honour, which I had to refuse. They were easy-going and quite unfazed by my presence, although interested in why I was there. I showed some of them the photograph of the camel wrestling (it was always in my notebook and a guaranteed way of breaking ice or engaging in conversation). Sure enough, they pointed, they laughed, showed it to their friends, some of them clearly puzzled at the logistics of how two camels could actually get into that position and many of them asked me how much money they would win. 'Nothing,' I replied, and tried to explain that it wasn't for the money but the enjoyment and the honour. They were most impressed with that, and chatted approvingly between themselves.

Back in the ring, two guys were trying to tempt me to go in with their friends for a major bet, which I agreed to do for a couple of dollars. But the fight dragged on for such a long time and as I find cockfighting boring the longer it goes on, I left before the end, having sampled typical Uzbek hospitality and watched them enjoy their typical weekend entertainment.

One of the men, Murat, asked me casually if I would be interested in seeing a dog fight. There was linguistic confusion at first, but by the manner in which he was bearing his teeth and making growling noises he was either suffering from a nasty disease or else miming a dog fight.

Murat invited me to join him the following morning – the venue another of those vague, no proper address, just a district by the sound of it from which it would be 'easy' to find the dog fight.

So, after getting hopelessly lost the next morning, asking people, snarling and growling in the hope they'd understand what I was looking for, a bus driver finally thought he knew what I was looking for. Three buses later I found myself in a very quiet suburb and so fed up with the whole venture that I was ready to get on the next bus back to town, when a man I had met at the cockfighting stepped out of one of the houses. He asked if I was looking for Murat and then gave a taxi driver strict instructions of where exactly to drop me off.

Judging by the venue where we eventually ended up, a deserted piece of land surrounded by a building site and a brand-new block of flats, it struck me that dog fighting couldn't be legal in this country. It was a most ungracious scrap of land, with a few trees around the edges, to which were tied up a few very ferocious dogs, different breeds but all large and bad-tempered. This confirmed it as the correct venue.

Murat arrived a while later, looking smug and a little smarter than he did the day before, in a well-cut jacket and trousers. He led out a large pit-bull called Rambo, who slobbered all over him. The opponent appeared and the two owners shook hands. I found a comfortable spot and sat on the grass. Over an hour went by and nothing happened, except that small clusters of men were talking enthusiastically about money. Judging by the amounts they were discussing, it seemed to be fairly high stakes. Most of the dogs were still tied to trees or trying to escape from their owners. But suddenly there was a lot of shouting and Murat's dog was in the pit, then its opponent appeared and they were pushed together.

If this was anything like the fights in Pakistan, I thought, then this would be a slow, gradual build-up ending with lots of blood and dismembered ears. But in a couple of minutes after the two dogs got on their haunches and into a clinch, there was a flurry of barking, snapping, half-hearted cheers from the spectators and then the owners stepped in, shook hands, and parted.

And that was it. All over in a couple of minutes. Such a performance and a build-up and attendance for a couple of minutes of a dog fight in which – to the untrained eye – it was unclear who the winner was. But a beaming Murat was having his back slapped and Rambo was getting patted, so it was clear who the winner was that morning. In the car, with Rambo stuffed in the boot, Murat told me that from that brief fight he had won $500.

Having failed to find ram fighting in Tashkent, I set off for Samarkand where, people in Tashkent told me, I would be more likely to find it. And of course, Samarkand is one of those places on every explorer's map to visit – its mere name evoking the spirit and romanticism of the Silk Road. But the most-visited destination in Central Asia seemed to me just another grey concrete sprawl. The city was nothing like the painting I had seen in the National Museum of Art in Tbilisi, which had an eighteenth-century oil painting of Samarkand depicting hazy yellow sunlight on camels and spice traders and a piercing blue Registan, where you could actually hear the noise of the bartering and activity.

Samarkand has enjoyed a colourful history being one of the oldest settlements in Central Asia, dating back to the fifth century BC. After it had been destroyed by Alexander the Great in 329 BC, the rebuilt city enjoyed a prosperous few centuries (even though under the thumb of a vast number of rulers – Arabs, Western Turks, Persian Samanids to name but a few) to be obliterated by Genghis Khan in 1221 and then revitalized, over a hundred years later, by Timur (Tamurlane), who made it his capital. Timur ravaged and plundered the riches of Iran, Iraq, Syria and Eastern Turkey which he poured into his new capital, Samarkand. There are larger-than-life statues of Timur in the city, the little that is left of his legacy. That, and of course the Registan, which is the main focus of tourism in the city.

But it was first and foremost rams I was after. I checked in to the Hotel Registan, in my guidebook described as 'truly awful' but, as one French tourist had said, cheap and friendly, and although one floor operates as a brothel, the other floors were actually quiet and safe.

So after taking a room, I headed to the place where I was most likely to find out about ram fighting. More than one person had said that the sport, a very old traditional game in many parts of Central Asia, was now no longer played in Tashkent but might be found on market days in Samarkand so the best place to try was the market in the Old Town. Finding information was a laborious procedure, but I eventually learned that it might just be possible to see ram fighting at the huge animal market held every Sunday on the outskirts of the city. Apart from that, cockfighting was a regular occurrence but no one quite knew where: I should return tomorrow and ask then.

For all that Samarkand is a famous historical site, the city became dead after dark at 7 pm. So it was back to my room where I drifted off to sleep early, turning a deaf ear to the noises coming from the working girls and their clients on the lower floors.

What woke me up several hours later certainly wasn't human, as the loud rustling and clattering came from inside the bucket under the sink. With a pounding heart, I guessed that the stale bread that I had thrown in it earlier had attracted the attention of a rodent, and judging by the amount of noise, it sounded like a very large one. A cold sweat made my body clammy and panic gripped me, as I realized that I couldn't get out of the door because that would mean putting my feet on the ground and the rat could bite my toes. The room was in complete darkness and I wondered just how I could get the thing out of my room without having to see it. I decided to frighten it away, and picked up whatever came to hand. Cassettes, batteries, books, all were thrown in its direction – and missed, but made a huge clatter; I reckoned that the guests on the lower floor must have thought I was having a better time than them.

I stood on the bed and then began to climb out of the window when I saw that it was a three-storey drop. I was trapped, powerless, at the mercy of a fierce rodent who had me in its clutches. The rattling had stopped; perhaps I had concussed it with a flying cassette, or perhaps it had finished all the stale bread and disappeared down a hole. Or perhaps it was waiting silently under the bed . . .

I passed the rest of the night hiding under the blankets, and at dawn I bypassed the prostitutes and the security guard who offered me a shower and checked out, determined that there really had to be something better. I did find something, a hotel on the edge of the peaceful Gorky Park.

Still determined on finding a ram fight, I spoke to the manager of a small souvenir shop close to the Registan, the only part of the city which caters to tourists. 'It used to be very common here,' he said, 'and every weekend in the market areas they organized it. People loved it. But a couple of years ago, the Mayor of Samarkand banned it. He was worried that if foreigners heard about it and it got on international TV, it would be bad publicity for the city.'

A further wild-goose chase in search of ram fighting – this time involving a fruitless trek to an out-of-town animal market and a ride on an enormous old motorbike with a drunken farmer and his massive chum to a ramless field – and I had had quite enough of Samarkand. I took a minibus to Tashkent, and from there a night bus to a chilly Bishkek.

24

The Long Road to Nowhere

It was a relief to leave Central Asia for a reason I couldn't define, except that the region had done little to inspire or entice me. Towards the end, I had been counting off the days till I reached India, a journey of several thousand miles and several days.

When I went to collect an Indian visa in Almaty, the officer informed me that Diwali was starting on 17 October and everything would be closed for four days. This meant I had to arrive in Delhi before then, in time to apply for a permit for Manipur – a north-eastern state of India, famous for its indigenous sports – or be stuck for four days until the festival ended. As Diwali was only eight days away I would have to hurry, as I also wanted to stop in Kashgar (sometimes called Kashi, in China's western Xinjiang) for two days to visit the famous Sunday Market.

When I left a gloomy Almaty bus station at 7 am for Ürümqi in China, taking the only practical route across-country and to passable borders, there were only seven other passengers in the bus – all young Chinese men – and it was a comfortable journey with plenty of room. A few hours later we stopped just before the Chinese border and used our remaining Kazakh som to buy big bunches of purple grapes from the roadside.

We crossed into China where in the immigration building an eager young officer practised his English on me, while other officers puzzled over my passport. Then the customs officer told me I couldn't take my grapes through, which they only saw because I had just washed them in the toilets.

'You are not allowed to take food or crops into China.'

'But where is the notice explaining that?' I asked, suspecting that he had made it up and he fancied them for his lunch. Chinese officialdom may be non-bribable but it is stubborn and the grapes were confiscated. (If they had looked in my bag they would have seen another kilo.)

One of the greatest joys of being in China was the food and at 5 pm, the bus stopped for dinner and I went with two Chinese passengers to a small simple restaurant. There I had the most enjoyable meal I'd ever eaten, my tastebuds reborn with the assault of garlic and chillies.

We travelled through the night to Ürümqi and arrived tired and groggy in the bus station, where I had to go and look for a bank to change money before returning to the bus station to buy a ticket for a bus leaving that evening for Kashgar.

The ticket queue was efficient and the woman at the counter was very polite. 'Are you a student here? Are you living in China? Then you must pay double-price for your ticket,' and she smiled sweetly. This is actually illegal in China, as foreigners' tickets were recently reverted to the same price as locals', but there was little point in arguing and I wanted to move quickly. I booked a sleeper-bus, double the price of a regular bus but ten times the comfort and half the time. Having endured a three-day bus journey to Kashgar in 1992 with every discomfort imaginable, I would rather eat broken glass than repeat the experience.

A sleeper-bus is a simple yet ingenious necessity in countries where long road journeys are common. The one I boarded was the same size as a regular coach but instead of seats there were three lines of bunks, an upper and lower level with four in each line, making a total of twenty-four beds, all with clean pillows and duvets.

I had asked for an upper sleeper by the front window, but the ticket seller never warned me that this bunk was so close to the ceiling it was impossible to sit up. Seeing this, I asked the driver to move me to another, empty one, but he laughed and told everyone on the bus how funny it was that the stupid foreigner had got the duff seat. Then he continued to sell tickets to other people and still refused to change my seat. It was impossible to stay there for thirty-six hours, with my nose two inches under the ceiling and unable even to turn. I survived until the morning and jumped into the first empty sleeper available.

We drove through the moon-like landscape of the Taklimakan

desert with its great grey rock formations, hostile and empty, and reached Kashgar on time, Saturday morning at 10 o'clock. I loaded my bags into a cycle cart (the sort only used for transporting goods) to take me to a hotel.

As we trundled along Renmin Xi Lu I saw that Kashgar was becoming like any other Chinese city, the most obvious change since 1992 being a new statue of Mao. It was ironic that while Bishkek was organizing the imminent removal of Lenin's statue from Ala-Too Square, China was bringing Mao to the very un-Chinese Uygur people.

The ethnic majority in Kashgar, and Xinjiang province of northern China (once called Chinese Turkistan) are Uygur Muslims, with a language said to be the original Turkish. But their occasional flair-ups with the Chinese authorities in their wish for independence, provoked the government into sending increasing numbers of Han Chinese to the area to quash the indigenous Muslim population. Kashgar's population totals over 300,000 of which 75 per cent are Muslim, a percentage fast diminishing.

Other obvious changes in this thriving old market town included the recent demolishing of most of the original town walls, destroying much of the essence of its historical atmosphere. I remembered it as a place with unique character and unlike the rest of the country but now shiny new skyscrapers reminiscent of Hong Kong, hotels and department stores have replaced many of the small shops. There was more traffic, more expensive cars replacing the small donkey carts which used to transport people and goods to and from the bazaars.

I checked into the Seman Hotel, of which the old block is the remains of the old Russian Embassy from the Great Game era, and went in search of food. In spite of the smart new department stores, the old town of Kashgar had retained much of its character and the Id Kah mosque and the bazaar were spiritually a huge distance from Mao's looming statue. From the wooden balcony of an old teahouse I could sit and watch the market below. Below me was part of the daily bazaar, narrow dusty lanes with small Uygur shops opening their wooden shutters to the street. Each street specialized in one product, and here were shoes and hats, men sitting at the back of darkened shops bent over sewing machines and raucous young boys scampering about with plates of tea.

Next to me sat two old Uygur men, small woollen hats pulled firmly over their heads, talking, watching, drinking tea from small, chipped bowls and bringing out stale bread – shaped a bit like a bagel – from their coat pockets which they dipped into their tea. They offered me some bread and their faces creased up with warm smiles as we 'salaamed' each other.

The next day was the Sunday Market, the one I'd been eagerly awaiting and the largest and most famous in Asia, where the population of Kashgar swells as people come from the surrounding regions to trade. From early morning, all available donkey carts transport people and goods to the market, an area of a few square kilometres in the east of town. For hours, the streets are full of buses, bikes, horse-driven carts, vans and motorbikes.

The market is divided into areas specializing in certain products, mainly livestock, fruit and vegetables, old clothes, tools, kitchenware, machinery, fabrics, shoes and boots. The crowds were dense, often impermeable as men and women, their animals, their cart-load of goods and children, scoured the streets for things to buy. There were traders on every scale, from major farming groups selling livestock and great quantities of goods, to the old men trailing a couple of sorry-looking sheep down to the animal bazaar.

The area with most activity was the one selling livestock, an enormous field divided into sections for each animal, filled with horses, goats, sheep, cows and donkeys. In one, horses were being 'test-ridden' with rather alarming enthusiasm, men leaping on their backs and galloping full tilt, suddenly stopping just short of a crowd of people.

The sheep-trading area was the largest, each farmer with his sheep in a double line, their heads tied together meeting in the middle, while the outside had two rows of woolly bottoms. They were a mixture of black and white, and the arrangement of colour, perspective and composition could not have been more perfectly choreographed by a designer. A shearer was doing an en-masse haircut, moving slowly along the line with electric cutters before they were sold.

The goats were arranged in a similar fashion, their small horns clattering in the middle where their heads met, looking unconcerned and standing patiently without so much as a bleat. The bulls in another corner were more boisterous, their owners trying to grab their ropes to control them.

The crowds thinned as the midday sun grew stronger, loading

up their purchases on wooden carts pulled by horse or donkey and trotting back home. On the main street, lined with pencil-slim trees, two flash young Chinese men in city clothes and with mobile phones handed out flyers written in Chinese and Uygur, attracting great interest. Every passing men took one, read it aloud laughing, told their friends and took another few. The two Chinese were embarrassed when surrounded by a dozen young chortling men.

That evening, I asked the man in the local noodle shop to translate it. '*Qiangjingbao Koufuye*', he read and looked awkward. 'It's, um, well it's for men to, um, well you know – to do it better, um . . .' 'Ah, do you mean it's like Viagra?' He looked relieved at not having to explain further. 'That's it!' he declared triumphantly. 'It is Chinese Viagra!'

The next morning I left for Sust, the tiny Pakistani border town over the Karakoram Highway. Also boarding the bus were a mixture of young Pakistani small-time traders, returning from their monthly trip to the market; and backpackers from Australia, America and Japan, most of whom had just returned from Mongolia where they had indulged in (what I considered to be) living hell – trekking and camping for six weeks in freezing tents with lousy food and no hot water.

After many delays we left Kashgar, winding our way slowly uphill through Upal, Ghez, Bulun Kul, and past Kara Kul Lake close to many Kyrgyz summer villages, along the Karakoram Highway.

The Highway emerged after a thaw in the frosty relations between Pakistan and China in 1966, leading to an agreement to build a two-lane highway from Kashgar to Havelian in Pakistan. The Pakistani side was completed in 1980 and formally inaugurated, which opened the Northern Areas to tourism. In 1986 the entire route to Kashgar was open to tourism, and the entire 1300-kilometre road paved by 1989. A mammoth feat of engineering, undoubtedly, given that the terrain passes through four major mountain ranges. Such an environment gives the route astounding natural beauty, rising up through jagged peaks of the Pamir, lush green valleys and the icy glaciers.

Several hours later after a customs check, we reached the highest point of the range at an altitude of 4,500 metres, and everyone trooped out of the bus; it was sunny but very cold and with a low oxygen level, so that it was difficult to walk quickly without getting out of breath. Soon afterwards we came to the first Pakistani check-point, with a warm welcome from the beaming guard who boarded the bus and shook the hands of his compatriots, greeting them like long-lost brothers.

At 4 pm we arrived in Sust, the first proper town, and here we were officially 'cleared' into Pakistan. 'Welcome, welcome,' said the smiling Chief Immigration Officer, a dignified grey-haired man looking remarkably English with his waistcoat and cravat. He lounged in an armchair in his office next to the customs yard, stamping our passports, unconcerned about the contents of anyone's baggage.

I left immediately on a minibus going to Gilgit, disappointed that as the sun had set, the route, possibly the most picturesque in the world, was plunged into darkness. We arrived five hours later and I spent the night at a hotel and then left early in the morning for the long journey to Rawalpindi, pulling into Pir Wadhai bus station after midnight. I jumped onto a slow, uncomfortable passenger bus just leaving for Lahore and was in Lahore the next morning.

Once over the border into India, a taxi to Amritsar railway station brought me with minutes to spare to a fast train to Delhi, where I collapsed into my first-class, air-conditioned seat. I bought four newspapers, a bowl of *channah masalah* and cup of chai from the platform, ate with my filthy fingers and felt happy, delighted to hear again the sweet music of noise and activity at an Indian railway station.

25

Straight as an Arrow

The next morning I left my hotel in the run-down area of Paharganj for the prosperous Channakapuri in south Delhi, home to most embassies and also Manipur Bhawan, Manipur state's representative in the capital. I had gone to the Bhawan in May to enquire about visiting Manipur which sounds simple, but reveals a process which brings out the best in Indian bureaucracy.

Officially, you apply for the permit at Manipur Bhawan, who sends a copy to the Home Department, who take 'about a week' to decide, then inform the Bhawan, who then informs you, and you get your permit from the Home Ministry. So, the kind Mr Vashist said, fill out the form twice and bring one to the Ministry of Home Affairs. But because they only give a permit to groups of four or more, I needed an invitation from the Manipur government. Luckily Mr Haokip, an ex-MLA (local politician) who was in the office, agreed to fax an invitation when he returned to Imphal.

'This may take weeks,' warned Mr Vashist, 'and maybe they don't give permission. But anyhow,' he shrugged, 'you can try. Then, you can telephone from another place and we can fax the permit wherever you are. You don't have to return to Delhi.' He said I could enter by road, which was useful as – if the permit was confirmed – it meant I could visit Shillong, in Meghalaya, on the way, as well as Assam and Sikkim.

The north-east region spreads like fingers from the main body of India, into a narrow strip wrapping around Bangladesh and then unfolding further east. The seven states of Assam, Manipur,

236

Meghalaya, Mizoram, Nagaland, Sikkim and Tripura are practically ignored by the outside world, meriting only a couple of pages in most guidebooks. Most of the states have been unstable for years with frequent insurgency and tribal wars, therefore unsafe to visit. Some have recently been opened to visitors but others – like Nagaland – are closed even to people from the rest of India. There are many reasons and theories as to why this is so. Perhaps the government does have a genuine concern for people's safety (the official reason); but some accuse it of being reluctant to allow the area to gain from tourism, financially and culturally, or of not wanting visitors to learn about their tribal life. The main concern is its geographical proximity to Burma, Bhutan, China, Bangladesh and Tibet. Ironically, the leaders of these states want them to be more accessible and open to visitors.

In the north-eastern states there are hundreds of different languages and dialects and the people have more in common – in looks, lifestyle and ethnic make-up – with the hill-tribes of Burma and Thailand, than they do with the rest of India. By the mid-1980s, widespread strikes and riots brought chaos to the area, developing into violence and terrorism, and the area was off-limits to outsiders. The people were angry about Central Government's lack of interest and support, with little being spent on transport links and infrastructure.

Two weeks away on 1 November was the Kut Festival in Manipur, one of the most important festivals of the year and, according to information, an occasion to witness some of their sporting events. Naturally, I was keen to get there in time for it so, with my Manipur permit submitted, I regretfully decided to forgo Diwali in Delhi (having only seen it celebrated in Bradford, where candles and lights are strung through the city's streets, as joyous an occasion as Christmas with less materialism) and take a train that night to Guwahati, Assam's largest city. I bought a ticket for the Assam mail train, scheduled to take an astounding forty hours to reach Guwahati.

Raj sat opposite me in the three-tier, air-con carriage; an arrogant young man from Delhi, he was on his way to an interview in Guwahati for a managerial position on a tea estate, one of many in Assam. A well-educated and privileged MBA, he was now looking for a better job. I asked him why he wanted to move from the country's capital to a less-developed region.

'It's too difficult to save money in Delhi. You can earn lots, but end up spending it. My friends go out every night to expensive pubs and discos, everyone has mobile phones and designer jeans. TV is so commercial now, all the advertising makes it so easy to spend. At least in the north-east I could have a more simple lifestyle and save money.'

I had witnessed, over the last seven years of visiting, a marked increase in available goods and a drastic change in attitudes of the young consumer, with a development of a pub-culture in major cities catering for young, wealthy fashion-conscious people. Desire for designer labels was increasing, fashions from America and Europe were more available, women's skirts were getting shorter and they were marrying much later. Hindi pop was booming, and people had a renewed pride in the country which could offer them more opportunities.

But as Raj explained, consumerism provides its own downswing with growing pressure from peers and TV alike. His solution was the reverse of that of most young people from the outer states, who are lured by the opportunities of the country's big cities like Delhi and Bombay.

Our immediate concern on that journey was, however, one of survival: a Patna-bound train which left Delhi just one hour before ours had overturned on the track just in front of us. Rumours spread that over 200 were killed. There was a long delay while they cleared the tracks (during which time the air-conditioning would not work because we were stationary), which we couldn't complain about too much knowing too well that it could so easily have been us.

It was eight hours before we moved and fell further and further behind schedule. Nearly two full days into our journey, we left West Bengal and entered Assam at 9 pm. 'Now we will be even slower,' said a cheerful young man from Shillong next to Raj. 'This is a very dangerous area. Terrorists in Assam have tried to blow up trains on this line, so we go slow and the driver can search the tracks for bombs. And there are dacoits. Last time I came on this train, it was exactly here that three men with guns jumped on the carriage next to mine and robbed everyone. They tried to shoot at some passengers, killed two and then escaped.'

The train slowed to a crawl and took five hours to complete the last hundred kilometres. In that time, torrential rain slashed at the window and we pulled into a sodden Guwahati station at 3 am after a 52-hour journey, twelve hours late and still in a downpour.

But you're never far from a hotel in India and a walk from the station across the road, through several inches of water took me to a room, and soon I was dry and asleep.

While making some initial enquiries, I met an old sports journalist who confirmed what I had suspected. 'It's true yes, that in this part of India there are many indigenous games which reflect the ethnic make-up of our people. But in Assam?' He shook his head. 'You know, you should really go to Manipur – they have unique games there. And have you seen the archery in Shillong?'

Following his, and others' advice, I left Assam and took the bus to Shillong, state capital of adjacent Meghalaya and an attractive hill station. This state, once part of Assam, was created in 1971 and is home to three main tribes – the Khasi, Jantia and Garo people.

As with most hill stations in the subcontinent, its appearance is very twee with English-styled cottages and gardens, though the town centre is terribly congested. There is a large market, many restaurants and hotels catering for Indian tourists making an escape from the uncomfortable heat of the plains.

The next morning, after a good sleep in the Pine Borough Hotel, I began my search for the famous archery. 'Four o'clock at the polo ground,' they told me, same time and place every day.

The polo ground was a mile away from the town centre, a field laid out in two halves. Near the entrance were five wooden shacks for refreshments, then dozens of smaller stalls for betting. At the other end was the playing area.

The first round of arrows was at 4 pm, and the field filled up with men, mainly to eat and drink. Next to the tea-stalls were two semi-circles of betting stalls, small wooden booths with a table and a couple of chairs. How anyone could have a flutter on the arrows was a mystery, and I intended to learn how. At each desk sat a man writing minuscule squiggles in an old exercise book, then tearing out tiny scraps of paper and handing them over to the punters. I asked an old bookie, who was filling out chits, how it worked. He patiently took out his pen and notebook, slurped his tea, spat out his *paan* and began a very confusing but fascinating account of the system.

'Over one hundred archers will shoot from there,' he nodded over to the other side of the field which was still empty. 'They aim for a large target, each man shooting twenty or thirty arrows. The punter must guess how many arrows will hit the target. They only bet on the last one, or two digits of that total. For example,' and like a maths teacher he jotted down some numbers, 'the total arrows which land on the target might be 456. But the punter bets only on the last digits, so he may have put 10 rupees on 6, so he will win 80 rupees. If he put 10 rupees on 56, then he wins 800.'

The first round pays a dividend of 80 rupees and the second 60 rupees. By predicting correctly the two digits in both rounds the punter stands to win 4444 rupees, for a 1-rupee stake.

Ready to gamble, my mind came up with the number 78 and I gave the man 10 rupees. Then I changed my mind and decided on one rupee on all the 'eights', thereby lessening the risk. He smiled at my caution. 'It doesn't do well to bet too much money. Little, little, is better. I have seen too many people losing all their money every day.' That was believable, knowing the ferocity of Indians' enthusiasm for gambling.

He tore a minute scrap of paper from his exercise book, and scribbled illegible marks which sufficed as my betting slip. 'But how do you recognize your receipt?' I asked, as all bookies have the same system. He smiled and then pointed to one of the squiggles. 'That's my signature.'

Fifteen minutes before kick-off the archers emerged from the tea-shacks and squatted on the grass, stringing their bows and chatting away, constantly munching on paan. The bows were very simple, made from a single piece of bamboo which bent into an arc as they attached the string, made from nettle fibres, across to the other end. The archers all wore very old, torn clothes which had been sewn and resewn and a chequered blanket over their shoulders tied under the chin. The bright reds and blues of the blankets were the only colours in the damp, dark green scene.

As 4 pm approached, they arranged themselves, squatting, in a large quarter-circle facing the target. The target was a large bamboo cylinder, roughly two feet by one, attached to a post in the ground so it was about three feet off the ground. Each man loaded one arrow, with a pile of arrows beside him on the grass. They were poised for the start and there was silence.

Exactly on time, a man called out a command and a section of fifteen archers began to shoot, the arrows flying through the air thick and fast in a steady stream. Each man shot continuously, experienced hands loading up another arrow as soon as one had gone. The target was becoming thick with successful arrows, while those that missed skimmed along the ground and into the muddy bank behind it. After a couple of minutes, the announcer called out another sharp command, the signal for those archers to stop and another group to begin. This continued for several minutes until everyone had shot.

As soon as the whistle blew, everyone stopped. Several officials came forward to take out the arrows from the bamboo and then take them to the members of the archery committee who stood at the front, the rest of the participants and punters behind a line.

The successful arrows were placed in a pile and spectators attempted the impossible task of trying to count them, in a line of fifteen men. A bunch of ten arrows were counted by the first man, who passed them down the line to be recounted by everyone else. Finally, an old man squatting on the ground at the end, jammed the bunch of ten into a metal rack, with holes arranged ten-by-ten on the ground.

Then the next group of ten were counted up, and so it continued until the pile came to an end, the crowd murmuring loudly, trying to anticipate the final number. The tens were all in the grid, and the odd ones left would be the most crucial factor, as the final digit in the total was the difference between winning and losing. The bunches of ten were counted and called out and it was written on a small slate on the wall. The number was 370.

The last few were handed over to a tall, regal man full of the importance of his task. Everyone's eyes were on him in the silence. He took the first arrow and threw it in front of him. '*Wei*!' Then the next. '*Ar*!' And he continued, throwing each in an arc in front of him. The tension was growing. '*Lai*! *Saw*! *San*! *Hynriew*! *Hynniew*!' And then the final one, which he announced with great solemnity. '*Phra*!'

The last number was eight, bringing the total to 78, and I was instantly annoyed that I had changed my bet after originally decided on 78. The punters shuffled around, the winners to the bookies' desks with their betting slips to claim their winnings. I returned to the old man who smiled. 'You are very lucky, eh? Beginners' luck maybe? Nearly you won 800 rupees, but you changed.' He cackled as he took my slip of paper, and gave me 80 rupees. Full of confidence at my intuition, I placed the lot on 'ending six'.

After a half-hour break the second round began and spectators, archers, officials and bookies returned to the field as the light faded and dark clouds loomed. They re-grouped, with a different archery club and a bigger target. The same routine began at 4.30, after the official announced the start and instructed which groups to shoot. The elaborate and formal counting procedure was repeated, and three arrows were thrown into the ground. More muttering and mumbling as losers cursed their bad luck and winners gave small smiles of victory as they collected their earnings. I, of course, lost the lot.

Archery has a longstanding connection with the culture of the Khasi tribe, and only in recent years has it evolved into a gambling pastime. For many societies the bow and arrow represent the most primitive of weapons, but to the Khasis they are part of their lives. For them, the arrow is a symbol of person's lifelong companion: shortly after the birth of a boy, three arrows and a bow are used during the naming ceremony. The first is seen as a guard for the boy, the second to protect the family, and the third to protect the territorial rights and integrity.

Three silver arrows in a quiver adorn the ceremonial dress of the male during the Thanksgiving Dance (*Shad Suk Mynsiem*), representing the blessings of God the Creator, the first ancestor and first ancestress. When a Khasi dies, three arrows are shot into the sky after the funeral pyre is lit, to guard the soul on its last journey to the Creator.

But the fourth arrow is associated with *Rong Biria*, or the game of archery. The most important rule in Rong Biria is fair play, for it is overseen not just by a referee but by a spiritual judge – the Lord Creator known as Ka Mei Hukkum. In a contest it isn't just the skill and accuracy of the shooter at stake, but the spiritual strength of the competitor or team. They must pray to the Creator, putting forward their arguments for winning and the more convincing the argument, the better chance they have. It's believed that these prayers also deflect the opponent's arrow from the target, and this belief gives the archer confidence. Enshrined in the heart of all archers are the guiding spirits, the tenets of fraternity, equality and justice.

With such a noble and spiritual history, archery has been turned into a betting game. As one journalist wrote, in an injured tone:

The game of archery has entered an era of commercialization, whereby it has been left bereft of its pristine charm.

Though the link with the past is sought to be maintained, the real taste of the game has become a thing of the past. The quest for earning wealth the easy way is symptomatic of our modern cultural ethos and we are sinking more and more into this unending abyss.

(These sentiments could be applied to most modern sports, including the very upholder of sporting values, the esteemed International Olympic Committee.)

Over several cups of tea in Shillong's oldest Chinese restaurant, Mr Laloo, the secretary of the Khasi Hills Archery Association, explained how it developed into a gambling phenomenon. 'We have gambled on archery for nearly fifty years. When we were part of Assam, the state government banned it in the late 1960s. We became an independent state in 1972 and the Meghalaya government legalized it ten years later, because people were still gambling illegally and we were still shooting every day. The government was sensible and realized the financial benefits in revenue, as well as creating over a thousand jobs.'

Every afternoon I spent down at the field, I saw only men participating, working and watching, except for a handful of women making tea. Typical of India, one would think, where the men have all the fun while the women work in the kitchen. But the Khasi people are actually one of the few tribes in the subcontinent which have a matrilineal society, so the women actually hold the purse strings.

The youngest daughter, the *khaduh*, inherits the family wealth and her responsibilities include taking care of the family and ensuring that grandparents and any poor relatives are looked after. And, quite unlike orthodox Indian society, when the khaduh marries, she controls her husband's wealth. Traditionally, she took charge of burying relatives and other religious duties but the advent of Christianity in many parts of the north-east (thanks to the mainly British missionary invasion), made many of her tasks obsolete, especially religious ones. Modernization in general means that fewer families now follow such traditions so faithfully. In recent years, small but vociferous groups of Khasi men have campaigned against the rules of their tribe, claiming that they shouldn't be losing control of the family's wealth. Many women, they declare, aren't worthy or capable of taking charge and the

Khasi social customs of lineage have been misused for their personal interests, which jeopardized the socio-cultural life of their tribe.

Or perhaps, as many cynics would agree, the men aren't happy with the women having a legal right to the family's wealth. The main pressure group, the Syngkhong Rympei Thymmai (SRT) argue that by allowing the matrilineal system to continue, the whole Khasi population is in 'danger of being diluted out by the offspring of non-Khasi fathers'. The male has no status in either his wife's or his mother's home, they bleat, and even his children don't 'belong' to him as they take the mother's clan name. A refreshing change, I thought.

The following Sunday I went with Mr Laloo to an archery festival in the rather run-down village of Mawjrong. I recognized many well-known characters from Shillong and some had already begun drinking. This village festival was an annual event, always on the same date, except no one knew the reason behind it.

It was raining when we arrived in the large field at the back of the village (we were not far from the former and the current wettest place on earth, respectively Cherapunjee, with an annual rainfall of 450 inches a year, and Mawsynram with 468 inches).

As late morning drizzled on, men started to straggle in for the competition. Over a hundred archers began the first round, all wearing their blankets tucked beneath their chin and looking intent. There was greater interest and tension today because there was a financial incentive. (In Shillong, the archers from the clubs receive a 'donation' every six months, made up from money collected every day from the bookies. The stewards get a fixed fee of 60 rupees a day.) Two teams were put together to shoot at the same target, so there were four contests going on simultaneously with the winners of each pairing up for the next round.

As the archers took aim, some muttered and mumbled under their breath, trying to convince the Creator that they deserved victory more than their opponents. Each man shot five arrows, with his team's arrows clearly marked. Between rounds, they regrouped with their friends and sat in the drizzle on the damp grass, chewing, smoking and looking quite bored. It wasn't the atmosphere I would have expected at a village festival, although Mr Laloo said that the real celebrations began at night. 'Then they start drinking and dancing, until the morning. Of course, none of the women will come.' So much for being in control.

During the final, the two remaining teams competing for a first prize of 8000 rupees, the rain still plopped onto blanket-covered figures squatting on the grass. After each team had shot separately, the successful arrows were counted up, the winning team announced and the prizes distributed with very little ceremony.

Then was the contest for the pairs, using the same target and all shooting simultaneously. It was down to a truck driver called Elas, a large robust man, and his diminutive senior partner Skin, who was a steward from Shillong. When they entered the final round, a shoot-off against another pair, both muttered their prayers. Whether this was to give themselves luck or to send their opponents' arrows astray, it worked and they accepted their first prize of 3000 rupees.

The final event was the mini-target for which archers entered individually, paying 5 rupees for every arrow they shot. The target was tiny – a four-by-one-inch cylinder mounted on a stick and standing three feet off the ground. It took great accuracy to hit it, with only about 10 per cent of arrows successful. When everyone finished, the referee retrieved the arrows from the target and calculated who had the most. Star of the day was definitely Elas who won that also, and he pocketed another few thousand rupees and immediately left in his truck before the real party began.

But the day lacked the vibrant atmosphere of other festivals I had attended in other parts of India where, whether religious, sporting or just for the hell of it, there was always a great spirit of merriment, music blasting out and the smell of a hundred types of snack filling the air. I was happy to accept a lift from the Archery Committee, who dropped me off at the bus stand in Shillong, just in time to catch the last bus back to Guwahati.

The next morning I phoned Mr Vashist back at Manipur Bhawan in Delhi, who had tried his best but with little success. 'We never received the fax from Mr Haokip. Without that there is little chance of the Home Department giving permission.' I telephoned Mr Haokip in Imphal and he told me that the fax machine had been broken and he would send a letter immediately with an invitation, but it would probably be too late. The whole procedure of getting to Manipur seemed remarkably ad-hoc, with different information depending on who you asked. I tested it out by asking the officer in Manipur Bhawan in Guwahati if I could turn up in Manipur without a permit.

'They would send you back from the airport,' he said emphatically. 'They would put you on the next plane out.'

'But I want to enter by road,' I told him.

'Impossible. There is no proper road to Imphal. It is too dangerous and they will not allow you. Your permit only allows you to enter by air.' Which was annoying as domestic flying was expensive, inefficient and not as much fun as by road, besides which, Mr Vashist had already assured me that I could.

I decided to go first to Gangtok, Sikkim's state capital, and if the Manipur permit didn't materialize in the next few days, I would just have to miss seeing games of rugby with coconuts and wrestling with hockey-sticks, and go down to Kerala. With those options in mind, I took the train to New Jalpaiguri in West Bengal, to begin the journey to Sikkim.

26

Sympathy for the Onions

This was my second time in New Jalpaiguri and I still found it dirty, unfriendly and unattractive. The adjacent town of Siliguri is a giant transport hub, a jammed crossroads for trucks and heavy vehicles. Not prepared to hang about, I came off the train and went straight to Siliguri bus station, where I planned to catch a bus to Gangtok, having first obtained a permit for Sikkim at the bus station – the procedure for this permit being infinitely easier than getting one for Manipur. Visitors to Sikkim are strictly controlled and allowed only two weeks in the state, with every move recorded. Such caution is provoked by its bordering Tibet, Bhutan and Nepal, and perhaps the presumption that foreign spies still infiltrate. But these restrictions have benefits and combined with its remote geographical location, mean a very small quantity of tourists.

I wanted to spend a few days in Gangtok to see their archery, having heard about village tournaments held when the farming season is at a low. They contrast sharply with the Shillong version, gambling playing no part in Sikkim's, while the sport has a noble presence in their culture and daily life.

It should have been simple to get the permit and straight on a bus to Gangtok. But these plans were dashed when the cycle rickshaw brought me from the train station to Siliguri bus stand. Instead of congested traffic and scrums of passengers there was a deathly hush in the station. Then, someone said the fateful word which strikes despair into the hearts of everyone in India. '*Bund.*'

A bund is a strike, a shut-down which can affect anything but generally transport. It usually lasts one day but always the day you need to travel. In this case, the strike had been called by the ruling party in West Bengal, the Communist Party of India (Marxist), protesting against the drastic rise in prices of basic commodities, particularly vegetables. A combination of poor harvest, bad politics, inept exporting and inane government policy had pushed the price of onions and tomatoes up ten-fold, causing havoc around the country. The CPI were stopping all traffic throughout West Bengal, with the threat of violence if anyone tried to break through a blockade. All public and private transport was banned and there was no other way of getting to Gangtok.

The staff in the bus station said that services would recommence at 6 pm. It was now 9 am, and staying in Siliguri until the evening, or staying overnight and leaving the following morning, were options less desirable than having my arm sawn off. I was prepared to cross the picket line to leave town.

I ended up with an unlikely trio of partners-in-crime. Inside the Sikkim Tourist Information Centre there were three men waiting patiently for a permit, who also found the prospect of a night in Siliguri quite horrific and were desperate to leave immediately for Gangtok. They were monks; two were temple lamas from Nepal dressed in jeans and T-shirts, taking their friend, a maroon-clad young monk from Thailand, around the monasteries of Sikkim.

In the bus station I was approached by an old man – obviously drunk – who offered to drive the four of us in a minibus to Gangtok for 1200 rupees, which worked out at double the official fare but worth every rupee if it saved us from the hell of Siliguri. The others agreed to this offer even though we doubted the driver's ability to see straight, and after an hour we collected our permits and set off on the road.

It all seemed so easy, a bit too easy really. We drove on empty roads in a comfortable jeep, quickly out of the polluted city and into the silent regions of West Bengal along the damp green hilly roads. This was far more relaxed and comfortable than most bus journeys in India, with no luggage squashed at my feet and no raucous Hindi pop.

Somboon, the Thai monk, had been travelling around India for several weeks visiting temples and areas of Buddhist significance, and the Nepalis were showing him round monasteries in Sikkim. I couldn't have wished for more peaceful, easy-going companions. But an hour into the journey, our well-laid plans nose-dived. On approaching Ramdi, a tiny village along the river,

A tchidowoba tournament – traditional wrestling –
in the shade of the village church near Tblisi, Georgia.

In hot pursuit of the headless goat during ulak tartish final
at the Hippodrome in Bishkek, Kyrgyzstan.

Left: A large crowd enjoys the ulak tartish at the Hippodrome, Bishkek on Kyrgyz Independence Day.

Above: Taking aim at the polo ground in Shillong, India, for the daily archery session.

Right: Counting up the all-important number of successful arrows in Shillong, which punters gamble on.

Students of kalaripayattu, the martial art of Kerala, India, practice advance leaps.

Less sophisticated but the same art: village boys
go through the moves at their simple kalari.

The experts of kalaripayattu demonstrate their skill on a beach near Calicut, India.

Village boys near Imphal, India, oil their bodies before beginning a game of yubi lakpi – rugby with a greased coconut.

The band leads out the players for a game
of mukna kangjei in a village in Manipur, India.

The final of a khang tournament – one of the oldest sports in Manipur –
in the village of Thoiba, India.

Essential to every zurkhane in Iran – the Moshad who recites poems and beats time as the pehlivans exercise.

To the readings of poetry, Iranian men take physical and spiritual exercise – with an audience – in a zurkhane in Esfahan.

we could hear an increasingly deafening noise from a loudspeaker and then our jeep was stopped by two teenagers wearing jeans, T-shirts and red bandannas. They politely informed us that we couldn't continue, and the road would re-open at 6 pm. It was now midday.

The monks accepted this news stoically and prepared themselves to meditate for the next six hours. We could do nothing but move away from the deafening monologue, obviously part of a political rally. Our driver sloped off and we went inside a small café which was someone's front room, ordered tea and noodles and discussed our plans.

'I think,' pondered Somboon slowly as he stirred his tea, 'that we have to wait here all day.' The Nepali brothers nodded thoughtfully. 'We have no choice, we just wait and relax.' Sometimes laid-back people who accept everything with good grace are highly irritating.

I stormed off towards the source of the noise. The speaker was highly excited and I pictured a fist-waving activist delivering his rhetoric to a few hundred angry political radicals. The reality wasn't so dramatic. A middle-aged man wearing brown trousers and thick glasses was yelling into his megaphone (unaware that there was no need to shout) to a couple of dozen young men lying idly on the grass by his feet. Some of his not-so-enthralled activists were reading papers, some eating, chatting and not looking particularly radical. I approached a young man who was reading a copy of *Sportstar*.

'Excuse me,' I smiled sweetly, 'could you please tell me the reason for your strike?' He explained, quite earnestly, that they were protesting against the government's excessive price-rises in consumer goods. 'We have demonstrated how this is affecting the lives of ordinary people.'

'We have a problem. I am a journalist for the BBC and have to make some interviews in Gangtok tonight. I hired a private vehicle to take me there.' 'What is your programme about?' 'Onions!' I said suddenly with a touch of genius. 'I am interviewing market-owners in Gangtok about the price of onions. After all, most Indians are vegetarian, so price increases in essential vegetables, like onions, are causing great financial strain,' I said, with sincerity. He looked impressed and went off to talk to a party official to see if we could leave.

A few minutes later, he returned with another man, who asked to see 'my particulars'. I produced a Press Pass from a cricket match in 1996, plus a letter on BBC paper (which didn't mention anything about onions) which convinced them. 'OK, we will escort you out.' We walked to the van, where the driver was in a drunken snooze and the three monks were meditating.

'Who are these men?' asked the man, frowning at Somboon in his flowing robes. I waved at them dismissively. 'They helped me hire the van because I don't know the area. I promised to give them a lift.' I wrote a sign saying 'Press' and stuck it in the front window, in case anyone decided to chuck rocks at us.

We drove off with an army jeep in front to escort us to Rangpo, the last town in West Bengal, with eight young men standing up in the back and fluttering their CPI flags. They were probably delighted that they didn't have to listen to many more hours of Party speeches.

We soon reached Rangpo, and our escorts tooted and shouted farewell. A little while later we came to Sikkim and registered our entry; from there the road grew more dangerous but luckily the driver had sobered up and kept a sensible speed around hairpin bends, through Sikkim's glorious deep green rolling landscape and mountainous terrain.

The slow, vehicle-clogged approach to Gangtok brought us down to earth. The others dropped me off at a hotel on the main road, and we said goodbye.

Since becoming India's newest state in 1975, Sikkim has had a steady influx of immigrants from other areas. My hotel was on the unimaginatively named Mahatma Gandhi Road, lined with Bengali sweet shops, Bombay snack houses, South Indian dosa restaurants, and small laser-disc movie-halls showing Chinese kung-fu movies. Gangtok must be the only Indian city which doesn't worship the banal sari-shimmying Bollywood babes, preferring something a bit more macho. The posters outside displayed blonde bimbos with short skirts, large cleavages and stilettos, and guys posing with sunglasses and AK47s. The manager of my hotel, who had recently entered the murky world of local politics, told me that Sikkim enjoys a lack of intervention from the authorities regarding importing and censorship.

Being a state dominated by remote, ancient monasteries and Buddhist temples, I had imagined the people of Sikkim to be pacifist, teetotal vegetarians. The violent movies had already given me some doubts and then I discovered the plethora of booze shops and cheap bars, with a diet consisting predominantly of meat.

As well as Indians, there is a massive population of Nepalese immigrants, now the majority ethnic group in the capital. Sikkim was originally inhabited by Lepchas, tribal people who were small-crop farmers following a Shamanism-type religion; Tibetans began to immigrate into Sikkim in the fifteenth and sixteenth centuries. The Red Hat sect of Buddhism was the official religion before Sikkim became part of India, but now the state is 60 per cent Hindu and 30 per cent Buddhists who co-exist peacefully, rather like in Nepal.

The hotel manager told me that archery practice was held near the Palace grounds above the town, up a snaking steep hill. The Palace, where the King used to reside, is on the right (now guarded and still closed to the public) and the grounds are down a steep path to the left where the King's soldiers used to practise every morning. These days, the local archers practise every Sunday especially in the winter months approaching Losar (Tibetan New Year) and Losung (Sikkimese New Year) when most competitions are held.

On Sunday morning I found around a dozen men practising their archery, ranging from teenagers to over-fifties. It was utterly different from Shillong's archery: each man took his bow and aimed the arrow at the other side of the ground, over 100 feet away. The target was a wooden rectangle around three feet by one with a small circle painted on, resting on the ground. For such a distance it was a tiny target and most of them missed, and on the rare occasion of success, there was a great cry of celebration from the winning archer's friends.

The men were divided into two teams and although this was just a practice, the same format was used for a competition. Each team consists of nine players with two reserves. A member of team 'A' shoots an arrow, then one from team 'B', then team 'A' and so on until everyone has shot. A shot on the target earns two points for a team, and if the arrow hits the ground within one foot of the target, one point. But a crucial rule is that if team 'A's man hits the target and then the next arrow from team 'B' is also success-ful, team 'A's points are cancelled out. At the end of the round, when everyone has shot, the target is moved to the other end of the field and everyone starts again.

The arrows are traditionally made from bamboo, with an iron tip, either coming from Bhutan or made locally. The best feathers come from the tip of a hawk's or eagle's wing. Recently, more archers have been using aluminium arrows which give a more consistent tension and flight. Most of them use bows made from lacquered wood, with strings made from boiled and stretched nettle fibres. However, many have been able to afford the expensive fibreglass bows, which are more streamlined, lighter and stronger.

Jigme Dorji, a government lawyer and a religious Buddhist, was one of Gangtok's star archers for years. He explained to me that archery originated in Sikkim and Bhutan and had always been the most significant and popular sport in the region. It is still played in the lull of the agricultural year, with the peak 'season' following the harvesting of the paddy fields in November. Inter-village archery competitions are held for a few precious weeks before farming recommences. Like many traditional sports in rural areas, such events are an important social occasion, the opportunity for two villages to meet up as well as an enjoyable competition.

'Today, we are training for next month's competitions for Losar and Losung. Even though we're all city people and not village farmers here, we still like to play and visit other towns to compete. We love our traditions, so everyone must wear the *kho* when competing.' The kho is the traditional Sikkimese dress, a heavy cotton tunic which these days is now worn only for festivals or religious ceremonies.

Jigme explained that archery has enjoyed a local revival over the last few years, mainly instigated by the Youth Tribal Association. It was felt that young Sikkimese people were losing their identity, few of them speaking the language and it was feared that the Nepalese population was diluting their culture. 'People don't speak our language any more and soon young people will forget their identity and roots.' As well as the Nepalese, and people coming in from other parts of India, modern living and commercialism were changing the Sikkimese lifestyle radically, and their culture and language were becoming a distant memory. Archery, once a major sporting culture, was demoted to a freak activity carried out by a minority of enthusiasts and only in the remote villages.

Urgent action was taken by the Youth Tribal Association of Sikkim to reverse the trend. A few years ago they re-introduced archery as a popular sport in Gangtok to revive the flagging local identity. Since then, the game has flourished and is attracting more and younger supporters. There is greater incentive with cash prizes and sponsorship for tournaments, but the overall principle of enjoyment remains its major attraction.

Some of the tactics used by a team to distract its opponents are colourful and highly original. In the rules of Sikkimese archery it's perfectly acceptable – even desirable – to shout abuse at a player whilst he takes aim; rude and crude insinuations to create maximum embarrassment. One senior player told me, 'Although women never play archery, they come to watch competitions and enjoy shouting obscene remarks to make the men lose concentration.' (Apparently the Bhutanese women have the most colourful range of insults.)

Another, more risky form of distraction permitted is for a player to block the target from view by standing in front of it as his opponent takes aim. Naturally, he must possess lightning reflexes as well as nerves of steel to dodge the arrow in time. Every self-respecting archer will bear arrow scars on their person.

I couldn't wait around the few weeks until Losung, to see the biggest tournament in all its glory, and other areas of Sikkim I would have liked to visit were mostly remote and off-limits. I made yet another phone call to Manipur Bhawan in Delhi which confirmed that no progress had been made to get the permit, so I very reluctantly abandoned all ideas of going to Manipur. Instead I decided to go straight to Kerala, in the opposite corner of India, to see *kalaripayattu*, the famous martial art unique to Kerala.

I had a train ticket from New Jalpaiguri to Madras on a waiting-list, and left the hotel early in the morning and walked down to the jeep stand, intending to catch the first available jeep back to Siliguri. There were a few buses and a couple of jeeps standing empty – and confusion. I asked the ticket man about a jeep. And there was that word again: 'Bund.'

Another strike in West Bengal, still over onions, which was making life extremely difficult especially as my train was leaving at 3 pm. After a long discussion and waiting around, one jeep driver decided to chance it. The vehicle filled up with passengers and a few miles down the road we broke down. No amount of tinkering with the engine could fix it, and after a while he lost interest and gave us a refund, pointed to the road, and implied that it wasn't his problem any more.

A small minibus soon came which dropped me just outside the

centre of Siliguri where there was also a bund, this one provoked by the death of a young boy killed by a speeding army vehicle. I took a cycle-rickshaw (the only permitted form of transport) to the station and tried to get a confirmed seat on the train. It took over an hour, during which the station manager was adamant that all quotas were completely full and I ought to have applied earlier, but I should wait until the train arrived to talk to the ticket collector.

The train came two hours late, but the ticket collector, who is revered a little above God, cheerfully allocated me a seat number as if he had quite a few spares up his sleeve, proving that there is no such word as 'full' on an Indian train.

27

The Deadly Dance

The other three sleepers in the cabin were occupied by a trio of men travelling from Guwahati to Bangalore. They made pleasant company, polite without being intrusive, and relaxed, spending most of the journey – over two days – playing cards and eating bananas.

The train terminated in Bangalore but my plan was to jump off at Madras and catch a train to Trivandrum, capital of Kerala, to spend a week in that state and see kalaripayattu.

Kerala is a narrow, fertile strip on the south-west coast, famous for its landscape, backwater canal trips, beaches increasingly crowded with holiday-makers, and its ethnic diversity. Although predominantly Hindu, the area also has the highest density of Christians in India, and Kochi (Cochin) has an old synagogue and the remains of one of the world's oldest Jewish communities. The state has a high standard of living, the highest literacy rate in India, a cosmopolitan spirit and boasts the first freely elected communist government in the world.

The train pulled into Madras Central which adjoins the commuter line, just in time for the 6 pm rush hour. I had a seemingly unending tide of thousands of Madrasis returning home to contend with, added to which were the noise, heavy baggage and the unpleasant humidity that always hangs over Madras.

A kindly ticket collector spent half an hour rummaging through timetables, unearthing the correct train, trying to bribe another ticket collector to 'find' a seat on an otherwise hopelessly crowded train, which failed. 'Better you get the fast train to Calicut which leaves in half an hour, and then change in the early morning for Trivandrum. There are plenty of seats available for that train.'

We sweated and toiled through the crush to the ticket office, where he bypassed the queue and got my ticket. We sat on the train and chatted for a few minutes before he wished me a safe journey whilst I thanked him profusely and tried to imagine a British Rail porter helping a foreigner for half an hour. I padlocked my big rucksack under the seats and flung my camera-bag above the seats, on to my upper sleeper.

Fifteen minutes before departure two smartly dressed young men got on and sat next to me, took out their laptops and underwent an animated conversation filled with balance sheets and share options. The train screeched and hooted and pulled out of the platform and soon afterwards the ticket collector came around, then the man giving out sheets and pillows.

A few minutes later I climbed up to go to sleep, reaching out for my camera-bag to lock it up, except it wasn't there. Not anywhere. Heart starting to race, I looked down at the seat which I had just left, and even under the seat, behind my big rucksack. It had gone. Even closing my eyes didn't make the bag reappear, and panic and horror hit that the whole bag had been stolen. Hearing a stream of expletives coming from their neighbour, the money-men lifted their heads from their computers and asked what was the problem. 'Someone's lifted my bag,' I replied very glumly. 'But we've been here the whole time,' said one. 'I would have noticed anyone trying to touch your stuff.'

There were obviously very clever thieves in Madras, who managed to creep in unseen and steal the bag before the train had left. I stumbled down the carriage in panic looking for it but as the train hurtled towards Calicut, it obviously wasn't carrying my camera-bag. Feeling very sick, I began a mental list: two Nikon cameras, lenses, a radio, a tape-recorder, personal stereo, a bag of films, money, wonderful Arabic and Turkish cassettes bought in Uzbekistan, notebooks and diaries, and my passport containing the precious Iranian visa which took so much trouble to obtain. By now the contents had probably been rifled and sold outside Madras train station for about £50.

I could do nothing but report the theft to the ticket collector, get off the train and return to Madras, in case anything had been found. Everyone was most sympathetic, but could do nothing.

Over three hours later, at 11 pm, the train made its first stop and I stumbled off. There were no trains to Madras for five hours – the longest five hours of my life. The Madras train came at 4 am and it was a dismal return to Madras Central at 6 am, at which time the Railway Police possessed not a brain cell between them and the half-wit in charge advised me to return at 10 am.

With only 600 rupees to my name, I would have just enough for one night in a cheap hotel and a second-class ticket back to Bombay the following morning. After finding a depressing hotel, I reported the passport loss to the British Deputy High Commission who processed the report and assured me I could get an emergency loan in Bombay whilst collecting the new passport there.

Back at the station, the Assistant Station Manager took the problem in his stride. 'My dear – how terrible for you.' He told the others in the office who tutted sympathetically. 'But tell me the most important thing – have you had your breakfast?' I gulped that I hadn't eaten since the previous afternoon and felt sick, and really not like eating anything.

'But, madam – you must eat something. Not even *iddly samba*?' Not even iddly samba, a typical South Indian breakfast dish. 'Well then, I will get you some juice.' And he sent out for a big glass of fresh orange juice and promised to arrange a ticket to Bombay for the next morning.

I wandered outside the station, peering into the many piles of rubbish, looking in the bins, scavenging around in case anything had been dumped. The person who invented the phrase 'needle in a haystack' had obviously been looking for something in Madras Central station. A search was impossible especially with the constant river of people and other scavengers, homeless, beggars and junkies with matted hair who were doing a cheap deal in heroin, also picking through piles of rubbish.

I returned to Bombay where I could get a new passport, stay with friends and try – for the fourth time – for the Iranian visa. I also decided that I would go back up to Delhi to re-apply for the elusive Manipur permit and personally supervise every step of the process so my application wouldn't be 'lost' in the pressured piles of paperwork.

The British High Commission in Bombay had received my application and report of stolen passport, faxed from Madras and already approved by the passport office in London. 'Fill your form in, submit photos and the fee, and it will be ready in two days,' said the woman. Then the farce began: I asked her for a loan.

She gave me a look, a combination of incredulity and disgust. 'But what do you need money for?' and she pretended to be very busy to distract my attention. 'Well I had everything stolen, and until money is wired out from England, I have nothing to live on.' 'But you said you were staying with friends? Can't you borrow off them?'

This went on for some time, until, with a bad grace, she vanished to reappear twenty minutes later. 'I managed to get 1000 rupees for you. You will have to pay this back before you pick up your passport,' she grudgingly announced, making it seem as though she had moved heaven and earth to procure me a total of £13.

Two days later my money had been wired successfully but I needed my passport to collect it. My new passport was ready, so I returned to my – er – friend at the Consulate. 'But we can't return your passport until you have repaid the loan,' she replied with a look of satisfaction. 'But how do I collect my money without it, to repay your loan?' 'We will give you a letter of identification,' was her solution and in spite of my shouting, fist-thumping and cursing the entire system to anyone who walked in, that was her final word.

I actually telephoned to make a formal complaint to the High Commissioner. I took great pleasure in telling him the official's name, hoping that her punishment was to be stranded in a foreign country with 1000 rupees.

When I enquired at the Iranian Consulate about the visa on my stolen passport, the chief secretary advised me to contact the Iranian Embassy in Bishkek, and if they sent a copy of my original visa to Bombay, it could be re-issued immediately. I faxed Mr Abbas in Bishkek but in case of hitches also filled out another visa form (now able to recite the damn thing in my sleep) and submitted that.

That night I took the train to Ernakulum in Kerala, a long journey due south, only too delighted to leave behind such nightmares in officialdom. 'How many hours does the journey take?' I asked the ticket-seller in Bombay's Victoria Terminus station.

'Well, madam, it takes thirty hours. But this Konkan line is single-tracked so many delays are there – maybe an extra twelve hours. And there is no food. No stations have refreshments and restaurant car is very bad. Good luck!' Faced with such an ominous send-off, I boarded the train with bagfuls of refreshments.

In the event, the journey was only delayed by seven hours, meaning a most inconvenient arrival into Ernakulum Junction at 3 am, with a two-hour wait for the first train into Trivandrum, the state's capital, where there were two centres I knew of where kalari-payattu was practised. It is like nothing else: 'part sport, part dance and drama, fight, movement – very dramatic, visual, unique and very sexy,' is how one South Indian friend described it.

Trivandrum is extremely hot and, for Kerala, quite noisy and busy but the pace of life is still more relaxed than in the northern cities. It is a city of palm trees and the smell of coconut, of white sarongs and temples and fishing, cool meandering rivers, green and fresh, rather than the suffocating smog and overcrowded chaos of much of India.

I booked into a hotel and after a short sleep, caught a rickshaw to arrive at the CVN Kalari in the East Fort area of the city, a small inconspicuous building, at 6 am. It seemed very early but I had remembered the pehlivans' early starts in the akharas. Inside, the pile of shoes by the door prompted me to remove mine and I could hear slow, calm instructions emerging from the *kalari* (the gymnasium) to the right. A young man wordlessly beckoned me to go up the steep wooden staircase, emerging onto a tiny balcony which overlooked the kalari.

Beneath was a plain, dark room with a hard red mud floor and stone walls. Seven young men with glistening, oiled bodies in small loin-cloths stood in a line and began their routine to the commands of the leader. They took three steps forward, swung one leg so their foot was way above their head, swung it back down, bent low, pivoted on one foot, and repeated with the other leg. They continued until they reached the other end of the room, then turned and did the same thing on their return with no lapse in their concentration or balance, their movements controlled, measured, calm yet with the fierceness of a panther. When they had finished, another group lined up and did the same.

After they had finished these warm-ups, they began the real exercises. Splitting into pairs, each chose one of several weapons – long spears, short daggers, sabres, wooden clubs, swords and shields – which were hanging on the walls. A series of deafening cracks then turned artistic grace into combat, fusing the art of dance with a potential killing machine. This is the real art of kalari-payattu, a deadly martial art using arms. Not that these boys could have harmed each other with their weapons, because they were carrying out routines so well co-ordinated that danger was virtually eliminated.

There was the thud of wood on wood as two teenagers swung their wooden clubs, striking with well-timed precision so that they never hit each other. In the opposite corner was the clash of metal, as two older men used sword and spear with breathtaking speed, turning and leaping and often clashing their weapons whilst in mid-air.

In the corner of the arena was a small shrine, with the deities of Siva and Sakthi who represent power, decorated with flower garlands and lit up with oil lamps. As each person entered, he first touched the ground, then kissed his hand and touched his forehead. He went straight to the shrine and offered prayers; then over to the *gurukkal* (who has the duel role of martial arts master and healer), to touch his feet and then kiss his own hand. After these preparations, he would join in the exercises.

The morning routine lasted a couple of hours. For most, this was their daily routine and after their early, energetic start they went to school, college or office.

Santosh, a twenty-six-year-old post-graduate student, had been training for over five years. 'I was learning karate for many years when a friend suggested I learned kalaripayattu, and because of my experience in martial arts I have learned these skills easily. But my personality changed after training here for a few months. I used to be more aggressive with my friends, but kalaripayattu made me more disciplined and calm and helped me with problems at home, and to feel more complete.' His observations reminded me of the akharas, where personal and psychological development is seen as important as physical.

The gurukkal went to the next-door room to his daily surgery of healing. Traditionally, kalaripayattu has a strong connection with herbal healing and massage, using a range of natural remedies. A young man lay on an old wooden bench which had undoubtedly been in service for many years and, taking a bottle from a shelf holding an impressive array of bottles of oils, lotions, potions and herbs, the gurukkal applied dark green sludge to the boy's leg and massaged it.

When he had finished his patients and we sat at his cluttered desk, he explained why healing is such an integral part of the art. 'Kalaripayattu is one of the oldest living traditions of martial art training in the world, with its roots in the Dhanurveda, the ancient Indian science of warfare. Apart from training to be a fighter, it is also a ritualistic and spiritual process of learning and is about harmony of the body. This is why there is a strong connection with the healing of the body also.'

Tall and stern, with the appearance of a headmaster – had he not been wearing a white vest and long white sarong – C.V. Govidankutty Nair Gurukkal has been the gurukkal here for many years, and involved in the art for over fifty years. He is the son of the late C.V. Narayanan Nair, one of a trio of practitioners who helped revive the art after it was near extinction. When the British were ruling in the late eighteenth century, they forbade the practice of kalaripayattu and the kalaris were dying out. A hundred years ago he, together with Kottackal Kanaran and C.V. Balan Nair, gathered knowledge from the dying schools to revive the heritage, gave it popularity with demonstrations and re-established many kalaris throughout Kerala.

Ask anyone how long kalaripayattu has been around and they look vaguely into the distance and say, 'for centuries'. No one can date precisely its origins, but historical evidence shows traces of it from the ninth century. Writings of fourteenth- and sixteenth-century travellers to Kerala, like Duarte Barbosa, and the popular 'ballads of Northern Malabar' describe it as an integral part of the medieval Kerala society, playing a vital role in the education of its youth and the training of warriors.

Originally, Kerala consisted of several small feudal principalities in constant conflict, and every village had a kalari to ensure a highly developed martial art training and prominent physical culture system. Later, it became a family tradition, parents sending their young sons for training in keeping with the regional culture and tradition.

Since its revival in the last century, the art has been popular with participants who appreciate its cultural importance, in addition to the benefits of regular physical exercise.

'We get no support from the government,' said Gurukkal. 'I run this place on modest fees from my students. Ideally we wouldn't charge anything, but we cannot live on good will alone.' They charge 100 rupees for children and 200 for adults. 'Treatment is free, as it is unethical to ask for money, but patients give what they can afford. We get a lot of publicity these days,' he said. 'Even though the government is not interested, the number of kalaris is growing again. Sometimes foreigners come to learn; a Japanese dancer comes every year to learn, and she gives shows in Japan with other Indian dancers.'

Today the motives are different but certain elements remain unchanged over the centuries. The kalari (the Sanskrit word for gymnasium) is always built in an east-west direction, the floor approximately four feet below ground level, and closed on all sides except a small door on the eastern side. The measurements are around 35 feet by 17, and 17 feet high. The deity is always placed in the south-west corner on a seven-stepped platform. Kalaris are considered a venue for physical training, but also a temple of learning, religious worship and spiritual growth where elaborate rituals play a central role.

The guru, or gurukkal, has great honour and respect bestowed upon him and the disciples surrender themselves totally. Such subservience is rarely seen in other sporting cultures, and I hadn't even seen it so prominent in the akharas. A gurukkal must be a student for many years, before undergoing decades of training and only then is he worthy of such an honourable position. He must be as knowledgeable about treatment and able to cure sprains, dislocation, fractures and even disabilities relating to neurological and muscular problems.

The training has a graded system of exercises which begins with the enrolment of the boy or girl from around seven years old. The first stage is the *uzichal*, where the student's body is smeared with medicated oil and massaged by the gurukkal to regulate the blood flow, preparing the muscles for vigorous training. The training is then divided into three sections and begins with *meythari*, which prepares the body for maximum control and strength with stretching exercises, balance, postures and total body control. Everyone begins their daily routine with this, even if progressing to more advanced stages.

When this stage has been perfected he progresses to *kolthari*, combat with sticks, canes and wooden clubs and staffs. The most important is the *ottakal*, a long, curved instrument which must be used with the correct cut and thrusts aimed at the marmas, or the vital points of the body on which the art hinges. The sixty-four marmas are not only the vital points of attack – it is said that a single blow to the correct point can immobilize or even kill – but is also central to the study of healing.

The final stage is the *ankathari*, training to defend and attack with fatal metal weapons. When kalaripayattu was originally used in warfare, this was the significant type of fighting, as duels with swords and spears would often settle disputes, ending in death for the losing side. 'Death was considered preferable to the shame of losing in a fight.' The most advanced instruments are the *kattaram*, or dagger, and then the sword and shield, which makes use of all the body movements, then flexible sword, then spear.

Each morning at 6 am, in every one of the fifty kalaris throughout Kerala, around 3000 students go through these same stages, actions, gestures, postures, rituals in the same lingering smell of ginger oil. A 300-kilometre trip north up the coast on a slow overnight train took me to Calicut where, early in the morning, I found the CVN Kalari Sangham run by Gurukkal Narayanan. There I witnessed the disciples as they trooped in, took their bottles of oil, wore their loin cloths and then began the meythari, identical to the one in Trivandrum.

The Calicut region is significant for kalaripayattu culture, especially the nearby town of Vadegara, birthplace of Tacholi Othenan. He was a much-feared warrior around 500 years ago, frequently rewarded by the local zamindar (landowner) with prizes and riches and a hero of every practitioner of kalaripayattu, for his skills were learned in the kalari. Next to the kalari where he trained is the Tacholimanikoth Temple, adjacent to his birthplace and built by his family in his memory.

Meppayil Raghavan Gurukkal has been in charge of the Tacholi Othenan Memorial Kalarisangam, for over ten years. Although it is a significant and historical venue, it doesn't have the facilities or publicity of some of the others I had seen. Watching the boys arrive there for their afternoon session, I was absorbed in the atmosphere of a village custom unchanged for hundreds of years, and far removed from the city CVN kalaris in Trivandrum and Calicut. The village was tiny and quiet, small dirt tracks led to the field containing the kalari and the temple. The kalari had no concrete and no 'office', but was a simple interior, its roof made of woven palm leaves and open at two ends so the breeze and light came through. You could see a wall of palm trees through the east end, and mountains in the distance.

Massages took place not on a 600-year-old table, but on a simple mat on the floor. But the exercises were exactly the same as those in the city kalaris, as were the motives. The gurukkal, not as financially secure as the others, was quite typical for a village kalari and asked only 25 rupees per month from each boy. But occasionally he struck lucky. 'I also do healing and massage,' he told me with a quick smile. 'A rich businessman from Madras just paid me 15,000 rupees for a massage.'

Back in Calicut, I visited the author of a prominent book on kalaripayattu, who wasn't the dusty academic I feared but a delightful retired government officer who possessed great intuition on the subject. Unlike most people who are keen to promote their traditional sport, Mr Balakrishnan had a realistic attitude. 'The basic skills of kalaripayattu are so important, so relevant to all sports people that it should be used as their basic training, then more Indians would excel in sports. For example, exercises like jumping up to kick the ball suspended high up, could then produce world-beating athletes at high-jump and pole vault!'

He had a valid point. The sport shouldn't be kept alive just for its own sake, but to be used for relevant training and authentic skills in many different contemporary sporting arenas. 'The revival in recent years has enabled groups to go to other countries in order to demonstrate it on stage. But that is not really the purpose. It was made into a stage art with good intentions but in doing so it has begun to lose its inherent value of defence and offence, because satisfying people became the main objective. The practice should remain authentic.'

Mr Balakrishnan saw a gloomy future, noting that whereas some kalaris are in good condition – mainly the highly publicized, well-supported CVN group – most have poor facilities. Unless everything is available, including the treatment centre and massage, then students won't learn the all-round skills. He fears that the standard is dying, that the art won't survive and the skills of the exercises will decline.

One solution he offers – a most realistic one – was to have kalaris supported by the government. Not financially, because if they became financially dependent, then the genuine will of the gurukkal would go and it would become an institution. But if kalaripayattu was introduced in schools as a training facility, then that would popularize it. It would be easy to get children to learn the basic exercises, not with weapons but as a way of keeping fit.' Perhaps it could also be used as training for other sportsmen; previously some Indian footballers had come to his kalari, and even the Bulgarian football team had undergone a course of exercises.

Many Keralites pointed out the connection between kalari-payattu and kathakali, the famous dance-art from Kerala, and several gurukkals told me that kathakali performers often train in the kalari to perfect their body movements and balance. In kathakali, the body is also prepared through a rigorous course of physical exercise, with daily massage using medicated oils to develop the suppleness and grace necessary for the expressive nature of the dance.

So my final destination was Cochin, famous for its kathakali and one of my favourite places in India. But the first problem was getting a hotel in the crowded and highly popular adjacent town of Ernakulum. Once I had found a hotel with a vacancy, the hotel refused to let me stay because I didn't have an Indian visa in my new passport; they wouldn't accept the police report nor a letter from the British High Commission that I proffered.

I eventually found a room in a shabby lodge on the railway tracks, filled with black-clad Hindu pilgrims from Tamil Nadu. I filled out the registration card myself, inserting a fictitious visa number to prevent a repeat performance.

There was enough time for me to take a boat across the Vembanad Lake to Cochin, the journey across the water being much quicker, cooler and more pleasant than going along the mainland. We passed a few other small islands along the way, and could just glimpse the Bolgatty Palace Hotel on the southernmost tip of Bolgatty Island.

The boat pulled into Fort Cochin and tilted and tipped as everyone rushed off, pulling bicycles and shopping and children. I followed most of the passengers and walked on the cobbles along the spice market in the Mattancherry district, streets which relive the town's important history of spice trading. The smell of ginger and cardamom brought alive the fact that traders have been sailing to Kerala for years. Tea-traders still conducted their business in tiny shops which open out onto the main street, whilst lorries loaded up sackfuls of grain, coffee, peppercorns and other dried goods. Dozens of seagulls circled overhead, pecking at sacks and squawking with delight.

Jewtown Road is the main road which leads to the old syna-gogue, the last remains of a once prominent community. The synagogue, which still conducts regular services, is the oldest in the Commonwealth, dating back to 1568. The Jews are said to have arrived as far back as AD 52, involving themselves in the trade and commerce of the Malabar coast. The interior of the synagogue is well-preserved and holds together the few dozen elderly members of the community.

After a brief stroll enjoying the sights, sounds and mainly smells, I returned to Ernakulum on the ferry and went to the See India Foundation for my evening of kathakali. The director, Mr Devan, promoted the show with flyers declaring, 'Director Devan's See India Foundation. Cochin's one and only traditional theatre. India's first daily Kathakali, 28 years [it was dated 1992]. By the family that danced over 100 years.'

The theatre was a simple wooden shed in a leafy garden. Rows of wooden chairs were still empty and the stage was bare. I took a front-row seat and at six o'clock two men emerged onto the stage. Wearing only a sarong tied at the waist, they began their elaborate make-up process, mixing the glowing colours with wooden sticks, then spreading them on to a dish like an artist's palette. By the light of one spotlight and two oil-burners, they applied the colour to their faces with small pointed sticks as the audience grew slowly.

A third man then entered the stage and prayed in front of a small shrine in the corner. He had a healthy paunch protruding from his long white sarong and white vest, with a plump face and magnificent thick black moustache which curled at the edges. He cleared his throat and spoke into the microphone, and the deep booming voice could have belonged to a Shakespearean actor. This was the famous Mr Devan.

'Welcome to this evening's show,' he began, then launched into an explanatory speech. '*Kathi* means story, *kali* is a play, and kathakali tells stories from the *Ramayana* and *Mahabarata*. The singer sings the dialogue, the drummer supports him, the dancer translates through body language and expression.' Then he explained the colours of the make-up and costumes, each having a different significance.

The actors' faces were now bright masks of colour: green denotes a good character (because green is also the colour of Kerala), red is bad, yellow belongs to ladies and saints. The lamps on the stage represent the fire god, which the performers bless before commencing to drive away darkness or ignorance.

The paints are made from natural products. The green is from tender coconut oil mixed with blue. The black is burnt coconut oil and soot which, according to Director Devan, can also be used for medicinal purposes to make the eyes strong and powerful, and placed inside the eyes can refresh them. Turmeric powder – also with medicinal properties – mixed with calcium paste makes red.

All the supernatural characters portrayed – gods, devils or demons – have pieces added on to their faces built up with plaster, to make their faces 'come out', as he described it, making them bigger than life. 'Around the world, theatres are the art of exaggeration. In the ancient Greek theatres, the actors wore masks.'

The stage lights went out and there was a drum beat, which signalled to the village – the traditional venue of the performance – the start. The two performers entered the stage, the lights came on, and the performance began. Kathakali performances depict a selection of 110 stories from Hindu mythology, using a total of 100 characters, and every trained dancer knows them all. They are usually performed in village temples especially during festivals, so it is considered religion, rather than theatre. This, explained our narrator, means that people take harmony and peace from watching; kathakali therefore being a medium to reach God.

Mr Devan narrated the story in English, the drummer changing tempo depending on the story's content. It reminded me of Chinese opera, with elaborate costumes and emphasis on expressions and intricate mimes. Both characters used every part of the face in a dozen different ways and each movement had, as everything in kathakali, a different meaning. The eyes can move in all directions as can the eyebrows, the lips, fingers and hands.

'It is the language of signs,' he said; twenty-four letters can be 'spelt' just using the hands, and the hand movement can make a total of forty words. I supposed that regular watchers could understand each one. The combination of eyes, face, hands and feet, communicates the entire meaning.

For our purposes, a quarter-full room of foreigners, mainly young backpackers clutching copies of *Lonely Planet* and wearing Velcro sandals, Devan narrated the story. Our eyes were glued to the faces of the two characters, who pulled and stretched their faces in ways I didn't think possible. The story lasted around half an hour, and told the tale of a Prince who gets tempted by the she-demon who disguises herself as a pretty maiden. With impure intentions she takes him home and dances for him; when he realizes her true identity he tries to leave, whereupon she gets angry and they fight, and he wins. End of story: good triumphs over evil or, in terms of Hindu ideology, resist temptation and all will be well.

The physical movements of kalaripayattu are linked to the moves of these performers; more in context of flexibility, control and suppleness. In both, the body is the sole means of expression, and rigorous training is necessary. Since the dance has been around for just a few hundred years, it has been influenced by the martial art which is centuries older.

After the performance, Mr Devan launched into an explanation of Hinduism and Indian philosophy. 'Why is the lotus flower [he pronounced this 'fulawaaaah'] the symbol of Hinduism? Because the lotus flower grows only in mud. There is no lotus in clean water. The flower fights through the dark age, blossoming in the open. The lotus inspires us, teaching us that anyone can come out and open up irrespective of background. The world is full of possibilities for all.'

And his father certainly made the most of his possibilities, dancing up to the age of ninety-seven and taking the culture to new heights. He performed Bible stories and *The Tempest* in kathakali. Recent experiments have developed the art into different formats and languages, proving Mr Devan's theory that 'in life, in Hinduism and especially in India, nothing stands still. The whole of our religion is full of art and creations; in our mythology, we have beautiful stories but nothing is fixed. We have lots of gods and plenty of time. And therefore our needs are few. The whole of knowledge,' he ended, 'is knowing what you don't need. Too much knowledge and the magic is gone. Better to have a little mystery.'

And so the mystery of Kerala's two most famous and important indigenous cultures experienced, I returned to Bombay (this time the train was only delayed by four hours) to learn the latest progress on the Iranian visa. The secretary at the Iranian Consulate said that Mr Abbas in Bishkek had not responded to my fax requesting information about my visa. I called him several times, each time he 'couldn't come to the phone', and eventually his secretary said, 'He is sorry but cannot do anything to help.' So much for the marriage and job offers.

28

Permit Blues

'They lost your form,' said an apologetic Mr Vashist – I had gone up to Delhi to chase, yet again, the Manipur permit – 'but if you go to the Department of Information, they may be able to help.' That took three solid days of running from one government department to another; letters of permission from one office and then going pleading and cajoling and begging with a wad of letters to another. There was lots of queuing, impatient sitting in overcrowded waiting rooms with screaming children and backpackers reporting stolen passports.

All those departments soon became a blur, with added confusion when one senior officer in the Home Department said I couldn't enter Manipur by land and had to fly, yet the officer next door said I was allowed to enter by land. After spending a total of nine hours on the Friday (my birthday), I assured myself it was all worthwhile when I eventually received a ten-day permit.

The next night I again endured the mammoth train journey to Guwahati, then got straight on the bus to Shillong. The following afternoon just before boarding the bus to Imphal, I saw that the route wasn't through Silchar in Assam but actually through Dimapur, in Nagaland. Nagaland is off-limits not only to foreigners but also to other Indians, which surely meant a police check at the border of the state, at which point they would throw me off. I panicked briefly, then decided to chance it.

The bus drew up in Dimapur, where I was about to pretend to be a nun (there was a group of convent-school girls accompanied by three nuns on the bus) if police interrogated me about my presence in this closed state. But there were no police, no army checkpoints and not a soul interested in seeing permits.

We left Nagaland as the sun was rising over rolling hills and took a slow, winding road over misty-topped peaks. I realized we were in Manipur and still no one had checked us. Perhaps when we arrived in Imphal, I thought, but a few hours later we arrived at the state capital and got off the bus. I took a rickshaw to the hotel; still there was no sign of a uniform. The friendly reception staff greeted me and said they had received my reservation, and showed me to a comfortable room. No one had yet asked for the precious piece of bloody paper which had taken so many painful hours to procure. I wanted to jump around the streets, with the permit stuck to my head and shout, 'It's here, it's here, and it took me four days of sitting in government offices,' but no one would have cared. I asked the receptionist if she wanted to see it, but she just said, 'Oh don't worry, we know you have one but we don't need to see it.'

With all the scary veil of secrecy and intrigue surrounding Manipur, I had imagined the streets to be filled with rioting mobs and armed soldiers behind sandbags guarding every street corner. But the city was easy-going, fairly quiet and slow, set in the midst of a green environment with few vehicles. I was excited to be in the only place in the world where *yubi lakpi* (rugby played with a greased coconut) and *mukna kangjei* (hockey-wrestling) were played.

I had been put in touch with a journalist who would help me find these unique games, and he instantly threw himself into the task. 'But first, you need to register with the local police. I think this will be quite useful – anyway he's my cousin and he could be helpful.' So Mr Iboyama Laithengbam, correspondent for *The Statesman* and *Eastern Panorama*, and his brother, drove me down to meet the local police chief to 'register'.

The officer looked amazed. 'But how did you get here? We have no record of your entry.' 'I came by bus from Shillong, this morning.' He slapped his hand to his forehead in disbelief. 'You did what? But *no one* comes here by road. All foreigners enter by air. That's why we have the police at the airport to register all foreigners and their permits.'

He seemed more flabbergasted than anything else, and was full of offers of help. 'If there is anything you need here, anything, please tell me and I will arrange it. Do you need your air-ticket? If you can't get a confirmed seat then tell me, I can arrange your seat. It is quite an honour for us that you are here, quite an honour.' He gave us tea, after which we left. Mr Laithengbam, a cheeky little man, gave a smile. 'It is useful that you visited him. You may need his help.'

He arranged for me to meet the Minister for Sports and Youth Affairs for the Manipur government, Mr Hemanta Singh, a young man who assured me authoritatively that he would 'arrange everything'. 'I can contact all these associations, and you can see all the sports you are interested in. All these games are played here but it takes a little organizing . . .'

Imphal's main drawback is a complete lack of activity after nightfall; when darkness fell, at 5 pm, everything shut and transport was severely limited. There are frequent power cuts – and without electricity the telephone system won't work, neither will the water pumps – and there are regular bunds [strikes] for all manner of reasons. But the friendliness of the people makes up for all that, and I found them to be gentle, kind and hospitable. The hotel was simple but well-run and clean.

Best of all – in a city with so many strikes, shut-downs, no-shows and no power – I was able to see everything I had hoped to. The first sport which I was invited to was a game of mukna kangjei in the village of Tayrempokpi, one hour's drive along an extremely bumpy and dusty track from Imphal. Mr Laithengbam's brother drove us out in his Ambassador, a huge black car, the same model as the old Bombay taxis. 'This belongs to my company,' he said with a grin, 'but I hardly ever use it for work. It is now our family car.'

The village, a small cluster of houses in farmland, seemed a haven of calm belying the ferocious image which has kept people away from the area. Chingakham Khomei was the organizer of that day's game and had been a player for many years. There were a few wooden chairs at the edge of the field, the sound-system was nearly completed (no matter how small the event or the venue, and however many miles from an electricity supply, it's considered crucial to have a loudspeaker system, even if it involves miles of cables running off a generator) and wooden tables arrived, carried on the backs of helpers.

Konthoujam Ibothombi was the other main organizer, wearing a long white sarong and calmly giving instructions to an army of helpers. Now in his seventies, he thought that in spite of some interest, mukna kangjei has nothing like the popularity of when he was a child. He played in his village from the age of twelve regularly for nearly thirty years. At that time, he remembered, it was the most popular game in the state. 'We never played football here,' he told me; in most rural areas football was a relatively recent development, popularized mainly through TV.

Mukna, Manipuri traditional wrestling, is the root of mukna kangjei (*kangjei* means ball). As the name suggests, this is a combination of Manipuri wrestling and hockey, introduced by the ancient gods who reigned in Manipur. The game is played especially on religious occasions like Lai Haraoba (festival of the deities). There are minor matches held between villages on a local level, but the biggest games of the year are still held during Manipuri New Year. In the traditional Panas (administrative units in Manipur) the King patronized the games and determined their length.

'In my childhood there was no public transport, so living in the villages meant we were much fitter, walking miles every day to school or to the farms. When we played a match against another village, we walked there. We played throughout the year, except in the rainy season, and competition was stiff and taken seriously. But in recent years, interest is not as great and popularity has been slowing down.'

Village elders and younger players are keen to revive the game, he said, to keep their cultural heritage alive, as most feel that Manipur traditions are dying. 'After all, it is not just important for our culture but a good way of keeping fit. I was able to throw any man onto the ground. In fact,' he said a touch optimistically, 'I could still throw a younger man to the ground.'

A couple of dozen people had walked up from the village to watch and soon there was the faint sound of music approaching. Coming around a small lake next to the path was a procession of people clad in white, approaching the field. Leading the march was a band of eight musicians playing their enormous brass instruments with gusto, and a couple playing bass drums which practically dwarfed them. Following them were two lines of young men, barefoot and dressed only in white cloths, tied at the waist and wrapped between the legs. They marched to the field carrying their sticks, similar to hockey sticks in size and shape but less polished and refined, each one resting on his shoulder like a soldier marching into battle.

On reaching the field, they made two rows – seven on each team – then each faced his opponent and handed him a garland in a very ritualistic, formal manner and the village chief came to bless each one. Then they gathered their sticks in their hands and raced onto the field. The ball, made from the root of the bamboo plant which has been shaped and polished, was thrown onto the field. The band had attracted a lot more onlookers, including many women.

The whistle signalled the start. The main difference from hockey became obvious when, within minutes, nearly every player got into a tackle with his opposite number. It followed the same principle as American football – you tackle an opponent to prevent him from getting the ball, rather than in rugby where you tackle only to retrieve the ball.

The field soon looked like a combination of a wrestling arena and *Come Dancing*. Most players were in arm-locked embraces with their opponents and leading them around the field trying to bring them down. The person who scores the goal has to be not just good with ball control and accurate passing, but also fast enough to dodge his opponent and win a bout of wrestling. Quite a skill.

It has a similarity also to hurling in Ireland, where the ball can be struck, thrown or kicked, but a goal may only be scored with the stick. There are no actual goal posts, but just a line marked on the grass where the ball must go over, as judged by the referee. Usually, it is the person who has resisted being tackled who manages to shoot. Not only are many skills necessary, but it's definitely not a sport for the faint-hearted. I was astounded that such energetic whacking and bashing with a very hard stick and ball didn't result in major injuries on bare ankles. An old player assured me that for mukna kangjei as well as physical stamina, speed and agility, an important requisite is an iron nerve.

The final score was 4-3, after the 45 minutes each half, and the players came off panting with luckily no injuries that day. There is an important tradition which dictates that every player must visit the temple to pray to the gods for protection before every game. Umang Lairembi, the goddess of the forest who receives their prayers, has probably saved more ankle bones than any other god.

This game once enjoyed royal patronage but changes in society where the tribal, village infrastructure is less important, means that it now has less relevance to their traditional way of life. And, as those involved in so many other indigenous traditional games have pointed out, only when such game has royal or wealthy support can it thrive.

This village was one of the few which still remained in a scheduled caste. They follow the Sanamahi religion, which is the original religion of the Meiteis, the indigenous people of Manipur. In the early eighteenth century, missionaries came to spread the Hindu religion to the tribal minorities, and the King forced everyone to adopt it. Although there was resistance, most adopted Hinduism and those that refused, the King called untouchables, forbidding social interaction. Today, the village still follows the Sanamahi religion with its original customs and religious practices, speaking the same Manipuri language but with a different dialect. They still worship the deities: gods of fire, forest and nature. Their village chieftain, the Khullakpa, still rules the village away from the jurisdiction of the police, presiding over disputes within his village, although more serious crimes are handed over to the police.

The band struck up another fanfare and both teams were presented to the Khullakpa. Then a man wearing a large wooden mask did a traditional dance in his honour, similar to a Chinese dragon dance. By this stage, the entire village stood watching the entertainment in the midday sun.

All the women wore the traditional dress, colourful, heavy material which was wrapped around the body and looked uncomfortable to walk in. They were extremely inquisitive and friendly, giggling between themselves at the sight of my black jeans and shirt. A few moments later, three young women who had scooted back to their house, came with a parcel of material. They wanted me to try it on, and have my photograph taken with them.

If anything is more difficult than wearing a heavy cotton wrapped tightly around the body to the ankles, it's wearing it over jeans and shirt. Feeling like an Egyptian mummy, or maybe a Japanese geisha, I had everyone in hysterical laughter and people crowded closer asking to have their picture taken with me.

Some of the players indulged in a few rounds of mukna, wrestling, in the bright green field surrounded by trees, in the golden light from the mountains. I felt that day-to-day life had altered little for decades. I was sure that few of these villagers had TV sets, and most had no interest in the Indian cricket team and little concern for the outside world. The village elders said that mukna kangjei was part of their life and society and although popularity has lessened over the generations, they insisted that it is still as important as it was 'in their day'.

A few days later I was visited by Sarangthem Manaobi, the Superintendent of Police, who invited me to a game of yubi lakpi, Manipur's other main sport, that afternoon. I really wanted to see this – mainly because of its description – rugby played with a greased coconut.

Perhaps this was the root of modern rugby? Most Manipuris are quite adamant that the modern world 'stole' the idea from them and made it into rugby. A journalist writing in *Naharal Gi Thoudang* newspaper, asked, 'When did yubi lakpi start in Manipur? Has it been taken from Manipur like polo has been taken? [Although I suspected he actually meant 'stolen'.] Or is the similarity accidental?'

He also quoted the incident of the visit from John Dubriskey from the Australian Embassy in Delhi. They showed him a game of yubi lakpi and the locals told him that this was the origins of rugby. 'He seemed quite impressed. We should try to bring yubi lakpi to international standard, because it is a very manly game and popular everywhere. The people of Manipur can exhibit the game in their own style. Players from other countries are famous for rugby, but if we exhibit yubi lakpi elsewhere, then players of these countries may also adopt our technique.'

Whatever its cultural bastardization in recent years, this game still exists in its pure and unadulterated form, and the evidence was the young coconut on a chair. We arrived in the small public square in a suburb of Imphal, where a practice game was due to get under way between local boys who were learning the game.

The ultimate aim of yubi lakpi (which translates as 'coconut snatching') is to present the coconut to the King, or the head of the tribe (as in the original games of buzkashi, where the goat was offered to the King after the match). In modern times, a 'king' is selected to receive the offering.

For this reason, it is a game of individuals where each player is vying to win the coconut and bring it to the King and get the reward. (In buzkashi also, the original format is individual-based, rather than a team game.) In the original games the King would watch the players to see who was the most skilful, and possessed qualities for the battlefield (as with mukna kangjei and polo). Every player therefore wants to impress.

The coconut was ripe, green and smooth, smeared with mustard oil making it slippery and difficult to hold. The boys wore only shorts or loin-cloths, and were barefoot. The referee gave last-minute instructions, and the 'king' was selected and went to sit in a wooden chair at the edge of the playing area. Just in front of him was a line drawn into the dry earth, to signify where the player must cross.

The 'king' (a local retired teacher) was dressed in his official regalia, with a long white turban wrapped around his head. Originally, when they played to the genuine king in a major match, each player would wear peacock feathers and a head-dress, removing them just before the game.

The coconut was placed at the opposite end of the playing area behind a line. The whistle blew and the boys all dashed for it. As first one, then another, tried to grasp the coconut, it slipped from their hands and slid along the ground. There was a great deal of hilarity from the boys, and I suspected that a grand final in front of the King in the 'good old days' was taken a touch more seriously.

It's not permitted to run holding the coconut to the chest, so the player must hold it under his arm. To take or retrieve the 'ball' from an opponent, a player is not allowed to kick, push or punch but he can tackle the other, wrestling if necessary. Unlike mukna kangjei, if a player isn't in possession, he cannot be tackled. A player cannot be knocked down, but may be blocked. 'The coconut is the aim, not the man,' as the Superintendent succinctly put it.

Played at full speed with grown men, this must also be quite dangerous as they play barefoot and on rough dried mud, so anyone falling would receive quite a bang. This game, which has been around for centuries, is so similar to rugby, which evolved a great deal later, that it must be more than a coincidence.

Mr Hemanta Singh, the Sports Minister, telephoned to say that the next day was the final of a *kang* tournament in his constituency of Thoiba. It began at 2 pm, but as he was the guest of honour, they wouldn't start without him.

I arrived in his office at 1.45 pm and at 3.30 when we were still there, I was worried that the finalists would be hanging around all night waiting for the Honourable Minister who never came. At 4 pm when I was sure it must be over, we set off in a dramatic entourage consisting of his car, three army jeeps in front and two behind.

'We have to be very careful in Manipur,' he said – a major understatement. We whizzed along for an hour, sweeping aside other vehicles and forcing them into ditches or swerving violently out of the way. The two front jeeps had red flashing lights and two armed soldiers mounted fiercely on the top, so drivers weren't in much doubt who was coming.

At Thoiba, there was a welcoming committee for us and I wondered if they were secretly cursing him for being so late. However, they had quite sensibly not waited for us but saved just the final round for him. Our arrival was announced formally on the loudspeaker, and everyone scurried around and the game was stopped. They stood up and applauded as we walked in and we were shown to big armchairs at the front. We removed our shoes and sat down as three women appeared with trays of tea, water, bananas and cakes. The rustle of interest caused by our arrival soon died down and play recommenced.

I was instantly struck by an ethereal calm, a hallowed hush inside what seemed to be a temple, with men playing a game which looked like bowls, except much more graceful. There were seven men at each end of the room, all dressed in white sarongs and white shirts. There was a lovely tranquillity amongst the dozens of spectators, all of whom were sitting on the ground or standing, and the grace of the movements of the men playing was astounding.

Kang is one of the oldest and most primitive games of Manipur, based on accuracy in hitting a target. There is a flat, egg-shaped 'disc' called the *kang*, made of plastic or lac (originally from bone), and smooth on the top and bottom. It has precise measurements as specified most emphatically in the *Kanglon of Kang Federation* handbook: 14-15 centimetres long and 8-9 centimetre wide; 120-180 grams in weight.

This kang is released from the hand smoothly in an action called the *lamtha*, skidding along the floor to hit the *chekphei* target, which is also made of plastic and is much smaller, shaped like a backgammon counter. This stands on its end at the opposite end of the 'court', whose length depends on the players. Seniors use a court of 40-45 feet, juniors or women one of 35-40 feet.

A team has seven members, and each player pairs up with someone on the opposing team and attempts to knock down the target. When one succeeds, he scores a point for his team and they turn around and repeat from the opposite side of the court.

As I watched, a man in the row at one end slowly bent down, aimed at the small target then released the kang slowly, steadily, out of his hand. It made a slight skidding noise as it slid across the polished wood floor, slightly roughened with scattered crushed rice.

This was the final of the Late Pukhrambam Chaoba Singh Memorial Knock-Out Kang Tournament, played between R.R.A.D.C.Tentha (A) and Ayangleima Leishangthem (A). I delved into the federation's handbook, containing many pages of rules and regulations, terminology and meaning, but found it confusing and complicated. As far as I could gather from watching the action, it is very straightforward: hit the target with your kang, win a point. Change ends and start again. The team with most points wins. End of game.

After the last round had been completed – they had already been battling this final for several hours – the formalities began. Mr Singh made a speech praising the organizers and thanking the participants and umpires. He spoke about the importance of kang, and the federation which tries to keep the game alive.

He told me that Manipuris consider this game – as all their indigenous games – of great importance, and that it is popular with old and young. Its origins are unclear but the Meiteis believe that Kang was originally played by the Seven Lainingthous (male deities) and seven Leimarons (female deities) to celebrate the creation of earth and the beauty of the rising sun and moon. It is derived from the Manipuri word Kangba, which means 'to start'. The game thus signifies the start of a new life after the creation of the earth. The playing area represents the field of life, and seven players for seven days of the week.

The deities played the game seven times, each time won by the Leimarons (which may explain why it is acceptable for women to play this game, not common in other indigenous sports). They used a round object known as Kangkhil, the seed of a giant creeper, which was considered advantageous to them, so in order for the Lainingthous to win they decided to introduce an oval-shaped kang. (I interpreted this as men's inability to accept defeat from women, and therefore introduce their own rules to give them a chance.)

According to the ancient Manipur Royal Chronicle, *Cheitharon*

Kumbaba, kang began during the reign of Raja Loiongba in AD 112. He was taking a stroll in the royal courtyard during the afternoon of Cheiraoba, the Manipuri New Year, and saw two kangkhils (the seeds) lying on the ground. He threw the first seed a fair distance, then aimed the other one to try and hit it. Apparently amused by such a simple yet entertaining pastime (or perhaps he was just bored) he introduced it to the rest of the royal family.

In the course of time it developed more rules and sophistication. The kang as a seed was replaced by wood for 'commoners' and ivory for royalty. The circular kang developed into an oval shape made of tortoise-shell or buffalo-horn. Several centuries later, in the reign of Raja Chandrakirti, a systematic playing court was developed and rules were specified, and teams of seven players formed.

They asked me to say a few words, and after I'd thanked them for their hospitality, the organizers challenged me to hit the target. The hall fell silent as they ceremoniously handed me a kang, its bottom newly waxed with black resin to make it smoother. I took aim, practised the throwing action, and let it glide out of my hand. It should have skimmed neatly over the floor, but it flew out at an obtuse angle and clattered to the ground, which caused everyone to shriek with laughter.

They asked me to try again, and this time the kang slid across the floor smoothly but stopped after about three feet. The third try saw me hit the target and there was a spontaneous burst of applause after which I was presented with my own kang, which was a touching moment.

Mr Singh then suggested we left, claiming it wasn't safe to be driving after dusk. (Considering we had four jeeps with a hefty amount of ammunition, I wasn't sure if he was being over-cautious or just emphasizing his own importance.) We made a dusty getaway with the entire village coming to wave us off as the AK47s were put in position and our gun-toting guards mounted on the leading two jeeps.

29

Not a Game, War

' It is a small State, probably until these events took place
    very little known to your Lordships, unless, indeed,
... some of you may have heard it as the birthplace of the
game of Polo . . .' said the Marquess of Ripon in the House of
Lords back in 1891. And he wasn't far wrong, at least as the
Manipur people would believe.

Polo, or *sagol kangjei*, is the real icing on the cake for the state's
indigenous games. By this stage of the journey I was accustomed
to everyone and their neighbour claiming to be the real pioneers
of polo, and finding its exact origins is a hazy subject. But the
Manipuris are as adamant as the Baltis, the Chinese, the
Mongolians and the Persians (and probably the Georgians, if you
pushed them) that they invented polo, and who was I to argue?

'International style polo is a game. Our Manipuri style is War,'
claimed Mr Buddhachandra Singh, a Secretary to the Manipur
government and the poor man on whose shoulders the responsibility fell for the National Games. These games, which used to be
called the Indian Olympics, are held every year and its venue
changed all over India. This year was the turn of Manipur, or
rather last year, but their preparations to build stadiums and housing blocks fell so far behind that the date had already been postponed three times. The Indian government warned them that if
they failed to be ready this time, they would lose the event to
another state.

That preparations were in chaos didn't come as any surprise,
considering the frequent strikes, poor quality of goods, the inac-
cessibility of the region, added to the alleged corruption within

the construction industry. The games were only three months away and I asked Mr Buddhachandra Singh if they would make it. 'Fifty-fifty,' he replied glumly. Some journalists, perhaps more cynical, said 'No chance.'

Mr Singh was a big polo fan and vice-president of the Manipur Horse Riding and Polo Association, not to be confused with the All Manipur Polo Association. (Both organizations deny the existence, or at least the authenticity of the other.) At the AGM of the latter, to which I was invited, one speaker got up to lament the fact that the Polo Association was all but defunct.

'We must organize more tournaments,' he said, 'otherwise it is pointless to have an association. There is apathy from members and the committee. And we have no money. Remember *arambai*? [Another old Manipuri sport of throwing a spear at a target from a running horse.] That used to be a way of life for us and now extinct. We cannot have the same thing happen with polo.'

The opposition camp also acknowledged that polo was in decline.

The Manipur Horse Riding and Polo Institute, Imphal, is the product of a crisis in the very existence of polo in the state. During the seventies polo matches were a rare sight in the state. Polo players and polo ponies, formerly the pride of the people, suddenly found themselves suspended in the tensions of a pull between the need for economic sustenance and the urge to get on the ponies and play polo. When one saw them doing the rounds of carrying around fodder to earn a living, the call for a revival of the game became stark.

And so the Institute was established in 1980, with twenty-four polo clubs affiliated.

People said polo is unique here because it's a 'common man's game', rather than an upper-class recreation, as ponies are cheap to maintain. Today's players are mainly from the valley's interior, predominantly farm-hands and small farmers, who practise during the farming off-season. The ponies are small, at a height of 11-13 hands, and the best age is around six or seven years old.

The two associations agree that polo began in Manipur and dates to a few centuries BC. Local historians claim that the game precedes history in Manipur, being so intertwined with the ethos of the people that the real facts have been clouded by myths, fables and rituals. Some believe polo originated during the reign of King Kangbaba a few centuries before the birth of Christ. The Kanjeirol, ancient writings on the sport, later records that it was played during the reign of King Nongda Leiren Pakhangba (33 AD) with seven players a side.

The *Cheitharol Kumbaba* chronicle details of matches, scores, injuries and even deaths during games at a time when intrigues and royal conspiracies were commonplace. Sagol kangjei played a perfect role in both sealing new friendships and eliminating an enemy with equal subtlety. Some Western historians claim that polo was picked up from the Chinese by the Tibetans, who named it *pulu* (the word for ball, the same as the Balti word) but the Manipuris have always called it kangjei.

Horsemanship is an integral part of the people in this state, growing from the strong relations between man and horse. The Meiteis, the predominant ethnic group in the Manipur Valley, domesticated this Central Asian breed, the Manipuri pony, for centuries. This pony had a distinctive role in the development of the Manipuri Kingdom as the expansion and consolidation of the kingdom depended on the use of the cavalry. The horse became a weapon of war and instrument in the expansion of the state in the seventeenth and eighteenth centuries.

Polo has been intertwined with the chequered history of the state, holding the essence of people's historic joys and sorrows. The polo mallet was used by ancient priestesses in their ritualistic dance to invoke the gods and goddesses of creation, as the mallet is a symbol of fertility. (It could be the root of the old custom of childless women bringing a polo mallet and ball to the best village player, asking him to bless her with children – and make them great polo players.) The best players received the King's royal patronage in the form of land grants and social status.

'We gave the world the Modern Game of Polo,' announced Mr Buddhachandra Singh in the programme for a tournament. The turning-point of Manipuri polo came with the arrival of the British, when the state lost independence in 1891 and came under their rule, and polo continued to get some support from the government. This was the point, claim Manipuris, of the ultimate sacrifice as the 'Britishers' took a liking to the game and spread it around the world.

The Manipur State Polo Committee was set up in 1948 to frame the rules, run an annual tournament, improve the standard of the game and increase its popularity. But one year later Manipur became part of the Indian Union in 1949, and polo took another beating: polo players were removed from government service and the ponies taken into custody of the government. The historical polo ground in Imphal which had hosted so many games, was denied to the Polo Committee for exclusive polo playing. Worse, financial assistance was withdrawn.

A dire economic situation and the breakdown of a tightly structured society in later years, slowly cut off the roots of the people's game and polo declined further. Without funds and with few ponies, the All Manipur Polo Club attempted in 1956 to rejuvenate the game. But it sank even lower in the 1970s, and the two associations have since tried to organize tournaments with visiting teams. For these tournaments, international style polo is played but thereby hangs a great disadvantage. Because the Manipuri pony is so small, there is no way it can compete with the the visiting teams' much larger horses.

The rules of the Manipuri polo are similar to those of northern Pakistan's polo. There are seven players each side, and each player usually plays in a specific position, marking his respective opponent. As the rule-book states, 'Sagol kangjei is not a game played at an easy canter.' The ball can be struck whilst in the air and a mounted player is allowed to pick up the ball from the ground, although it must be hit with the mallet for a goal, and pushing and barging are part of the game.

In recent years, slight modifications have taken out the more dangerous elements. The original rules were delightfully indifferent to any kind of foul. The conduct of the players was governed by *thaksi-thaksi*, social etiquette which compelled a player to play fair. But in 1928, the Maharaja forbade *sagol tupnaba*, riding across an opponent's path or into a player with deliberate intent to cause damage, and also *hairou*, the deliberate hooking above pony height.

On my final day in Imphal, I was lucky to see a short practice match, which was actually an opportunity to show the polo ground to a Minister deciding the ground's suitability for the National Games. 'Isn't it a bit late to be showing him now?' I asked the president of the association. But they were convinced there was still a chance to get some assistance from him to level the ground.

On a cool sunny Thursday afternoon, two local teams rode up to the marquee, put up especially for the committee and visitors. The main difference which made Manipuri polo unique was instantly obvious: rather than the players wearing shirt, breeches and boots, they wore a white dhoti (a long cotton loin-cloth), a big white turban held by a chin-strap and a short-sleeved cotton jacket to match the chin-strap with the team's colours. Their feet were bare, but some wore a leather ankle-covering called a *khun-ningkhang*, and padding to protect the calves.

Perhaps it was their uniform which added a theatrical air to the game. Play was as rough as in Pakistan, ferocious and dusty, players darting their horses in front of their opponent, taking wild swipes with the mallet. And like in the mountains of Pakistan, it was fast and skilful. Most of the players were young men from Imphal, marking a change in recent years to more participation from the capital.

The Manipuris are more prominently proud of polo than of their other indigenous games. I found it sad that the two polo organizations, with the same aims and principles, didn't communicate or co-ordinate and when one organized a tournament, the other knew nothing about it. If their efforts and resources were pooled, polo would have a greater chance of surviving. The greatest 'war', in Manipuri polo, was not on the field but political.

When it was time for me to leave, Mr Laithengbam brought me to the airport but when I checked in, the man said, 'Sorry, you are still a wait-list passenger. We don't know if there's a seat. Anyway the plane is at least three hours late.' The Superintendent of Police had assured me that he had arranged everything but after I'd harassed him with a flurry of frantic phone calls, he admitted that actually he had not made the arrangements himself but had left them to a peon and assumed it had been organized.

To make matters worse, all the previous day's flights had been cancelled because of fog. This caused havoc to the major air-routes and airports, and all the passengers scheduled to travel the previous day were now expecting to fly today. My only option was persistence and I followed the airport manager around the building (he even tried hiding in the engineers' room to escape my regular half-hourly requests), figuring that I could make him so sick of me that he would gladly shove me on the next flight.

Some hours later I was summonsed to the manager's office.

'There is a flight leaving for Guwahati, but you must wait there a couple of hours for a connection to Calcutta. Will you take it?' I had the choice between a definite arrival in Calcutta that evening, or wait for the direct flight which would be quicker – but no guarantee of a seat.

I picked up my bags and checked in. Before I boarded, a friendly young chap came and, checking his clipboard, asked me what date I flew in. At last I had found the official check on permits! Sergeant Singh was horrified that I had managed to fool the foolproof system by coming by bus. 'But no foreigners have ever come by bus . . .' he muttered as he recorded my exit in an exercise book with green felt-tip.

'Merry Christmas!' he said as I walked out to the plane. 'It is very nice to have you here. We don't have many visitors here. It is a shame, I could practise my English and we could learn about each other, yes? But government, you know, it doesn't want us to learn about other people,' he added as he escorted me to the plane. 'I wish you and your family a very merry Christmas, and a happy new year!' he shouted as I waved from the top of the steps. Guwahati, here I come.

Soon I discovered that the only thing worse than several hours in Imphal airport was Guwahati airport, crammed to the brim with hundreds of very irate passengers from many cancelled flights. The Calcutta flight was due to leave two hours later. Then came the announcement that the flight was another three hours late.

In the airport restaurant it was like being in a buffalo stampede. The poor staff who were bringing out trays of free food couldn't keep up with the pace of such a frenetic swarm, everyone piling their plates up and then rushing back for seconds. Dollops of dhal, ladlefuls of rice and chicken, mounds of naan bread and vats of chai were some consolation for an eternal wait. The mood lifted as everyone tucked in, and I remembered that there's only one thing worse than impatient Indians waiting for anything, and that's hungry impatient Indians.

Mr Buddhachandra Singh had kindly arranged for me to stay one night in the Manipur Bhawan guesthouse in Calcutta, and a driver was meeting me at the airport. I tried to phone the Bhawan to update them on my flight change, but the man running Guwahati airport phone office informed me there was a bund, and all lines were down.

News then filtered through of a car bomb, killing eight people including three Assam government ministers, which added further to the chaos and delayed everything again. After a total of seven hours waiting, we eventually boarded and I spent the journey worrying that there would be no one to meet me at the airport and no accommodation booked for me. There was the additional worry that the Bombay train ticket Mr Singh promised had been arranged by the Bhawan leaving the following evening wouldn't be there and I would have to spend the entire day extracting a ticket in the pre-holiday crush.

I was wrong on the first two counts and correct on the third. The driver was waiting and took me to a very comfortable room in the Manipur Bhawan guesthouse. And the next morning I spent a total of six hours to wait and queue and beg and plead with the supervisor to get a ticket on the emergency quota for a seat on the train that night to Bombay.

The various quotas are life-savers in the extremely complex system of Indian Railways. On most main rail routes there is a quota for foreign tourists, making it relatively easy to get a seat. The confusion comes when some systems work differently from others, some stations requiring booking in advance for tourist quotas, some not; some having no tourist quota, which means the last resort – the emergency quota.

In Calcutta, this entailed turning up to an office at 10 am on the day you wished to leave, waiting two hours with a dozen other hopefuls until the officer eventually decided to turn up. There were six other workers in a huge floor, swamped with dusty files on dustier desks. Someone handed me a sheet of paper on which to write my 'reason for requiring emergency quota' and, like cheating in an exam, I peeked a look at the others in the pile to see what my competitors were saying. After all, there was statistically a very small chance of getting a seat. There was 'urgent government business' , an urgent heart operation, an important interview, funerals, a crucial exam, a life-saving operation . . . I put that I needed to catch a flight back home in the wake of urgent news from home. Not true of course, but I was desperate to get to Bombay to collect my (fourth) Iranian visa, then scoot up to Delhi to collect the Pakistani visa and – I hoped – leave before Christmas. Today was the 19th.

Several hours of pleading, pacing around and running from one office to another, brought me the desired ticket, three hours before the train left. I got to Bombay just in time to pick up the Iranian visa and then leave for Delhi the following night.

30

Where Fitness Meets Ferdowsi

Once again, I was rushing to get out of Delhi before it shut down for the holidays, this time Christmas. Before that, I had to apply for and collect my Pakistani visa for the overland journey to Iran which, in spite of dense fog enveloping northern India causing delays, I managed to do. Just.

It was a freezing cold Christmas morning when I arrived in Amritsar to catch a bus for the Attari border, thankful it was for the last time. Once through the the border I hurried to Lahore railway station, anxious to be on a train to Quetta by the end of the day. I enquired about the 1 pm train, due to leave half an hour later.

'Madam, the train will leave eight hours late. You see,' explained the kindly Assistant Station Manager, 'we are waiting for the train from Rawalpindi to add his bogeys onto ours. But there is bad fog and anyway train is always late so . . . and then the train has not yet left Rawalpindi, maybe it leaves after some time and so . . . maybe it gets here at 8 pm and then, miss, you will leave for Quetta.' I wished I'd never asked.

In sleeper-class, there are six berths to a compartment, with a private toilet and sink. Two elegant old men were chatting when I went inside. Also in the compartment was a young man working for Pakistani customs; a tall turbaned man with a dozen sacks of garments for his brother's shop which he was trying to wedge, unsuccessfully, under the seats, and a Japanese tourist who refused to speak but frequently coughed up his insides. When 5 o'clock came and it was time for Iftar (Ramadan had begun six days earlier), we all brought out food and shared it out. Hours later the train moved off and it began to get cold. The others had blankets and thick clothes but my sheet and Kashmiri shawl were woefully inadequate. Apart from the cold it was a comfortable and friendly journey, unusual in that my fellow passengers didn't fire constant predictable and personal questions at me, but kept a polite distance. The Japanese man coughed constantly and still didn't speak, regularly jumping off his berth and standing outside to smoke a handful of cigarettes. Then he would re-enter and continue hacking up lumps of phlegm. Eventually one of the old men lost his patience.

'Why do you keep smoking when you have cough? Huh? This is most annoying.'

Asif, the customs officer, discussed politics with the others and when they got to nuclear testing, I was reluctantly dragged into their conversation, which progressed quickly to the predictable anti-British and American rhetoric.

'Why do Mr Blair and Mr Clinton feel they can dictate to the world? They can have nuclear weapons but not us? Huh? Can you answer that, Miss Emma? And why is there one rule for the rich countries and one rule for the poor? And don't you agree that the problem in Kashmir is all the fault of the Britishers? And do you think that people are afraid of us just because we are Muslim?'

I managed to give polite, brief answers and hope he'd get bored.

'I am proud to be Pakistani and I would die for my country. Your country tries to tell the rest of the world how to live, yet why are you any better than us? You are all hypocrites,' said Asif emphatically. I stuck my nose in my book. Shortly afterwards the train stopped at a station and the other passengers in the compartment went off to buy tea, including the gut-wrenching Japanese. Once they had gone, Asif, having been inveighing against the West, lowered his voice and asked me if I could help him get a Green Card for the States, or a visa for England. Astounded, I pointed out to him that if he wanted to live in England he shouldn't criticize it so much.

We approached the barren stretch of Baluchistan and it was suddenly warmer. After another night on the sleeper, we arrived in Quetta at 8 am. At 5 pm I boarded my bus for the Iran border and soon realized that I had made a poor choice in the bus company. The journey was noisy, cramped and uncomfortable, and it was a relief to arrive at Taftān at 8 am.

This border town between Pakistan and Iran is everything a smugglers' den ought to be. At the edge of an inhospitable desert, barren, windswept and yet dramatic with sheer rock formations, it looks as if a sharp gust of wind would blow the wooden shacks over. The 'town' is a maze of tiny alleyways lumped together in the vast emptiness; cramped stores and smuggled legal goods are piled outside – mainly electrical goods, plastic buckets, watches and clothes. The illegal stuff is more discreet. A few dozen trucks and buses ferry passengers with mountains of baggage to and from the border.

Mingling in the general chaos is a gaggle of money-changers, mainly young Afghani men who swarm enthusiastically up to every arriving and departing passenger with brick-size wads of Pakistani, Iranian and Afghani notes and dollars. The black-market rate for Iranian rials is almost double the official bank-rate, so every tourist to Iran knows to bring dollars cash to change on the street.

I was now so close to embarking on the challenge to enter a zurkhane. It was a tough proposition, especially as in Iran women are forbidden to watch men playing sport. They weren't allowed to watch Iran's qualifying matches for the World Cup, but forced themselves into the celebrations in the Azadi Stadium in Tehran when Iran eventually qualified. Supposedly, the authorities will soon relax these laws but as it stood, it was highly unlikely they would allow me inside a zurkhane to see the activities. But I was here to try.

There was a long wait before the border opened. I looked desperately for tea but it being Ramadan, there were no refreshments; I would have given my front teeth for a glass of fresh orange juice. Then a young customs officer, Akbar, took me to a hidden teahouse and ordered me a pot of green tea. I was most embarrassed as he sat and watched me drink it, refusing any himself yet insisting on paying.

'Can I make friendship with you?' he asked as we returned to his post after the tea. Did he mean sex? Pen-pals? Both? 'But I'm leaving in ten minutes,' I said, in case he intended sex. 'Oh no,' he said, confused, 'I want to write to you. Can I have your address?'

I managed to avoid handing over my address, cautious now of well-meaning pen-pals after a couple of difficult situations, making some excuse to him. We then said '*Hudar hafiz*' before I changed into my *chador* (which means 'tent'), the all-covering outer garment which all women must wear in Iran. It's usually a long, loose coat buttoned from neck to ankle, the style favoured by younger women in the cities, and a scarf covering all the hair. In more traditional areas, women wear a large black wrap which goes over the head.

Mine was a cheap and nasty black nylon coat, resembling a badly-made dressing gown, from the Muslim bazaar in Bombay, which served the purpose but was certainly no fashion statement. It was made from a flimsy, static material that gave me a minor electric shock every time I moved. To top that masterpiece, a heavy black scarf covered my head.

The main problem was that this outfit was definitely not designed to be worn whilst carrying a rucksack. As soon as I picked up my rucksack, the headscarf slipped and when that was straightened, the neckline of the coat went all indecent and the buttons started popping open.

Crossing the border went smoothly; there was a queue for the Pakistani immigration desk but women were ushered through first, and then we simply crossed the road to the Iran border post. The Iranian immigration and customs check was more organized and formal. I was worried that they would see that I had a 'journalist' stamp on my Pakistani visa and ask questions, but none of them could read English. The customs officer asked everyone to open their luggage and searched quite thoroughly.

'You are in Iran first time?' He smiled at me. 'No, second time. I love your country and especially Azizi!' That was a certainty to end the search. Azizi is one of the heroes of the Iranian football team, scoring the equalizing goal in the dying minutes against Australia, which enabled them to qualify for the World Cup.

I was quickly out of the border post and into the city of Zāhedān, then on an express bus westward to Bam, an attractive town with a citadel only a few hours away. There was enough time to get there before nightfall, and then probably move on to Esfahān the next day. As a city quite accessible to tourists, Esfahān would be the best place to start on the search for a zurkhane.

The bus was comfortable and unbelievably cheap. It had all the comfort, organization, choice and regularity of a Turkish bus, but was cheaper than in India. The five-hour journey on an air-conditioned bus with comfortable push-back seats cost less than a pound. The back-row seats contained the 'naughty eaters', those who were officially allowed to eat though it was Ramadan (because they were travelling) but did it secretly. So, as I surreptitiously scoffed cake on the back seat hiding behind a four-day-old newspaper, a hand from the seat in front came around, holding a small bun. I took the bun and the man in front sneaked a conspiratorial smile and threw his orange peel in the bin next to my seat.

It was dark and the streets deserted when the bus dropped me off on the outskirts of Bam. I then took a taxi to Ali Amiri's hostel and went into reception. I figured that the owner would be a pretty friendly chap if his reputation in that great bible of backpackers *Lonely Planet* was anything to go by. He looked up, bored, and said yes, he had rooms and yes, they were clean and cheap and when I asked to see them he looked as if I had just ordered two pints of lager and half a kilo of hash. But the rooms were clean and so were the showers.

Things soon looked up, however, with the appearance of a large Afghani working there. He possessed the most wonderful pair of ears, blown up and exploded into a mashed piece of hard flesh which could only belong to a wrestler. 'Ali,' I said. 'Sen pehlivan?' [Turkish for 'are you a wrestler?' He gave me a look of sheer joy and shook my hand. Not just a pehlivan, he was a coach in kushti, traditional wrestling, to young boys at the local sports centre.

I asked him about any zurkhanes in town. He, the manager, and I talked and concluded that there were several and the manager's friend could help arrange for me to visit one. This was the best news for days, and I was even prepared to be more pleasant to the slightly sleazy manger, who promised to call his friend in the morning.

Thoughts of leaving for Esfahān were postponed and I visited the manager's friend around the corner. Bam is a pleasant small town, and the hostel was near a busy main road lined with eucalyptus trees with small water-channels running down between the pavements and the road. The friend called up another friend who was a teacher and spoke good English, was meticulously polite and saw nothing strange about my request to see a zurkhane.

'I can take you to see my friend who runs a zurkhane and plays the drum.' We visited a large bearded chap who worked in a cultural centre. 'Come tonight at half-past six,' he boomed. 'But is it possible to see the men exercise?' I asked, thinking this was too much to hope for. 'Come at half-past six, and we start at seven. We must eat Iftar at home, then we come.'

'But,' I was getting a little worried that perhaps he had not understood, 'I want to come and see the men exercise. But I am a woman. Is it OK for a woman to come?' I pointed to my headscarf, a stupid thing to do as he probably thought it was bloody obvious I was a woman. 'Yes, yes, fine – you come tonight.' He gave a smile which lit up his large bearded face as we left and I was stunned with joy and anticipation.

That evening I set off for the Pooryaē Vali Zurkhane and stopped by two young men squatting on the pavement eating a couple of kilos of oranges, to ask for directions. They looked delighted and said they were also going there and would take me. They took me into a courtyard and through a huge wooden arched door, at exactly 6.30. As we entered, there was a roar of a motorbike and there was the bearded drummer, who welcomed me inside.

The interior was breathtaking; it was white, huge and high-ceilinged, with most of the vast wall space covered with faded black-and-white photographs and calligraphy of Persian poems. It was illuminated with enormous light-bulbs hanging low from the ceiling. In the centre was a sunken octagonal pit, with the floor patterned with black and white tiles. There was a stage with prayer-mats where a few men were kneeling and reciting their evening prayers.

Strange objects were lined up against the wall, and hanging from hooks on pillars: wooden clubs, metal chains, heavy black iron instruments which were impossible to identify. More people arrived by motorbike and on foot, and disappeared behind the stage to change. Those that noticed me gave a look of initial surprise then a welcoming smile. They emerged in their attire; long track-suit pants, T-shirts and a nappy-like checked cloth tied between their legs.

There was no one around who spoke English, so with no explanations possible I could only sit back and watch the activity unfold, like being at the theatre. There were things, symbols, sounds, actions and objects which were baffling. A few people came to watch, sitting at the sides on rickety wooden chairs and benches. It seemed a surprising spectator sport.

Several men stepped down into the pit to warm up. They touched the ground, then kissed their hands and touched their forehead, the same action the sportsmen of India or Pakistan perform on entering a fighting arena. About fifteen men entered the pit, their ages ranging from early teens to middle-ages.

They bowed to the bearded man, now wearing a white vest and a large sarong wrapped around his legs, sitting high up on a tiny raised platform lit up with a strong spotlight, with a large drum across his legs. It looked like a shrine in a Hindu temple, with a shiny copper bell over his head and flowers decorating the outside of the stand.

The room fell silent as the drummer began a slow beat and chanted into the microphone, his voice booming clearly around the large hall. They faced the same direction and followed the lead of one man (possibly the equivalent of an aerobics instructor) who was wearing an Ozzie Osbourne T-shirt and was the only one wearing a pair of rather splendid tan leather breeches with heavy green embroidery, reminding me of the Turkish kispet.

Each of them got a small wooden board, about two feet in length and stood a couple of inches off the ground. Placing their hands palms down and stretching out their legs, they did an exercise very much like press-ups with their hands always on the wood. They repeated this thirty times.

These were done to a non-stop reading by the beard, his steady drum beat and occasional ring on the golden bell. I didn't know what he was reciting but he read from a huge book resting on a stand. After every few lines, the gathered troops in the pit rested from their press-ups and recited a line together, usually the same line repeated, from the heart and sung to the heavens. It was a most moving and spectacular experience.

After their press-ups, they put away the wooden boards and each selected a pair of wooden clubs from a row of different sizes and weights, choosing ones to suit his strength. The younger, slimmer men took smaller clubs, the older, broader and more experienced men took the large ones. With one in each hand, they curled the clubs around their shoulders, above their heads and back again the opposite direction, never once allowing the club to touch their backs. This was done in unison, led by the leather-trousers and again in rhythm to the recitations.

The next stage was more unusual: hanging on a pillar were objects a bit like bows, made of heavy iron with a sturdy chain across. Three men took one each – also of varying sizes – holding it above their head with one hand on the metal, one hand on the chain. Then each swung it from side-to-side over their heads. They looked heavy, so presumably this was an arm-strengthening exercise.

It was frustrating not understanding the reason and concept behind the actions, yet the beauty, grace and calmness were exotic and deliciously confusing which added to its intrigue. The next item of apparatus looked like a huge wooden door: an arch-shaped, heavy piece of wood about four by two feet, with a small square hole in the middle with a metal bar across to grip it.

A few men then took turns, lifting one in each hand while lying on the ground. Raising each arm, each man held the wood above his head for a few seconds, then down to the ground while lying on his side and half-twisting his body. Then he repeated with the other arm. Only a few attempted that exercise, as it looked to be the most physically demanding.

Finally, there was a winding-down slow jog around the pit, led by leather-trousers and then, standing in a circle around the edge facing the middle, each one in turn performed a spinning routine. The younger ones began, each spinning round and round, twisting on the spot with their arms outstretched at incredible speed for several minutes, keeping their balance better than any ballet dancer. One by one, they performed this high-speed pirouette, ending with the oldest and most experienced.

That over, they stood and together recited more verses while looking to the heavens, then shook hands with each other and kissed the ground before leaping up out of the pit and backstage to change.

I found the routine mesmerizing, puzzling and mysterious, and I was determined to learn about its meaning and significance. Since my dream of visiting a zurkhane had been fulfilled so soon, I could leave Bam and go to Esfahān. If a zurkhane was quite simple to visit, it would surely be possible to do the same thing in Esfahān and, I hoped, get more explanations.

The hostel manager was especially nice to me the next morning when I was leaving. 'Why are you leaving us so soon? I could find you a job here. We can find you a good man to marry. Why not live here? Stay a little longer.' I told him I was returning to Istanbul. 'Ah – you live in Istanbul? Then I will come and visit you. I really want to see the city but I have no one to stay with.'

'I don't think my Turkish fiancé would approve, actually. We're getting married this summer.' 'Oh – marriage to a Turk? Oh . . .' Looking thoughtful he delved inside the cupboard and unearthed a box of Bam dates, the soft, plump and delicious variety that are grown locally and exported world-wide. He handed me the box with a smirk on his face. 'You will need these, if you're now going back to your Turkish man.' He pointed to the side of the box, where it was clearly written: 'Full of vitamins and energy'. (For energy, read aphrodisiac.)

I accepted the dates, grateful for some nourishment for the journey, doubting very much that the dates would last until Turkey. A shared taxi and then an overnight bus took me to Esfahān, famously described as 'half the world'. And it was.

The reception area of the Naghshē Jahan Hotel was pleasant and bright, with a marble and chandeliered interior and a short bargaining procedure later, I had a warm room, small bathroom with endless hot water, a telephone and breakfast.

To get more information on the zurkhanes in Esfahān, I went straight to the Ministry of Culture and Islamic Affairs, situated in the centre of the Maidanē Emam Khomeini, a most magnificent example of Persian architecture. It is the second largest public square in the world – after Tiananmen Square – with the Masjedē Emam at one end, the Ali Ghapu Palace at one side and smaller mosques around a grassy and spacious lawn.

Inevitably, most of the ground floors of the buildings around the square are souvenir shops, mainly selling carpets, good-quality handicrafts and books. It was wonderful to return to the square, which had made such a tremendous impression on me on my last visit in 1994. Then, there were virtually no foreign tourists but on this overcast grey winter's day which threatened snow, I thought I was hallucinating when a coach-load of Japanese tourists got out at the Masjed, moving in short-stepped clusters with their multitude of electronic gadgets, like a walking audio-visual store. There was now a small ticket office on entering the Jami, whereas earlier anyone could walk in. It was good to see the place making something from tourism, as Iran has much to offer but is viewed with suspicion, many people suspecting it to be a nation of dangerous terrorists and fundamentalists.

The mysteries of the zurkhane were soon solved by Mr Saiid of the Ministry of Culture and Islamic Guidance, who launched enthusiastically into explanations about the origins, the practices and the symbols on which the zurkhane are based.

'Zurkhanes were first constructed seven centuries ago when the Mongols attacked Iran, defeated and then occupied us. Iranian men had to be powerful to overcome the Mongols but it was forbidden to exercise. In order to become strong, they had to build cellars, or underground places where they could gather secretly. Today, we still use these places. Even new ones are built in the same style to remind us of its origins.

'The zurkhanes became very popular, where many people went to learn the rules and tactics of fighting. But the most important aspect is not just physical strength and being a sportsman. It is about being a man. Being honest, concerned for the poor, never imposing your strength over the weak, to be humble and modest. Practising good behaviour, generosity and helping everyone – these are the characteristics of a real man.'

Even the construction reflects the importance of being humble: 'The main door is low so you have to bow to the people who are sitting, even if you are the best, most senior person. The same reason is for the exercise pit, the *gode*. It is octagonal, based upon the shrine of the Prophet Muhammad, and sunken so people are physically lower. Being eight-sided means that every side is equal and there is no head.'

He described how every single item, detail and custom of the zurkhane related to inner strength and modesty. 'The man who beats the drum is the *Morshad*, the Arabic word for Preacher. He sits high on the platform to allow the men to look up to him, to give respect to the words he is reciting.'

Most of the readings are verses from classic Persian poets like Ferdowsi, Hafez and Sa'adi. A favourite is the famous *Shah Nahma* by Ferdowsi written over a thousand years ago, an epic of about 50,000 couplets, which took over thirty years to complete. Extracts are read, especially those which reinforce the spirit of the zurkhane.

Verses from the Holy Koran usually tell stories and teachings of Imam Ali, the fourth khalif of the Sunnis and the first Imam of the Shias, who was the first and best exponent of 'pehlivanism', the art of the pehlivan. (In this context the word means not just 'wrestler' but relates to the man fulfilling the exercises.)

'All people are the same, created from one precious thing.

If it happens that one of the members feels pain, or has problems, the others cannot keep still, all are worried. If you are not worried about others, you are not a human being . . .' as Iman Ali once said.

Mr Saiid helped me to find, and get permission to enter, local zurkhanes, which was achieved after a phone call. 'My friend will be happy to help you. She will make enquiries and meet you tonight, and she can explain everything.' This was terrific but I wondered who the woman was and her willingness to help. I told Mr Saiid that I would gladly pay her for her time.

'No – she will not accept any money. She is a teacher and is very happy to help foreigners when they come here, as a friend.' Later that evening I met Zohreh, a tiny young women in her early thirties, swamped from head to toe in a black chador, long black coat and black gloves. Her broad smile and sparkling eyes were full of character and chatter.

'I have the addresses of three which we can visit. I couldn't get through on the phone but we can just turn up.' She was obviously a religious woman and I was concerned about her going inside a zurkhane, an all-male environment with lots of sweaty half-dressed men. Would she be embarrassed or offended? 'Er . . . Have you been inside a zurkhane before?'

'No, never, but I'm very much looking forward to it. I don't know much about them at all . . .'

It was snowing when we arrived at the zurkhane, smaller and more modern than the one in Bam. Its walls were completely covered with photographs. There were chairs all around the edge, still empty as we were early. The men slowly began to arrive and changed into their kit, identical to those in Bam. The chequered cloth tied between their legs, called a *long*, signifies that everyone is equal, regardless of age or status.

The zurkhane reminded me of the akharas in India and Pakistan but whereas the akhara culture is slowly dying in the face of the glamorous TV sports, the zurkhane happily co-exists alongside the country's football craze. A young pehlivan told me the cultural importance to Iranian people.

'There are so many advertisements about different modern sports now and football is on every TV channel. But this is traditional and shows the connection between people and their history. There are no advertisements, no media or prize money. The people who have come here for thirty years don't like the televised sports. A footballer plays professionally for only a couple of years, and in that time receives so much money and always on TV all the time . . . But this zurkhane is part of our lives, and every Iranian should be proud to come here.'

Like the akharas, young boys from ten years old are often

brought to try and 'improve' their character. But if a boy shows no signs of improvement, they remove him in case he influences others. Another similarity is the lack of government support, resented by many people. 'The government is only interested in supporting football, because that's where the money is. They don't offer financial help or encourage the zurkhane's popularity. All the money comes from us, people donate money every time they come which pays for the upkeep and renovations,' said one Morshad.

Before the Islamic Revolution, there was less interest in the zurkhane. One man said to me, 'In the time of the Shah, there was too much recreation and not much interest.' (He was referring to the lure of casinos, alcohol and pornographic films.) 'People were coming smelling of alcohol and had to be sent home.' Since 1979, when such activities became illegal, people had more incentive and opportunities to come here. And, presumably, fewer 'distractions'.

The tenets of the zurkhanes meant that the Shah's regime was held in some disapproval by the pehlivans and in every zurkhane hangs the portrait of a young pehlivan called Takhti, who was seen as the embodiment of true pehlivanism: strong yet religious and pure, heroic but also humble and wise. Since childhood he went to the zurkhane and achieved a high level of competitive wrestling. But he didn't respect the Shah's authority. In one stadium where he was competing, the Shah's brother came as a guest of honour and the crowd rose to greet him – but Takhti refused to stand. Shortly afterwards the pehlivan died through poisoning and his followers say (although it was never proved) that the Shah had arranged his death as punishment for his defiance.

At eight o'clock, a couple of dozen men arrived and a few spectators sat around the walls; many of them came regularly. Apart from its spiritual values, a zurkhane is the most popular meeting-place after the teahouse for men to get together in the evenings.

The exercises followed the same pattern as in Bam. Since Mr Saiid's explanation, I could now understand each action, its specific reason and origin. The first routine was a simple warming-up or loosening-up exercise, led by the *miandah*, who is usually one of the most experienced pehlivans. It began with a gentle jog, then shaking the limbs, then all in unison would go down on bended knee; first one leg and then the other, holding that pose for a few seconds. This is called *khamgiri*, and strengthens the legs, especially for kushti.

Then came the press-ups using the wooden blocks, or the *takhtē shenoh*, (literally 'swimming wood') to strengthen the upper arms. The huge wooden clubs were next, called *mil* (or, in Esfahān, *gaburgeh*), which reminded me of the gurz in Indo-Pak, the silver or gold mace of honour offered to the champion wrestlers. The origins of this exercise, as for every fighting sport, lie in defending one's country in times of war. The mil is said to be a derivation of the gurz, an instrument of honour in attack. Exercising with the mil is a reminder of the honour for those who defend their country. They are also heavy enough to strengthen shoulders and upper arms.

The most bizarre-looking piece of apparatus, the metal bow-like one, is the *kabodeh*, which, as its appearance would suggest, was designed to improve skills in using a bow and arrow. There are different weights and sizes, depending on a person's ability.

Next was the door-like wooden shield, called *sang*, used lying on the ground. This was originally to train men to fight off an attacker or an animal who had them on the ground. To use the sang effectively, one has to be able to push up the wood, which sometimes weigh as much as 70 kilos and is therefore as heavy as a man.

Finally came the individual spinning exercise where each man spins round as long as possible. This is the *chah-ki dan*, which Mr Saiid had explained: 'If a man can spin quickly and steadily, it means when faced with several enemies, he can kill them all with a knife.' So, our lone spinner with knife or sword in one hand, can hope to inflict severe damage on a group of attackers, spinning quickly so as not to be caught.

Crucial to the spirit of the zurkhane is the utmost respect the pehlivans hold for each other and although there is equality, there is a hierarchy based on experience. If a man is young but has been going to the zurkhane for many years, he is higher on the 'ladder' than an older, less experienced man. To reflect this, the least experienced ones go first in an exercise. In a reversal of the usual polite exchanges, one hears pehlivans arguing: 'I'm going first', 'No I'm going first', 'No I insist on going before you', because going first acknowledges that you are less experienced than the other.

It also dates back to the events of Ashoura, when Imam Hussain and his followers were massacred in a brutal battle. His followers insisted on going in before him, knowing that they were all going to die but all trying to spare him the suffering, respecting his seniority and position.

The Morshad chanted verses throughout, banging a steady drum beat and ringing the golden bell above his head to emphasize the important passages, and Zohreh translated them: 'Good friends – if you have no friends you have no reputation.' 'Sit with inferior people so that you can improve yourself.' 'Sometimes walk slowly and know how the slower people live.' 'If you sit with a wise person for one minute, it is better than spending a whole life by yourself.'

Then, from a poem by Sa'adi: 'Oh beggar, go and knock at Imam Ali's door, because he will give you his ring, The ring which indicates his governing.' Imam Ali, the most revered pehlivan, had a strength so great it was unnatural, proof that it was God's gift. A story of a war between the enemies of Islam and Imam Ali's troops tells of how his enemies fled into a castle to escape him but Imam Ali was able to pick up the door of the castle and use it as a bridge over the moat to help his troops across. But he was also said to be extremely humble, doing great acts of generosity whilst concealing his identity. People spoke of how he took food to poor Arabs but remained anonymous by covering his face.

Zohreh and I left, to the good wishes of all the members, and she looked up to me, eyes shining. 'Would you like to go to another one tomorrow? We could meet at the same time.' And so it was arranged, both of us buzzing. I wondered how she felt. 'I was worried that you may feel uncomfortable watching these men do their exercises. After all, women are not really supposed to go inside. Did you feel comfortable?'

She was smiling. 'I didn't really know what to expect,' she replied. 'But there is so much religious feeling present, it makes me feel very happy. Even though women don't go inside, the men treated us with great respect and modesty. Did you notice that when they spoke with us, they wouldn't look us in the eye? This is the proper way a man must address a woman.'

So, the next evening, we went to Kamol zurkhane, named after the founder and Morshad, Kamol Attori. Mr Attori greeted us and brought tea and sweet pastries. Kamol has retired his duties as

Morshad after forty years, recently handing the reins over to his nephew, one of many he taught to be Morshad.

Sayed Mehdi Attori was nineteen and a volleyball coach. 'I first came when I was ten years old, because all my brothers came. I gradually learned all the skills and now come every night. Although it's not really useful for physical skills in volleyball, I come because of the ideology. It is an Islamic culture and you can pray as well as take part. It is the only sport which is truly Islamic, and you are constantly reminded of who you are. What other sport can give you that feeling?'

On our final evening, we visited our third, out of a total of sixty-three in Esfahān. The Arhan zurkhane was the biggest I had seen, with proper tiered seating for spectators, which made it look like a small theatre. Once again, the walls were covered with ornate old photographs, poems written in graceful calligraphy, paintings of Holy Imams Ali and Hussain above the door, and of course the portrait of Takhti.

A Morshad and trainer, Mujtabor Pehlivani, had his little son on his lap. 'I bring him here every night and hope that he will grow up wanting to be a pehlivan. He always asks me to bring him. I came with my father when I was three years old.' I asked him about financial support from the government. 'A football match can make money for the government but we can't. Why should the government bother to support us? If they gave us some money, obviously it would be better for us. We do need money to exist, but don't like to ask and only request donations from members. The older people don't want to ask the government for help, as many of them hate talking about materialistic things.'

Esfahān is one of the more liberal Iranian cities, accustomed to seeing foreigners especially before the deposition of the Shah, when it was a popular tourist destination. But while in 1994 there was little evidence of tourism, Iran is returning to the overlander's trail from Europe to India, as well as welcoming more coach parties from Japan.

There are still hints of the fundamentalists and extremists who remain, but as a small minority. The faces of Khomeini, Khaminei, the current Ayatollah and Khatami are in every shop and public place, and gigantic murals on the sides of tower blocks depict the stern image of the Ayatollah and messages to his people. My favourite mural was near Ferdowsi Square in the centre of Tehran, which depicts the American flag but with skulls instead of stars, and the stripes are falling bombs. Underneath is written in English 'Down with USA'. In Farsi it is a little more extreme: 'Death to America'.

31

My Baby My Chocolate

Visiting four zurkhanes was already better than I could have hoped, so I decided to spend a few days in Tehran before taking the bus to Istanbul. Once in the capital, I would try and see one more. But in Tehran it was more difficult to achieve anything; more bureaucratic, officials were more suspicious of me and requested letters of permission explaining everything. I tried to get permission to attend a football match in the huge Azadi stadium, which was an unlikely prospect.

It was hard to find out about zurkhanes and I was sent on a wild-goose chase invoked by the enthusiastic but clueless receptionist at my hotel. Then by chance I found a sports office, but everyone was busy and not particularly friendly. One man told me that I would need permission. 'Tehran is not the same as Esfahān. We are more strict here.' He advised me to contact the President of the Federation of Traditional Sports.

As I was leaving, a dapper man in suit and tie entered the office, the first Iranian man I had seen in a tie, for it is branded as un-Islamic and un-Iranian by central authorities. He introduced himself as Dr Dawoody and asked would I like to go to his office to chat? Well, thanks, I said, but actually I have to get to the Ministry of Culture and Islamic Guidance to get some information. No problem, he said, I can drop you there.

It was the beginning of a short but eventful friendship with Dr Dawoody, a vivacious and charismatic Azerbaijani who spoke a fair smattering of English. On the way to the Ministry we went to do his weekly shopping, then back to his office where his two daughters cooked lunch and when he opened a bottle of vodka and sloshed a fair slug into my Fanta, I realized that there would be no visit to the Ministry that day. And all this during Ramadan.

We spent the afternoon watching videos of concerts he had organized of Azeri folk musicians in Tehran and Tabriz, and videos of his musician friends giving small, informal performances in his office with a crowd of his cronies. 'Look, look, this bit is good . . .' and he pointed to himself on the screen in a state of mild drunken euphoria, arms outstretched and dancing to the music to the delight of his friends.

'You must come and visit my family, my beautiful wife, my baby my chocolate, my little son, my daughters . . . Come for dinner one night.' We planned to meet and go to his house on the outskirts of the city near the Alborz mountains.

That evening I met Dr Sadjjadi at my hotel, the tall dignified President of the Federation of Traditional Sports and Heroic Wrestling. The Federation had been going for twenty years, and although mainly involved with the zurkhane, it also organizes kushti, the traditional wrestling.

He said it would be difficult to go inside a zurkhane without permission. 'People are more strict here and more afraid of the authorities. But I can arrange for you to visit my friend's zurkhane tomorrow night, at 11 o'clock. He will be very happy to help, and I will give you a letter of introduction. This is a very old traditional one, very different from the others you have seen.'

The next evening after my taxi driver had got thoroughly muddled, we at last pulled up outside a dark building with a thin young man in jeans and a battered leather jacket standing outside, and I showed him the letter. I said there was someone inside who was expecting me, but he just looked confused and said that this man hadn't come. 'I don't know if we can let you in.' He went inside to check, and after an eternity reappeared and reluctantly let me inside. About 150 pairs of suspicious eyes gazed upon my long black coat and headscarf. Everything fell silent. The spectators, aged between five and ninety-five, looked astonished. The pehlivans stopped in their tracks – except for an old one-eyed man who hadn't noticed the intrusion – and even the Morshad froze mid-sentence. Trying to hide my face behind the scarf in embarrassment, I was ushered to a seat at the front and gradually the drumming and the action recommenced.

The interior was spectacular, worth coming just to see it. It was much bigger and older than the others and in its historical atmosphere it was easy to envisage the Persians trying to overcome the Mongolian invasion seven centuries ago. It was brightly lit by huge light-bulbs hanging from the high ceilings and, here too, large black-and-white photographs of wrestlers, classic Persian poems written in graceful calligraphy in ornate frames covered the walls while paintings of the holy Imams Ali and Hussain were positioned over the doors and windows.

I sat on the edge of my seat next to the wooden racks with everyone's shoes, and felt uncomfortable. There was still no sign of Dr Sadjjadi's friend who was expecting me. At the back of the zurkhane on a raised stage, young men were practising kushti which really made me feel as though I had gone back in time. There was the occasional 'thump' as a wrestler was flung on his back. I had permission to take pictures, so I took a few very discreetly until the doorman returned, eyeing my camera uneasily.

'You can take a couple more pictures but then you must leave quickly,' he whispered apologetically. He hovered over my shoulder. 'I'm sorry – but if the police come and see you, there will be trouble.' He pointed at the door. 'I'm very sorry but they could complain and then everyone will be in trouble.' 'But why will there be trouble if I have permission to be here?' I asked. 'But these are the Komité – religious police – you are woman and non-Muslim. And it is Ramadan. This is first time woman is coming inside here. It's not really allowed.' He saw the look of disappointment on my face and as if to soften the blow, he handed me a glass of tea and a syrupy pastry. 'Here – have tea.'

As I was reluctantly preparing to leave, an authoritative-looking man with an impressive grey moustache came over. He had a few sharp words with the doorman and eyed me sternly. 'Why are you here?' he asked and I showed him Dr Sadjjadi's letter in reply. He read it thoroughly and then his eyes lit up with pleasure.

He took the letter triumphantly and showed it to some of his friends, then went over to the two Morshads and requested them to stop speaking. Much to my embarrassment he then stood up in front of the spectators, who were now watching with fascination, and with large, theatrical gestures spoke for over twenty minutes.

'We should welcome this lady from England. It is of great pride to us,' he boomed in Farsi, 'that she is learning about our great culture and traditions and will write about them in the West. It is an honour for us to have her as a guest.' (Although my Farsi is minimal, it was possible to understand the general sentiments.)

Spectators and pehlivans alike drank in every word, first looking at him, then at me. As he spoke, the atmosphere changed and there were warm glances of approval from around the room. A few men put their hands on their heart and waved towards me as a gesture of acceptance. It was an official welcome.

It was after midnight when the exercises came to a close.

As I was leaving to get a taxi, a heavily sweating and panting pehlivan, just emerged from his exercises, staggered over and introduced himself. 'My name is Ahmed and I am a wrestling coach. We welcome you here, very glad to see you. Please, I would like to take you back to your hotel.' I refused politely, thinking it was a long way for him to drive, especially at this hour. But he mistook my hesitation. 'No, no, I have asked my teacher if I can take you home, and he says it is fine. Please, you must.' I was very touched not only by his offer, but his thoughts to 'check up' whether it was OK.

It took him a few minutes to change, so I said my goodbyes and thanks to my hosts and then we left to his car. 'Would you like to see my friend's zurkhane now? I think they are still there – maybe till one o'clock. You will enjoy it.' After a split-second's thought I decided that he was a trustworthy chap and agreed to go.

It was snowing when we stopped outside a building which looked boarded up. 'I will check first that you can come,' said Ahmed and several minutes later he beckoned me in. This was an older and much smaller zurkhane, with all the trademarks that I was now getting accustomed to seeing. A couple of men were standing around chatting, one man was making tea and two more were praying. 'They have finished now but please drink tea and they welcome you to come tomorrow.' We stood around amicably until way past 1 am and drank sweet glasses of tea, whilst they repeated the invitation for me to return the next evening. 'We would be glad to welcome you,' beamed the old Morshad.

Ahmed dropped me off at my hotel, where I found frantic messages from Dr Dawoody wondering if I wanted to go to Ghom at 2 am, which provoked major disapproval from the receptionist (who needed little encouragement to meddle in my business). He had apparently interrogated Dr Dawoody, ticking him off for making 'improper' invitations.

The next day one mystery was cleared up. I met with Dr

Sadjjadi again, and told him how much I had enjoyed the experience the previous night. 'But where did you go?' he asked looking puzzled. 'My friend was waiting for you until midnight and you never came.'

I had actually been taken to the wrong place by the taxi-driver and the others had misread the address on the letter. No wonder the people inside were confused. I apologized profusely to Dr Sadjjadi and asked him to pass the message on to this friend.

Tehran is a hugely polluted and unattractive sprawling city, so with little else to keep me I bought a bus-ticket for Istanbul. On my final day, instead of visiting one of the many much-heralded museums, I went to the shrine of Khomeini just outside the city, approximately halfway between Tehran, the city where the Islamic Revolution began, and Ghom, where he underwent his theological training.

The magnificent building which houses the shrine is visible for miles, its striking golden domes reflecting the sunlight. It will take several more years to complete and promises to be one of the greatest Islamic buildings in modern history. As the bus dropped us off at the driveway in front of a rather inconspicuous entrance, the scaffolding and half-built walls around the back were very much visible.

The shrine is a long walk from the roadside, a walkway consisting of several shops selling copies of the Koran, together with an eclectic collection of cassettes, postcards and posters of the Imam Khomeini. I saw a large post office, a bank, a supermarket, a Refah department store and a small arcade with restaurants and refreshments. It was surprising to see so much consumerism in a holy site, but apparently the Imam had said that he wanted his shrine to be a public place where people could enjoy themselves, rather than a mosque.

And enjoying themselves they certainly were. Women went through a separate entrance and after being frisked and searched, bags, cameras and shoes were left outside and we entered slowly into the vast, cool marble-floored room. The atmosphere was surprisingly relaxed, rather than sacred. It was spacious and airy, and once inside men and women weren't segregated. Several groups of schoolchildren were praying together, including many schoolgirls who were given lessons on how to pray. They wore pale, flowery chadors over their school uniform, which was dark blue trousers and a long knee-length tunic with matching scarves.

Families lay casually on the carpets, children ran around laughing and rolling coins across the floor, young men sat in small groups chatting, old women got out their bread and snacked, people prayed together or alone, and old men curled up on the carpet sleeping. It was most tranquil.

The cloth-draped coffin was inside a small room with glass walls, so it wasn't possible to touch it. Around the wall was a narrow gap about three feet off the ground and a few inches wide, where people could drop money through. There was a pile of notes of all nationalities and denominations around the circumference of the shrine. Some people were wailing and praying with emotion, hands reaching out to his coffin. Weeping old women tied small pieces of string on the bars to the shrine of the man who twenty years earlier had changed the country.

Dr Dawoody invited me to lunch at his house before I left Tehran on my mammoth bus journey to Istanbul. The bus was leaving at 2 pm, and scheduled to take two days of continuous travel to get there. I had already been to his house one evening and met his beautiful wife (whom he called 'my baby my chocolate') who cooked great vegetarian food, although she spent most of the evening in another room whilst he and I ate and drank vodka.

Today, he again opened the vodka ('We have to drink to your safe journey' was the excuse this time) and after lunch his wife prepared food for my journey: a container of salad, apples, cheese and *kuku sabzi*, an Iranian omelette with potato, cut into thick wedges. With only minutes to spare to get to the bus station, I had literally to beg Dr Dawoody, who had promised to drive me there, to leave; and five minutes before the bus was supposed to leave, he was still considering popping into his cousin's place on the way.

When we arrived at Maidanē Azadi, the massive and highly confusing meeting of several highways, locating my bus stand in amongst over twenty different bus companies all with buses going to Istanbul at the same time was a nightmare. With exactly one minute to go, we dashed up dragging the pile of baggage. 'See, see, I told you I'd get you here on time,' gasped Dr Dawoody as he and his son struggled with my bags. 'We're not there yet,' I growled wishing I'd come alone. Luckily, the bus was leaving one hour late so there was time to spare.

While waiting, Dr Dawoody announced that he was coming

with me on the bus. 'I will buy a ticket and come with you as far as Tabriz. It will be nice, no? I can visit my relatives there.' 'But what about your son, and your wife?' 'I will send my son home in a taxi and I will telephone my wife and tell her I will come home in a few days.'

To someone as eccentric as Dr Dawoody, it was probably normal to get on a bus for a twelve-hour journey in January with thick snow on the roads, dropping in on relatives for a couple of days, carrying nothing but his briefcase and wearing a suit and tie. 'I don't have much money on me and no food, or passport, but no problem. I know all police around here anyway. Will you pay for my ticket?'

When the bus left at 3 pm, Dr Dawoody had already acquainted himself with the other passengers – twenty young Iranian men most of whom were returning to their jobs in Istanbul. He began singing loud and tuneless folk songs in celebration. I was rather glad to have some company for a few hours and whatever else, he would never be boring. Soon he was reciting poetry to the young men who were gazing at him in awe. He gave dramatic recitals of Persian classics, followed by a mini-lecture on each one, taking out notes from his briefcase. His audience was eating out of his hand.

Night fell as did the temperature, which aggravated a bad cough I had which sounded quite alarming. Dr Dawoody then began his art of persuasion, begging me to stay in Tabriz with him instead of going to Istanbul. The first couple of times it was amusing, but this continued for hours and hours whilst he tried to clutch my hand, and I pretended to be asleep. 'My baby my chocolate, why are you going to Istanbul? You must stay in Tabriz and I will show you everything . . .'

The temperature plunged further and we were stuck in a blizzard, thick driving snow which made visibility practically zero. 'You cannot go to Turkey in this weather, you should stay in Tabriz until weather gets better. Driver said that even the petrol tanks are freezing up and buses not moving over in Turkish side. My baby my chocolate, my love.' Oh shut up, Doctor, and let me sleep.

It took over twelve hours to reach Tabriz but he made no move to leave. 'It would be problem now to get out as it is too late. I will come to border with you.' A terrible thought crossed my mind, that of Dr Dawoody following me to Istanbul crying 'my baby my chocolate' and never going home. 'I don't have my passport with me but I know the border guards and maybe they will let me go into Turkey.' Then he stood up. It was 3 am and everyone was asleep, until he began to recite a long and emotional poem that he'd been writing frantically a few minutes earlier in Farsi.

Everyone woke as his voice boomed, waving his arms around dramatically and causing the lads to watch him with awe, not knowing whether to laugh or cry. He punctuated certain lines by turning and pointing to me, and I heard my name mentioned several times. 'This is a love poem, for you. I translate: "I follow her to the end of the road, but I know not where the road ends. I know not why I follow her, but I cannot leave now. I watch her sleeping peacefully in the moonlight . . ." ' I pleaded with him to stop and the lads gave him an enthusiastic round of applause.

Everyone was now awake and began chatting. There was Hassan behind me who worked as a carpenter in Istanbul, but didn't like the Turks because, he claimed, they were money-grabbing. He asked if I could get him a visa for England. Ahmed, the poet across the aisle, announced: 'I am going to America. I am a poet but I am artistically persecuted by the Iranian authorities. I will get a visa from Istanbul.' Then, a little later, at our breakfast stop, Ahmed asked, 'Do you think I should go to America or stay in Iran and write a book on the young generation of opium addicts?' I said I thought it was a close call. But were there many addicts in Iran? 'Oh yes, all the young generation. After all, everything is banned. They cannot drink, no parties, no discos, no girls. Opium is cheap and everywhere.'

At Maku, just before the border, we stopped to change money in an oven-hot teahouse. It had stopped snowing but there was thick ice everywhere and the driver told us it was minus 15 degrees. Dr Dawoody was still talking about coming to Istanbul. 'Look,' I said wearily, 'I have my baby my chocolate waiting for me in Istanbul. He won't be very happy to see you. He's a wrestler.' He sulked for a while, until the bus reached the border post of Bazargan at around 9 am, where we had to wait in freezing conditions for an hour. Then we took our bags off the bus and started the long walk through buildings which contained the immigration, police and customs on the Iranian side, and the same in reverse order on the Turkish side. It took over an hour of standing, waiting in locked rooms, dragging bags to be searched. I said goodbye to Dr Dawoody, quite relieved that he had decided to go home.

The next room in the building was officially Turkey, so I could legally remove my chador and headscarf, which created hilarity among the Iranian lads, who were taking good care of me in accordance with the Doctor's strict instructions. We were about to buy a couple of bottles of brandy from the Duty Free shop, when I was summoned by a stern Turkish soldier. 'Madam – please come back to Iran.'

He led me round the outside of the buildings until we came to the barbed-wire fence which divides the two countries. The mountains were snowy and desolate, the barbed-wire coils menacing, and the multitude of soldiers looked intimidating. And there, like a scene out of *Doctor Zhivago*, was a man clutching the fence, his eyes streaming with tears.

'When will you come back to Iran?' whispered Dr Dawoody, with a small crowd of guards watching earnestly. If it wasn't so funny it might have been dramatic. Stifling a laugh, I replied, 'Maybe one day, maybe never,' shrugged heartlessly and walked slowly to the bus.